# SPIRITS OF THE BORDER III:

# THE HISTORY AND MYSTERY
# OF THE
# RIO GRANDE

By

**Ken Hudnall**

**Omega Press**
**El Paso, Texas**

**Spirits of the Border III: The History and Mystery of The Rio Grande**

**Copyright © 2005 Ken Hudnall**

OMEGA PRESS
An Imprint of Omega Communications Group, Inc.


For Information address:


Omega Press
5823 N. Mesa, #823
El Paso, Texas 79912

Or

http://www.kenhudnall.com


First Edition


Printed in the United States of America

## OTHER WORKS BY THE SAME AUTHOR
## UNDER THE NAME KEN HUDNALL

### SERIES

### <u>MANHATTAN CONSPIRACY</u>
*Blood on the Apple*
*Capital Crimes*
*Angel of Death*
*Confrontation*

### <u>THE OCCULT CONNECTION</u>
*U.F.O.S, Secret Societies and Ancient Gods*
*The Hidden Race*

### <u>DARKNESS</u>
*When Darkness Falls*
*Fear The Darkness*

### <u>SPIRITS OF THE BORDER</u>
*The History and Mystery of El Paso Del Norte*
*The History and Mystery of Fort Bliss, Texas*

### <u>THE ESTATE SALE MURDERS</u>
*Dead Man's Diary*

### As ROBERT K. HUDNALL

No Safe Haven: Homeland Insecurity

The Northwood Conspiracy

# DEDICATION

As with all of my books, the one whose support has been most important to the completion of the project has been my lovely wife, Sharon. Without her assistance, all of my ideas would remain just ideas.

# TABLE OF CONTENTS

# PREFACE

I was talking to someone about my books the other day and the comment was made that it was sad that a particular location would become known because of ghost stories and not for the actual history of the location. This comment started me thinking about how I needed to present the stories and legends that I collect about the area. Then it dawned on me that the many stories and legends of hauntings of El Paso and the buildings within it are actually a part of the history of the particular location being discussed and it would be wrong not to discuss it. To leave out the allegedly paranormal happenings is to delete a part of the actual history that makes the places that I write about so well known. It also shows the narrow mindedness and short sightedness of the persons that have made such comments.

Books are meant for enjoyment and education. However, not everyone feels this way and with the ardent fervor usually shown by the ignorant and self righteous, they create a problem where one does not exist. As a classic example, I was uninvited from a Church Christmas Fair in Clint, Texas that I had been invited to attend as a result of such narrow mindedness. Many were looking forward to being able to get my books, but it seems that one prominent lady of the church felt my books about the ghosts and unexplained happenings in the surrounding countryside sent the wrong kind of message to the reading public. She had set herself up as the keeper of the public morals.

I am not sure what message this woman wanted to send, but I could not refrain from pointing out to the messenger[1] that informed me that I was not welcome in Clint that the Holy Bible, in which both she and the woman who did not want me to come to Clint, professes to believe so strongly, is a book full of ghosts, demons, spirits, the Devil, incest and prostitution. However, it is

---

[1] This fine upstanding keeper of the public morals did not have the intestional fortitude to talk to me face to face to tell me that I was not welcome, but demanded that others do her dirty work. I am sure that she is proud of having protected the morality of Clint from the likes of me and my books.

interesting to note that this woman does not feel that the Holy Bible sends the wrong message as well so are we dealing with a clear case of a double standard? The pitiful thing is that such people who want to direct what their neighbors can or cannot read seem to get their way through sheer arrogance and the desire on the part of others not to make waves. It is such self righteous "I know what is best for you" attitudes that in the past have led to the Salem witchcraft trials and Prohibition. Both of these shameful events were clear violations of the rights of others, but all done in the name of what is best for society.

Sadly, such an attitude is becoming more and more prevalent in the Protestant faith so that when someone professes to be a Christian, I know without a shadow of a doubt that I am usually dealing with someone who is closed minded and self righteous in the extreme. It is such fanatical types that have led us in the past to such enjoyable events as the Spanish Inquisition, the complete destruction of the Incan and Aztec civilizations and the Crusade in the South of France that decimated over half of the population in that region. All of this was done in the name of Christianity.

For this reason, I make no apologies as I relate the strange and unusual material that I have collected for this second look at the little discussed side of the History and Mystery of the Rio Grande. Parading about, making unreasonable demands and deciding for others what they should or should not read does not make these events go away.

Sadly, out of nothing more than consideration for the very difficult position in which the organizer of this Christmas Fair had been put by the unreasonable demand made upon her, I was forced to not attend the Clint Christmas Fair. So I guess the woman that demanded that I not come to the Clint Methodist Church Christmas Fair feels vindicated and thinks she saved the citizens of Clint from reading my evil works. I guess she does not care that she kept a totally disabled veteran that served his country to protect her rights from earning a living form his writings. Such closed minded self righteous people never care about anything or anyone other than themselves.

However, it will be interesting to see what happens when this same "keeper of the Public Morals" decides that she does not like something that a church member does, says or wears. Such is the fear in which this unreasonable woman seems to be held by the other church members that I am sure that the offending person will be thrown from the church and chased out of Clint. As the only one who is apparently in direct touch with God, I am sure that she is the only one who knows what others should be doing. I feel very sorry for the members of the Clint Methodist Church that they do not have the courage to put this woman in her place. I thought this was a free country, but apparently this does not apply in certain areas of El Paso and in the community of Clint, Texas.

Ken Hudnall
El Paso, Texas
2005

# PART I

# LOOKING BACK AT SOME HISTORY

# AND

# SOME MYSTERY

# CHAPTER ONE

## ANOTHER LOOK

When I wrote *Spirits of the Border: The History and Mystery of El Paso*

**Figure 1: The City of El Paso.**

*Del Norte*[2], I never dreamed that there would be such unbelievable interest in the

---

[2] Hudnall, Ken and Connie Wang, <u>The Spirits of the Border: The History and Mystery of El Paso Del Norte</u>, Omega Press, El Paso, Texas. 2003.

topic of ghosts and hauntings in this staid, quiet city. When I sat out to write the first volume, I was rebuffed by many that I approached for information on the events that had happened to them, who were afraid that they would be ridiculed for their stories. Now, I am inundated with stories of supernatural events that have happened to various people in El Paso. I guess the overwhelming reception of the first book by the reading public has made a difference in the minds of all but a few.

In addition, I am continually being approached by those who wish to know much more about both ghosts in general as well as specific instances of hauntings. The most common question revolves around the ability of a ghost to hurt a living person. I am of the belief that a ghost can only injure someone indirectly, such as instilling fear or causing the viewer to commit some dangerous act in an attempt to escape the ghost.

I have always been a history buff, but I know that history tends to put most people to sleep. In fact, I have heard many people remark that El Paso has nothing going for it and no reason that tourists should come spend any time here. This statement could not be further from the truth. I discovered a unique approach that has made this first volume of the series a major success and started people looking at El Paso in a new light. **It turns out that the region around El Paso, Texas is one of the most haunted parts of our country!**

Though most find this statement hard to believe since there are so few well known stories emanating from El Paso, there is no doubt that there a large number of haunted buildings in this city. The only problem is that no one has ever gone to the trouble of telling the many stories of the many hauntings of El Paso. The few books that have gone into these stories have only given a thumbnail sketch of the events, without looking at the history of the location, or trying to identify the ghost. Hopefully, this series will go a long way toward rectifying this oversight.

In this third volume of this unique series, *Spirits of the Border*[3], we will take another long look at some of the little known history and mystery of this very old city and the surrounding countryside. There will be some addition information presented regarding some of the topics discussed in volume one and we will also talk about some new haunted locations and some new treasures for those who enjoy the great out doors. Literally, El Paso has something for everyone.

---

[3] Volume I - Hudnall, Ken and Connie Wang, <u>The Spirits of the Border: The History and Mystery of El Paso Del Note</u>, Omega Press, El Paso, Texas. 2003 and Volume II - Hudnall, Ken and Connie Wang, <u>The Spirits of the Border: The History and Mystery of Fort Bliss, Texas</u>, Omega Press, El Paso, Texas. 2003

## IT BEGAN WITH ONATE

I also want to correct some mistaken ideas about El Paso. I included a section on lost treasures in this area in the first book and afterwards was informed by several self-styled amateur treasure hunters that there was absolutely no possibility that lost or hidden treasures existed in El Paso, Texas. The very idea seemed to almost offend them. After all, if there were any treasures hidden in or around El Paso, surely they would have found them long ago. There was no doubt in their minds that one had to travel long distances to find real hidden treasure.

However, I would point out that the Spanish invasion of the North American continent began as one vast treasure hunt and it all started in El Paso. There are those that would have the student of history believe that Don Juan Onate came north into what is now Texas and New Mexico in the year 1598 looking only for land where he and his followers could establish homes. However, the truth is that from the outset, Don Juan Onate had high hopes of being able to find vast deposits of silver[4] and return home a wealthy man.

Juan de Oñate, (1550 – 1626) was an explorer and founder of the first European settlements in the upper Rio Grande valley of New Mexico, son of Cristóbal de Oñate and Catalina de Salazar, was born around 1550, most likely in the frontier settlement of Zacatecas, Mexico. His father was a prominent Zacatecas mine owner and *encomendero*. In his early twenties Oñate was leading campaigns against the unsubdued Chichimec Indians along the turbulent northern frontier around Zacatecas and prospecting for silver. He aided the establishment of missions in the newly conquered territory. He married Isabel de Tolosa Cortés Moctezuma, a descendant of the famous conquistador Hernán Cortés and the Aztec emperor Moctezuma. They had a son and a daughter.

On September 21, 1595, Oñate was awarded a contract by King Philip II of Spain to settle New Mexico. Spreading Catholicism was a primary objective, but many colonists enlisted in hopes of finding a new silver strike. After many delays Oñate began the entrada in early 1598. He forded the Rio Grande at the famous crossing point of El Paso del Norte, which he discovered in May 1598, after making a formal declaration of possession of New Mexico on April 30 of that year. By late May he had made contact with the first of the many pueblos of the northern Rio Grande valley.

In July 1598 he established the headquarters of the New Mexico colony at San Juan pueblo, thus effectively extending the Camino Real by more than 600 miles. It was the longest road in North America for several subsequent centuries. While awaiting the slow-moving main caravan of colonists, Oñate explored the

---

[4] Hernandez, Ph.D., Rick, *Searching for Lost Padre: Eighteenth Century Mining Claims in the Organ Mountains and Greater El Paso del Norte Area*, Password, The El Paso County Historical Society, Volume 46, No.2, El Paso, Texas. Summer 2001.

surrounding area and solidified his position. Construction of the mission at San Francisco and a mission for the Indians of San Juan soon began. Mutiny, desertion, and dissent plagued the new colony when riches were not instantly found. Oñate dealt with these problems with a firm hand. Some of his men explored east beyond Pecos pueblo towards the Texas border in search of buffalo; they probably reached the headwaters of the Canadian River, twenty-five miles northwest of the site of present Amarillo. Oñate visited Acoma pueblos as well as the Hopi and Zuni pueblos far to the west; one party in his group went as far as the San Francisco Mountains in Arizona, finding silver ore and staking claims. Upon Oñate's return to Acoma he put down a revolt that left eleven colonists dead. He severely punished the rebellious Indians.

Prospecting expeditions continued in an attempt to bring prosperity to the colony. The colony was reinforced in late 1600, but hardships, including cold weather and short food supplies, continued. On June 23, 1601, Oñate began an expedition to Quivira in search of wealth and an outlet to the sea. He followed the Canadian River across the Texas Panhandle and near the Oklahoma border headed northeast. Probably in the central part of what is now Kansas, Oñate's expedition arrived at the first of the Quivira villages. The great settlements of Quivira proved to be a disappointment to men who had come looking for easy wealth, however, and they soon turned back. While Oñate was on this expedition, conditions deteriorated in the New Mexico colony because the land was poor, the Indians were troublesome, and there were no silver strikes. The colony was subsequently abandoned except for some of Oñate's most devoted followers. The deserters spread the news of conditions in the colony when they returned to New Spain, and the government soon initiated an inquiry into the situation in New Mexico and Oñate's treatment of the Indians. At the same time Oñate launched his last major expedition, from the Zuni pueblos to the Colorado River and down it to the Gulf of California.

In 1606 King Philip III ordered Oñate to Mexico City until allegations against him could be investigated. Unaware of the order, Oñate resigned his office in 1607 because of the condition of the colony and financial problems. He remained in New Mexico to see the town of Santa Fe established. King Philip III decided to continue supporting the colony. A new governor was appointed, and Oñate was summoned to Mexico City in 1608. In 1613 he finally faced charges of using excessive force during the Acoma rebellion, hanging two Indians, executing mutineers and deserters, and adultery. He was fined, banished from New Mexico permanently, and banished from Mexico City for four years. He spent much of the rest of his life trying to clear his name, with some evident success. Eventually he went to Spain, where the king gave him the position of mining inspector. He died in Spain on or around June 3, 1626[5].

In the broad scheme of things this was certainly a strong possibility that Onate's explorations could have made him a vastly wealthy man as his father had

---

[5] http://www.tsha.utexas.edu/handbook/online.

discovered a major deposit of silver at La Bufa in Zacatecas and been honored by the Spanish Crown for his valuable discovery. Unfortunately, by the time Don Juan Onate became of age, all of the major deposits that had been mined by the Aztecs and the Incas that the Spanish could find were already producing great wealth under the control of others. Therefore, he and others like him turned their eyes to the north.

From the arrival of Onate's expedition until the Pueblo Revolt of 1680, no matter what other activities were being undertaken by the Spanish conquerors, mining for gold and silver were never far from their thoughts. Unfortunately, the fantastic riches of Incan Empire in Peru and the Aztec Empire in Mexico were not duplicated by efforts north of the Rio Grande. What mineral deposits that were found were quickly exhausted.

Spanish adventurers searched for many locations thought to contain vast riches, eagerly following up every Indian legend brought to their attention. There was the mountain known as the Sierra Azul, thought to be a mountain over 200 leagues long made entirely of silver, which certainly fired the imaginations of the explorers. Then there was the Cerro Colorado, which was thought to contain large amounts of mercury, worth a king's ransom and let us not forget the fabled Seven Cities of Gold thought to lie just over the next mountain range. Even though several adventurers claimed to have seen and visited this fabled kingdom of gold, none of the Spanish expeditions ever found it. Thousands died searching for these vast riches thought to lie somewhere in the uncharted lands of the new world.

In fact, the thought of these vast riches believed to lie in New Mexico being in the hands of the ignorant savages after the deadly Pueblo Revolt was one of the primary reasons that led Don Diego de Vargas organized the successful reconquest of New Mexico in 1690. Once Spanish control had been firmly reestablished in New Mexico and the worst offenders suitably punished, the victors immediately returned to looking for some of the many fabled lost or hidden treasures for which New Mexico is famous.

## THERE IS GOLD AND SILVER IN THEM THAR HILLS

Historical records leave little doubt that the early Spanish miners and explorers did find riches in the form of gold and silver in the Organ and Franklin Mountains. There are hundreds of legends about great wealth being hidden as miners scrambled to escape the rampaging Pueblo Indians in 1680. According to the records maintained by the Spanish Government, a number of producing mines were lost or destroyed as a result of the death of those that were working them at the time of the revolt. Doubtless, one of the mines lost as a result of the Pueblo Revolt was the fabled Los Padre Mine thought to be located in the Franklin Mountains above El Paso that still lures treasure hunters even to this day.

In 1751, Valez Cachupin, the Governor of New Mexico ordered those purporting to own land in the El Paso Del Norte area to produce titles for their holdings. Among the many documents produced by land owners to confirm ownership of their land was the registration of a mining claim dated September 2, 1738, the earliest known claim[6] on record. In 1751, five additional mining claims were filed by Juan Jose de Rojas, Juan Antonio Perez Valarde, Bernardo de Miera y Pacheco, Cristolbal Sanchez and Francisco Garcia Carabajal.

Then on January 9, 1774, Francisco Moradillos registered a claim for a mine in the greater El Paso Del Norte area which he called Santo Tomas Cantuariense. Due to problems that arose, Moradillos was delayed in taking possession of his mining claim and, as a result, possession was given to Vicente Bravo. In 1787, Moradillos registered a claim for another mine called Nuestra Senora Santa Ana which was located on the northern side of the Rio Grande near the Franklin or Organ Mountains. The records also maintain references to shipments of gold and silver from these claims, so there does not appear to be much doubt that gold and silver deposits were found close to what is now El Paso. Based on the description of the location of this particular mine, it comes close to being a fit for the legendary Lost Padre Mine that once furnished riches for the Spanish Mission in Juarez.

In addition to gold and silver, it is also common knowledge that there have been tin deposits found in the Franklins, as some of the abandoned tin mines are located very close to Tom Mays Park and can be seen by anyone taking the time and trouble to walk through the canyon. Located within the boundaries of the Franklin Mountains State Park is copper bearing vein mineralization.

Additionally, it is claimed that there was once a producing silver mine located in the southern tip of the Franklin Mountains. This mine was described as being situated at the southern point of the Organ Mountains (the Franklins) about 1500 feet high and two and one half miles from the City of El Paso. It was alleged that this mine was a lode or vein of black chloride of silver, containing sulphurets, the outcroppings being about 40 feet wide. The vein was described as running north and south, dipping to the west at an angle of 45 degrees. The silver lode was found in a bed of old, red, sandstone and the overlying face was igneous, with traces of ion.

In the 1980s, a crew digging a sewer line under Murchison Street in west El Paso encountered a large, previously unknown cavern, which they subsequently covered over to keep the local children from entering. It is thought by many researchers that this cavern may have been the *Nuestra Senora Santa Ana* mine and perhaps, earlier, it was also known as the *Lost Padre Mine*, but thanks to the haste of city workmen to seal up the accidentally discovered entrance, we shall never know.

---

[6] Ibid.

I might also add that there are also stories alleging that this same cavern could once be entered by going through old tunnels running from nearby Southwest General Hospital. I have had several friends who were given to opportunity to tour that old building, assure me that there are indeed old tunnels running from the basement in the general direction of the mysterious cavern. There are also many stories of mysterious tunnels running from the basement of El Paso High School in the general direction of the cavern. Perhaps, this cavern system is much more extensive that anyone has yet believed possible. Only time will tell.

With all of this said, there is no doubt that at least at one time, riches could be taken from the Franklin Mountains. I would have to believe that there is absolutely no reason that the mountains surrounding this city could not once again give forth riches for the lucky finder. In the next chapter, we shall look at some more recent reports of vast wealth for the taking.

# CHAPTER TWO

## MORE INFORMATION ON THE
## LOST TREASURES OF THE EL PASO AREA

In the previous book, I wrote about a number of lost treasures in and around El Paso. Less there be some idea that there are only those few lost or hidden treasures in the El Paso area that I described in *Spirits of the Border: The History and Mystery of El Paso Del Norte*[7], let me add the following stories.

## LOST MINES

There are a large number of treasure stories about lost mines and hidden Spanish gold throughout the southwest United States. Though many of these so called lost mines are the things dreams are made of having come from the dreams of failed treasure seekers, some are as real as can be. Extensive research makes it very clear that one or more of the illusive lost mines are to be found around El Paso.

Though I wrote of the legendary Lost Padre Mine in *Spirits of the Border: The History and Mystery of El Paso Del Norte*[8], many that I have talked to still feel that this particular mine is only a myth. However, there is actually considerable evidence that one or more lost mines do exist in or around the city of El Paso. Records show that a considerable amount of gold and silver was

---

[7] Hudnall, Ken and Connie Wang, The Spirits of the Border: The History and Mystery of Fort Bliss, Texas, Omega Press, El Paso, Texas. 2003.
[8] Ibid

actually mined in the Mountain above El Paso. Confirmation of the existence of these mines can be confirmed though records maintained by no less an authority than the Catholic Church archives in Mexico City[9].

In the 1880s a researcher confirmed in these archives that a very rich gold mine was once operated by the Spanish priests from the mission *Nuestra Senora de Guadalupe* located in Juarez, Mexico. The documents made reference to the mine being located in the Franklin Mountains across the river from the mission. Continued research further confirmed that the priests would periodically send shipments of gold amounting to hundreds of burro loads to the mother church in Mexico City. It was also confirmed in these old records that when the mine was hidden during the Pueblo Revolt that over 250 burro loads of gold were hidden in the shaft before it was closed[10]. These attributes are identical those of the legendary Lost Padre Mine that so many have sought, but only a few have been able to find.

Several searchers for the Lost Padre Mine have discovered old mine shafts in the mountains above El Paso that are filled with the red dirt of the Rio Grande. Many legends of the Lost Padre Mine state that before they abandoned the area to flee to the safety of Mexico City, the Padres of the Nuestra Senora de Guadalupe Mission had their Indian workers haul dirt from the Rio Grande up the mountain to securely seal the mine shaft before abandoning the mine. The finding of shafts filled with this red dirt has excited more than one treasure hunter, certain that he was close to the mother lode. More than one attempt has been made to remove this fill dirt from the discovered mine shafts and reach the treasure. To date no one has been able to succeed in reaching the treasure believed to be hidden deep within the sealed up shaft of the old mine.

It was discovered however, that at one suspected location that was extensively explored, the main mine shaft actually ended in a "T" shaped junction, with two side passages leading away. Both of these passages were securely blocked with tightly packed adobe bricks[11]. There is no question that someone went to a great deal of trouble to hide something deep beneath the Franklin Mountains.

## ANOTHER LOST PADRE MINE

In addition to the better known Lost Padre Mine believed to be located in the Franklin Mountains, there is apparently at least one other mine hidden in the mountains near El Paso. This particular story begins in the year 1791 and

---

[9] Savoy, Carlos, <u>Texas Tales of Lost Mines and Buried Treasure</u>, Republic of Texas Press, Plano, Texas. 2002.
[10] Ibid.
[11] Ibid

involves a Catholic priest by the name of Father LaRue[12], whose assigned flock was located at a hacienda near Chihuahua during the latter years of the Spanish Colonial Period.

Though the Indians and peons under his care were relatively few in number and his area of responsibility a poor one, Father LaRue took his duties as priest very seriously, working to do his best for the many members of his small flock. It was his custom to visit the sick and dying each day in order to give them what comfort that he could. One fateful day, he was summoned to comfort an old soldier who had become quite ill. While sitting with an old dying soldier, the earnest man of the cloth listened while the soldier told him of a rich gold-bearing deposit alleged to be hidden in the mountains north of El Paso del Norte (El Paso, Texas today.)

The soldier explained to LaRue that the wealth he had personally seen in this mine made him sure that it was the actual mother lode that had been searched for by explorers for hundreds of years. This king's ransom in gold could be found by traveling one day north of El Paso until three small peaks could be seen in the distance. When the peaks came into view, according to the old soldier, the journey would turn east across the desert to the mountains. In the first mountain range, there would be found a rock basin containing a spring at the foot of a solitary peak. Upon this mountain was to be found a rich vein of gold.

Shortly after making his confession to the kindly priest, the old soldier died leaving Father LaRue in possession of information that could make him richer than Midas. However, the location of the mine had been made to him as part of the old soldier's confession and what is revealed in the confessional is traditionally kept secret. It is very likely that Father LaRue would never have made use of this information had not the poor Chihuahua settlement for which he was responsible been devastated by drought and famine. Father LaRue sent word to his superiors at the mother church in Mexico City, hoping for assistance for his followers, but none came. Finally, believing he had no choice if anyone was to survive, the Padre called the villagers together asking if they would follow him north to a better climate and more water. They agreed and the party migrated to the north.

**Figure 2: Spanish Conquistador**

After crossing the river at El Paso del Norte, they followed the course of the Rio Grande to the small village of La Mesilla near what is now Las Cruces, New Mexico. North of there, they sighted the three peaks and turned east across

---

[12] Bentley, Mark T., *The Padre Silver Mine*, The El Paso County Historical Society, Volume XXXVI, No. 2, El Paso, Texas, Summer 1991.

the dreaded Jornada del Muerto desert, finally arriving in the San Andreas Mountains.

After a couple of days of exploration, they located a basin in which there was a spring at the base of a solitary peak, just as the old man had said. Settling the new colony at Spirit Springs in what most have long believe is the current Dona Ana County, LaRue sent the men that had followed him on this long journey out to search for the gold he had been told would be near. Just as the dying soldier had promised, on one side of the peak, they located a rich vein in a deep canyon southwest of the springs. They tunneled into the mountain and followed the vein downward. The deeper they went, the richer the ore became. As the dying old soldier has promised, there was a king's ransom in gold, theirs for the taking. The priest assigned dozens of his followers to mine the gold, form it into ingots and stack it along one wall of a natural cavern inside the mountain. For two years LaRue extracted the gold from the mountain, stockpiling it, taking only enough out to trade for what his flock needed to survive.

As LaRue had long dreaded, the absence of his flock was finally noticed and reported to Mexico City. The Army was searching for the missing villagers. Unfortunately, word leaked into Mexico that LaRue had set up his own little empire and he was extracting large quantities of gold. The Church was angry that La Rue had not turned his newly found wealth over to his superiors and the Governor was angry that the King's Fifth[13] was not being paid as required. The Spaniards wasted no time in rounding up an expedition to send north to punish this upstart priest and confiscate the gold.

When a small group of La Rue's followers were in at a trading post near what became known as La Mesilla they learned a Spanish search party was on the horizon. Hurrying back to their hidden camp, they spread the alarm. The nearness of the Spanish naturally party caused great alarm among La Rue's flock. It was one thing for Padre La Rue to leave his post without the permission of church officials in Mexico City, but it was quite another for the group not to deliver the Royal Fifth (or Quinta) of the gold they had found for shipment to Spain. Failure to pay the required one fifth to the government was an offense punishable by death. The Church leaders, of course, felt that he should turn the rich mine and all of the gold over to them so that they could use the wealth to fatten their own coffers as they spread the word of God.

Unwilling to let those that had failed to send help when his people desperately needed it profit from their hard work, Father La Rue immediately set about concealing all traces of the mine, hiding a vast fortune in the shaft before closing it for the last time. Working day and night, knowing the soldiers were drawing ever closer, he had his little group labor to seal the entrance to the mine and erase all trace of its existence. When the soldiers finally arrived in their camp and demanded to know where the gold came from which was used to

---

[13] The King's Fifth referred to the Spanish law that required one fifth of all mineral wealth found to be turned over to the King.

purchase the supplies in La Mesilla, Padre La Rue and his followers refused to answer. Since he was a member of the clergy, Padre LaRue was initially treated with some respect by the Spanish soldiers, when he refused to turn over the secret of the gold mine to the soldiers their greed overrode their fear of God. Father LaRue died under torture, as did many of his followers. The soldiers searched the entire area, but found no clues as to the location of the hidden mine. Finally, they returned to Mexico empty-handed, leaving only the bloody, mutilated bodies of La Rue and his followers to mark the location of the small camp.

Although the historical facts suggest LaRue and his followers were in the Organ Mountains between present day Las Cruces and Alamogordo and believe his mining operation was deep in the San Andres Mountains north of Las Cruces, this many not have been the case. Believers in this version of the story swear that according to legend, north of Las Cruces, in what is now New Mexico was the location where the treasure was concealed[14].

However, there is another version to this story, one that is surprisingly supported by facts. It may come as a chock to many, but both civilian and U.S. Topographical Engineers' maps of the El Paso area in the mid-nineteenth century show a mine called the "Padre's Silver Mine" located at the south end of the Hueco Mountains. Additionally, there is plenty of evidence at the location marked on the map to confirm that a mining operation was conducted at this location long ago[15]. From some of the relics unearthed at this location, it was very clear that the miners were Spanish.

Located on the crest of a red outcropping at the base of the Hueco Mountains are the ruins of what was clearly a stone fort. The old fort has always been there, no one has any idea who built it, but approximately 50 feet down slope from the ruins of the old fort is a mineshaft typical of the type dug by early Spanish miners as well as other traces of a fairly extensive mining operation.

Evidence located at the site dates this mining operation to the period of time between the years 1789 to 1821, roughly the time period that Father LaRue was believed to be tending his flock. So it would appear that the legend of Father LaRue finding gold north of Las Cruces may have been wrong. It is just as possible that Padre LaRue and his flock were in the Hueco Mountains. The primary question left to be answered is where the good Father and his followers hid the large amount of mined gold that they refused to turn over to the Spanish soldiers? According to legend, it would appear that this incredible fortune still awaits some lucky soul who can find the hidden mine shaft.

There are other stories relating to the fabled Lost Padre Mine which differ so much from each other it would seem that they speak of yet another Lost

---

[14] LegendsofAmerica.com
[15] Bentley, Mark T., *The Padre Silver Mine*, The El Paso County Historical Society, Volume XXXVI, No. 2, El Paso, Texas, Summer 1991.

Padre Mine. According to Professor G.A. Feather, formerly an instructor at New Mexico State University in Las Cruces, New Mexico, the Lost Padre Mine of legend was originally found by Yaqui Indians in the year 1734. Legend says that they removed a chuck of silver ore weighing 2,730 pounds[16]. Still another legend holds that some Jesuit fathers found the mine in the middle of the 1700s in the Organ Mountains outside of Las Cruces, New Mexico. Unfortunately, the Jesuits, a fairly military religious order if there ever was one, were chased out of the mountains by the even more fierce Indians who considered the mountain area theirs. The Jesuits hid their mine shaft prior to leaving, concealing within the abandoned shaft, bars of gold and silver as well as some jewelry previously stolen from the Aztecs in Mexico that was too heavy to be carried to the safety of Mexico.

A United States Geological Survey map shows a Padre Mine Canyon in the Hueco Mountains, some thirty miles east of El Paso. Not far from the mouth of the canyon is a U.S.G.S. marker labeled Padre Mine[17]. According to local legend, there was an ancient stone hut located at the mouth of the canyon and nearby is a mine shaft about thirty feet deep. Perhaps this was the actual location of the Lost Padre Mine, or perhaps, the location of a third lost mine in the El Paso area.

In 1927, a man by the name of Tex Clifford visited the tumbled down hut and stated that there was some wood work still in place and that above the door of the hut was an inscription that read "Padre Mine." Local legend has it that this mining operation was undertaken by the Padres of the Mission of San Elizario, however, the records of the San Elizario Church make no mention of any mining operation being conducted by anyone affiliated with the Mission. The mysterious hut was no longer standing in the mid-1950s, though no one knows when or by whom the old hut was torn down. Perhaps hidden in or around the old hut was a treasure just waiting to be found by some lucky person. However, to date no one has discovered any records regarding the mining operation that took place such a short distance from El Paso.

## TREASURE IN THE STOCKYARDS

Though it is little known outside the ranks of a few of the old timers in El Paso, there is, or was, an ancient ruined church located within the old Union Stockyards near the Rio Grande that is rumored to be both haunted and to contain a rich treasure[18]. This ruined church is reputed to be the oldest Catholic Church in El Paso, though its history is somewhat hard to ascertain.

---

[16] Jones, Harriot Howze, El Paso, A Centennial Portrait, El Paso County Historical Society, Superior Printing, El Paso, Texas. 1972.

[17] Ibid.

[18] Spence, Margaret, *El Paso Has haunted Church Where Treasure Is Said To Be Buried*, El Paso Herald, March 7, 1931.

According to research conducted by a former welfare worker turned historian, Cleofas Calleros, in the 1930s, this old church hidden in the railroad yards can be traced back to at least the 1870s. However, the ruined structure was rebuilt from an even older church that was known to have been used during the time when Fort Bliss was located at Concordia. Many of the older generation of El Paso in the 1930s recalled that this early church was called *San Jose de Concordia el Alto*[19], a name that has continued down through the years with each incarnation of the original church. Additionally, they all agreed that it had been standing longer than anyone could remember.

What is known about a church of this name was that in 1854, a chapel and cemetery were built at the Hugh Stephensons' ranch. This huge section of land had been named Concordia by its owner after the town in which he was born. So it was natural for the cemetery that was shortly to be started to also bear the same name.

The chapel construced by Hugh Stephenson was named "San Jose de Concordia el Alto" which seems to be the first time that a church by this name was constructed. It is the ruins of this early church that may stand lonely and neglected in the stockyards.

On February 6, 1856, a pet deer gored Juana Ascarate Stephenson, and she became the first person to be buried in the Concordia Cemetery. Stephenson lost his land after the Civil War, but his son-in-law, Albert H. French, purchased the Concordia property at a federal marshal's sale in 1867. French sold each of the Stephenson's heirs an equal portion of the property for a dollar. By the 1880s, various groups interested in establishing cemeteries were contacting the heirs. The city of El Paso bought its first part of the cemetery in 1882 as a burial ground for paupers.

If the ruins in the stockyard is of this original church as some believe, no one knows how the rumors of ghosts and buried treasure became associated with this ancient structure. Perhaps there is some basis to these stories that has been long forgotten, or perhaps it is the mystery of the church's founding that has prompted the many stories of unsolved mysteries and long hidden wealth. It is known that in frontier days, during times of danger, it was a custom to hide valuables either within the church itself or within the church yard. Whatever the reason for the stories, there is no doubt that many believe them and a few adventurous souls even searched for the hidden treasures.

Treasure seekers have dug great holes beneath the altar and in front of the niche that held that baptistery there is another deep excavation. However, as far as is known, none of these eager treasure hunters have found the gold that they sought. Of course, lack of results does not keep others from searching for the treasure that so many believe was hidden on the Church property. Was there

---

[19] Calleros, Cleofas, *Ruins of One of Oldest Churches in El Paso Are Now Included in Union Stockyards Near Rio Grande*, El Paso World Wide News, June 4, 1932.

treasure hidden in or around this historic old church? Only the dead know for sure!

# CHAPTER THREE

## MORE MYSTERY

### OTHER ILLEGAL ALIENS

In *Spirits of the Border: The History and Mystery of El Paso Del Norte*[20], I wrote extensively about the El Paso area being a hotbed of UFO activity as early as the Great Air Ship Mystery of 1897. After the publication of the first book of this series, the following story came to light that certainly supports my premise that the El Paso region is a UFO hot spot. I had heard about this incident earlier, but only recently did I find a report on the Internet.

On Aug 25, 1974, at 10:07 PM, US Air Defense radar detected an unknown approaching US airspace from the Gulf of Mexico. Originally the object was tracked at 2,200 (2530 mph) knots on a bearing of 325 degrees and at an altitude of 75,000 feet, a course that would intercept US territory about forty miles southwest of Corpus Christi, Texas. After approximately sixty seconds of observation, at a position 155 miles southeast of Corpus Christi, the object simultaneously decelerated to approximately 1700 (1955 mph) knots, turned to a heading of 290 degrees, and began a slow descent. It entered Mexican airspace approximately forty miles south of Brownsville, Texas. Radar tracked it approximately 500 miles to a point near the town of Coyame, in the state of Chihuahua, not far from the US border. There the object suddenly disappeared from the radar screens.

---

[20] Hudnall, Ken and Connie Wang, <u>The Spirits of the Border: The History and Mystery of El Paso Del Norte</u>, Omega Press, El Paso, Texas. 2003.

During the flight over Mexican airspace, the object leveled off at 45,000 feet, then descended to 20,000 feet. The descent was in level steps, not a smooth curve or straight line, and each level was maintained for approximately five minutes.

The object was tracked by two different military radar installations. It would have been within range of Brownsville civilian radar, but it is assumed that no civilian radar detected the object due to a lack of any such reports. The point of disappearance from the radar screens was over a barren and sparsely populated area of Northern Mexico. At first it was assumed that the object had descended below the radar's horizon and a watch was kept for any re-emergence of the object. None occurred.

**Figure 3: Could this sight have greated our earliest ancestors?**

At first it was assumed that the object might be a meteor because of the high speed and descending flight path. But meteors normally travel at higher speeds, and descend in a smooth arc, not in "steps." And meteors do not normally make a thirty-five degree change in course. Shortly after detection an air defense alert was called. However, before any form of interception could be scrambled, the object turned to a course that would not immediately take it over US territory.

The alert was called off within twenty minutes after the object's disappearance from the radar screen.

Fifty-two minutes after the disappearance, civilian radio traffic indicated that a civilian aircraft had gone down in that area. But it was clear that the missing aircraft had departed El Paso International with a destination of Mexico City, and could not, therefore, have been the object tracked over the Gulf of Mexico. It was noted, however, that they both disappeared in the same area and at the same time.

With daylight the next day, Mexican authorities began a search for the missing plane. Approximately 1035 hrs there came a radio report that wreckage from the missing plane had been spotted from the air. Almost immediately came a report of a second plane on the ground a few miles from the first. A few minutes later an additional report stated that the second "plane" was circular shaped and apparently in one piece although damaged. A few minutes after that the Mexican military clamped a radio silence on all search efforts.

The radio interceptions were reported through channels to the CIA. Possibly as many as two additional government agencies also received reports, but such has not been confirmed as of this date. The CIA immediately began forming a recovery team. The speed with which this team and its equipment was assembled suggests that this was either a well-rehearsed exercise or one that had been performed prior to this event.

In the meantime requests were initiated at the highest levels between the United States and Mexican governments that the US recovery team be allowed onto Mexican territory to "assist." These requests were met with professed ignorance and a flat refusal of any cooperation.

By 2100 hrs, 26 Aug 74, the recovery team had assembled and been staged at Fort Bliss. Several helicopters were flown in from some unknown source and assembled in a secured area. These helicopters were painted a neutral sand color and bore no markings. Eye witness indicates that there were three smaller craft, very probably UHl Hueys from the description. There was also a larger helicopter, possibly a Sea Stallion. Personnel from this team remained with their craft and had no contact with other Ft. Bliss personnel.

Satellite and recognizance aircraft overflight that day indicated that both the crashed disk and the civilian aircraft had been removed from the crash sites and loaded on flat bed trucks. Later flights confirmed that the convoy had departed the area heading south.

At that point the CIA had to make a choice, either to allow this unknown aircraft to stay in the hands of the Mexican government, or to launch the recovery team, supplemented by any required military support, to take the craft. There occurred, however, an event that took the choice out of their hands. High altitude overflights indicated that the convoy had stopped before reaching any inhabited areas or major roads. Recon showed no activity, and radio contact between the

Mexican recovery team and its headquarters had ceased. A low altitude, high speed overflight was ordered.

The photos returned by that aircraft showed all trucks and jeeps stopped, some with open doors, and two human bodies laying on the ground beside two vehicles. The decision was immediately made to launch the recovery team but the actual launching was held up for the arrival of additional equipment and two additional personnel. It was not until 1438 hrs that the helicopters departed Ft. Bliss.

The four helicopters followed the boarder down towards Presidio then turned and entered Mexican airspace north of Candelaria. They were over the convoy site at 1653 hrs. All convoy personnel were dead, most within the trucks. Some recovery team members, dressed in bio-protection suits, reconfigured the straps holding the object on the flatbed truck then attached them to a cargo cable from the Sea Stallion. By 1714 hrs the recovered object was on its way to US territory. Before leaving the convoy site, members of the recovery team gathered together the Mexican vehicles and bodies, then destroyed all with high explosives. This included the pieces of the civilian light plane which had been involved in the mid-air collision. At 1746 hrs the Hueys departed.

The Hueys caught up with the Sea Stallion as it reentered US airspace. The recovery team then proceeded to a point in the Davis Mountains, approximately twenty-five miles north east of Valentine. There they landed and waited until 0225 hrs the next morning. At that time they resumed the flight and rendezvoused with a small convoy on a road between Van Horn and Kent. The recovered disk was transferred to a truck large enough to handle it and capable of being sealed totally. Some of the personnel from the Huey's transferred to the convoy.

All helicopters then returned to their original bases for decontamination procedures. The convoy continued non-stop, using back roads and smaller highways, and staying away from cities. The destination of the convoy reportedly was Atlanta, Georgia.

Here the hard evidence thins out. One unconfirmed report says the disk was eventually transferred to Wright-Patterson Air Force Base. Another says that the disk was either transferred after that to another unnamed base, or was taken directly to this unknown base directly from Atlanta.

The best description of the disk was that it was sixteen feet, five inches in diameter, convex on both upper and lower surfaces to the same degree, possessing no visible doors or windows. The thickness was slightly less than five feet. The color was silver, much like polished steel. There were no visible lights nor any propulsion means. There were no markings. There were two areas of the rim that showed damage, one showing an irregular hole approximately twelve inches in diameter with indented material around it. The other damage was described as a "dent" about two feet wide. The weight of the object was estimated as approximately one thousand, five hundred pounds, based on the effect of the weight on the carrying helicopter and those who transferred it to the truck.

There was no indication in the documentation available as to whether anything was visible in the "hole."

It seems likely that the damage with the hole was caused by the collision with the civilian aircraft. That collision occurred while the object was traveling approximately 1700 knots (1955 mph). Even ignoring the speed of the civilian aircraft, the impact would have been considerable at that speed. This is in agreement with the description of the

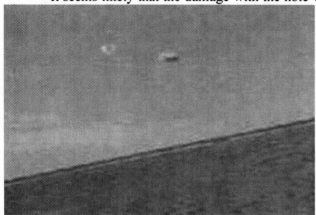

**Figure 4: One of the mysterious metallic disks seen in the sky.**

civilian aircraft as being "almost totally destroyed." What was being taken from the crash site was pieces of the civilian aircraft.

The second damage may have resulted when the object impacted with the ground. The speed in that case should have been considerably less than that of the first impact.

No mention is made of the occupants of the civilian aircraft. It is not known if any body or bodies were recovered. Considering the destruction of the civilian light aircraft in mid-air, bodies may well not have come down near the larger pieces.

Unfortunately what caused the deaths of the Mexican recovery team is not known. Speculation ranges from a chemical released from the disk as a result of the damage, to a microbiological agent. There are no indications of death or illness by any of the recovery team. It would not have been illogical for the recovery team to have taken one of the bodies back with them for analysis. But there is no indication of that having happen. Perhaps they did not have adequate means of transporting what might have been a biologically contaminated body.

Inquires to the FAA reveal no documents concerning the civilian aircraft crash, probably because it did not involve a US aircraft[21]. However, the mere fact that there is no written report on file with the FAA does not keep the incident from being real.

---

[21] Source: www.ufobbs.com/txt4/3263.ufo ; http://www.about.com; Vince Johnson, alt.paranet.ufo.deneb

## WERE THE ANCIENT INCANS TEXANS?

**Figure 5: Hueco Tanks Today.**

In addition to the mysterious lights in the sky that seem to have been part of El Paso for centuries, there is another mystery about this area that has puzzled men for decades.

There is no question that early man lived around what we now know as Hueco Tanks, however, no one is really sure how long ago the first settlement was established in this area. Representatives of the prestigious Smithsonian Institute have gone on record as stating that the earliest settlers in this are were Pueblo Indians who they believed lived here long before the Spanish arrived in their search for riches[22].

In fact, as unlikely as it may appear, there is evidence that the ancient Incan civilization that ruled what is now Peru may well have originated in the area around Hueco Tanks[23]. According to an article found in the El Paso Times, important data linking prehistoric civilizations of the American Southwest with the predominant ancient culture in Peru are to be found as a result of investigations conducted by Dr. John Winthrop Sargeant, of the El Paso Archeological Society in conjunction with Dr. W.H.K. Staver of the British Museum.

---

[22] Author Unknown, *Scientists Think Cave Indians Were Pueblo*, El Paso Post, September 15, 1927.

[23] Author Unknown, *Evidences Found At Hueco Tanks That Ancient Incan Civilization Started Here*, El Paso Times, February 6, 1928.

Identical pictographs and petrographs have been found in both ruins from the Incan civilization and at Hueco Tanks and other areas used by primitive races. One example is the symbols found on the scepter of the Incan ruler. Identical symbols are found to have been used by the rulers of some of the very early primitive races that settled in this area. Even fringed headbands such as were worn by the Inca royalty have been found in the El Paso area by relic hunters around Hueco Tanks.

Hieroglyphics have been found on rocks and ancient pottery that have a significant bearing on the history of successive invasions of South America by nations from the north. Surprisingly many of the symbols were found to be identical to symbols used by both Incan and pre-Incan peoples known to have inhabited the area claimed by the Incan Empire.

Dr. Sargeant was quoted as saying that all of the traditions and evidence uncovered in his investigations around Hueco Tanks in tracing the course of civilization in South America points to colonization and invasion of the southern regions from North America. He also said that proof can be given that this invasion from the north was so long ago that civilization was already old in Peru when that of ancient Egypt was young. One after another, ruling dynasties in Peru rose to great heights only to fall into decay. This means that the destruction of the Incan Empire by the Spanish was only one of many such disruptions.

He also made mention of one group of invaders who landed at Lambeyque, Peru who brought with them a large emerald shaped like a parrot that they worshipped. They called their emerald god, the "Great God Chott." As a result of wars of conquest, the worshipers of the emerald god conquered large areas, before they, too, fell into the black hole of history. No one knows what happed to these early little invaders of Peru or their "Great God Chott." Perhaps buried in some long forgotten deserted city in the jungles of Peru is a great emerald shaped like a parrot.

Dr. Sargeant also discussed an intricate road system that had been ignored by many of his fellow researchers. He felt that the very existence of this road proved that there had been intercourse between the races to the south and those in the northern areas of the Americas. According to Dr. Sargeant, he had traced two roads, separated by a break of 65 miles, that he believed had at one time been joined as part of one road system. The road began in Tucaman, Argentina, went through Bolivia, Peru, Colombia and into the country of Panama. This unusual road system, after the 65 mile break, continues through the country of Panama, into Costa Rica, Nicaragua, Honduras, Guatemala, ending in the Uxmal country of southern Mexico. During his research and physical investigation of this unusual ancient roadway, he found the same hieroglyphs, pictographs and bas reliefs all along the way showing that there was undoubtedly a heretofore unknown extensive civilization stretching for an unbelievably long distance.

This discussion of such an extensive road system also raises the question of why such a complex road system was built when established science has long maintained that even as advanced a civilization as that of Incas in Peru had never made use of the wheel in their transportation system. Even with such a sophisticated road system linking the ends of their empire, the ancient Peruvians were too primitive to have developed the wheel. Of course, these same scientists are not able to explain why ancient Peruvian children played with wheeled toys very similar to those of modern children.

## WHO INFLUENCED WHO?

Dr. John Sergeant is not the only one who finds pictographs and drawings similar or identical to those at Hueco Tanks in other parts of the world. The extensive pictographs at Hueco Tanks tell an amazing story of a number of early peoples.

Hundreds of years ago, probably during the time of the Roman Empire, there was a smallpox epidemic among the basket weaver people who lived in the area of Hueco Tanks[24]. We know this because an unknown early writer painted a picture of a spotted human on a rock near Hueco Tanks. After all, a picture is worth a thousand words and unless there were leopard spotted humans eons ago, this is a very good representation of someone with smallpox. Other records so that this epidemic was so severe that the elders feared extinction of the tribe, so this permanent record was prepared to tell any survivors what had happened.

It is also interesting to note that many of the symbols used by these early story tellers were very similar to those used by the early Egyptians. The early Egyptian hieroglyphics used animals to indicate directions and both the unknown writers who lived at Hueco Tanks and the early Egyptian priests used the symbol of the cat to indicate the direction of west. With such amazing similarities in what passed for a written language, could it be that the people that we call the American Indian actually originally came from Egypt and not over the mythical land bridge to Siberia or vice versa[25]? Whatever may be the real answer, the evidence discovered to date is certainly startling in its implications.

It is also interesting to note that even though mainstream science adamantly believes that the American Indian came to the North American Continent across a land bridge from Siberia thousands of years ago, many of the tribes have their own legends that contradict the Ivory Tower scientists. Several tribes maintain that their ancestors came to this continent in large ships from a land to the east. Unfortunately, giving in to peer pressure, most researchers

---

[24] Author Unknown, *Hueco Tanks Pictographs Tell Graphic Stories of Early Days*, El Paso Times, November 24, 1930.
[25] Author Unknown, *Pictograph Discovery Stirs E.P. Scientists*, El Paso Times, December 23, 1930.

ignore such native American legends, assigning them to the scrap heap of "Myth and legend."

There have also been many unexplainable items found at archeological excavations that do not fit in with established scientific theories. Rather than write about them or place them on display in museums, these are the items that fill the storerooms of museums instead of being on display. After all, the scientific establishment would not want to "confuse" the paying public nor have anyone's pet theory shot down in flames.

## EVEN THE AFRICANS CAME BEFORE COLUMBUS

It is becoming more and more clear that our accepted history of the discovery of the New World may well be totally incorrect. It is generally accepted that Columbus did not discover the New World as was taught in our schools for generations. Ancient records show that the Phoenicians made regular voyages to what is now North America. The unfortunate part of this is that each new discovery of early contact between the old world and the new brings new screams of hoax and fabrication from the accepted mainstream historians.

In 1982, a treasure hunter in southern Illinois named Russell E. Burrows found a hidden cave containing gold sarcophagi, statues, gold medallions and weapons. There were also hundreds of stones inscribed with various symbols and letters as well as the profiles of Roman soldiers, ancient Jews, early Christians and West Africans[26].

The established history of these items found in the hidden cave show the involvement of Cleopatra Selene, daughter of Cleopatra, and her husband King Juba II, the rulers of the semi independent Roman province of Mauretania. King Juba II revolted against Roman rule when his son Ptolemy was executed by Roman Emperor Caligula. In the ensuing warfare, the Roman legions eventually crushed the revolt, but King Juba II and his people built a fleet and with the help of native West Africans, set sail for the one safe haven known to them. This safe haven was North America, where they landed some 15 centuries before tardy Columbus.

It is my belief that our "established" history is full of errors and mistakes, supported only by those with the most to use by the truth coming to light. Early man was clearly not as primitive as established science would have us believe.

---

[26] Joseph, Frank, The Lost Treasure of King Juba: The Evidence of Africans in America Before Columbus, Bear and Company, Rochester, Vermont. 2003.

# PART II

# HERE THERE BE MONSTERS!

# CHAPTER FOUR

# WHEN MONSTERS ROAMED THE EARTH

In the first volume of *Spirits of the Border*[27], I wrote about a monster that legend maintained lived in the Franklin Mountains. Naturally, many readers laughed at the very idea that anyone thought that a monster might roam the mountains around this city.

However, on the other hand, since the original publications of the first book in this series, I have had a number of people approach me not only to confirm the existence of the creature I originally wrote about but to tell me about other mystery animals that seem to like to call El Paso home.

## THE MYSTERYIOUS CHUPACABRA

I was at a book signing when someone approached me and gave me a folded piece of paper. This individual had read he story I had written about the humanoid lizard man alleged to be living in the Franklins and wanted me to know about another monster thought to make El Paso his home. Inside this mysterious missive was the following story about another fabled monster of this region that seems to be more real that we have previously believed.

Stories about monsters and mysterious creatures roaming the nights have long been assigned to the category of myth and legend. However, there is a body of evidence that supports the existence of the creatures only whispered about at night as humans gathered around the safety of the hearth. Only a fool chanced the darkness, as who knew what might be lurking in the shadows.

## EL CHUPACABRA

---

[27] Hudnall, Ken and Connie Wang, *Spirits of the Border: The History and Mystery of El Paso Del Norte*, Omega Press, El Paso, Texas. 2003.

**Figure 6: This is alleged to be a dead Chupacabra.**

If the truth be known, I have heard about the mysterious El Chupacabra since first moving to El Paso. The name El Chupacabra actually means "the goat sucker" in Spanish, so named because of the way it allegedly sucked all the blood from Puerto Rican goats. The creature called El Chupacabra has been leaving fear in its tracks for many years now, but was always thought to be safely contained on the island of Puerto Rico..

First spotted in Puerto Rico in 1994, the Chupacabra has since migrated off the island and has recently been spotted in many locations in the jungles of South America as well as the wilder, more unsettled areas of the United States. Although it was originally named because of its choice of goat-blood as a meal, the Chupacabra has reportedly attacked and devoured the blood of a wide variety of animals including dogs and sheep. As far as we know, there have yet to be any human fatalities, but who is to know if the last sight that lonely amperes and herders has seen are the glowing eyes of the Chupacabra as it closes in for the kill.

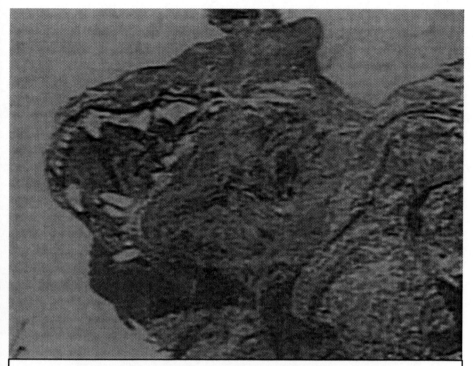

**Figure 7: Imagine those sharp teeth sinking into your flesh.**

Due to the distinct technique the strange animal has of killing its prey, it is very easy to tell if the Chupacabra was involved in an animal's death. Animals that have fallen victim to this mysterious creature are always found with puncture wounds in their neck and most of their blood removed. Often, the victim's vital organs have disappeared as well even though the only wound is a small hole in the animal's neck. Reports of laser-like cuts on the victim's ears are also common. Although some people say they have seen the Chupacabra's tracks, in many cases there are absolutely no signs of blood or tracks around the dead animals.

Research into the mysterious Chupacabra reveals that it is unknown to science even though it has long been systemically killing animals in places like Puerto Rico and Mexico. The creature's name originated with the discovery of some dead goats in Puerto Rico with puncture wounds in their necks and their blood allegedly drained from their bodies. These mysterious deaths are not rare, as according to UFO Magazine (March/April 1996) there have been more than 2,000 reported cases of animal mutilations in Puerto Rico in the last two years attributed to the mysterious creature known as the Chupacabra.

Puerto Rican authorities have long maintained that the unusual animal deaths are due to attacks from groups of stray dogs or other exotic animals, such as the panther, illegally introduced into the country sometime in the island's past. The director of Puerto Rico's Department of Agriculture Veterinary Services Division, Hector Garcia, has stated that there is nothing unusual or extraordinary about the cases they've observed. One veterinarian said "it could be a human being who belongs to a religious sect, even another animal. It could also be someone who wants to make fun out of the Puerto Rican people."

It should be noted that similar explanations were given by "local authorities" regarding killings by the African Great Ape. Until finally photographed in the early 20th century, the great ape was a creature of myth, its activities explained away as being the result of over active imaginations on the pat of the witnesses. In spite of claims to the contrary, science has not yet identified every creature that walks the face of the earth.

Like other creatures in the cryptozoologist's barnyard, the Chupacabra has been variously described. Some witnesses have claimed to have seen a small half-alien, half-dinosaur tailless vampire with quills running down its back; others have seen a panther like creature with a long snake-like tongue; still others have seen a hopping animal that leaves a trail of sulfuric stench. Some think it may be a type of dinosaur heretofore unknown to science. Some are convinced that the wounds on animals whose deaths have been attributed to the Chupacabra indicate an alien presence. However, they do not attribute the "mutilations" to the aliens themselves, but to one of their pets or experiments gone awry. Such creatures are known as Anomalous Biological Entities [ABEs] in UFO circles.

Those who think the Chupacabra is an ABE also believe that there is a massive government and mass media conspiracy to keep the truth hidden from the people, probably to prevent panic. This view is maintained despite the fact that the President of the Puerto Rico House of Representatives Agricultural Commission, Mr. Juan E. [Kike] Lopez, has introduced a resolution asking for an official investigation to clarify the situation. The television show Inside Edition sent a crew to Puerto Rico to investigate the ABE story. According to all accounts, rather than conducting a serious investigation into the issue, these fearless television reporters allegedly ridiculed the Mayor of Canavanas, a witness to the Chupacabra, and basically made fun of the whole idea. However, in spite of the ridicule heaped onto the subject and the witnesses by these intrepid reporters, there have been and continue to be numerous published stories and reports regarding the Chupacabra.

Jorge Martin, a Puerto Rican journalist, reports that it has been brought to his attention that the U.S. and Puerto Rican governments have captured two of the creatures. Perhaps there will soon be a film on the ABE autopsy to rival the discredited alien autopsy film. Martin cautions us not to exclude other reasonable possibilities.

Martin theorizes that the ABEs can also be the product of highly sophisticated genetic manipulations by human agencies. A Chinese-Russian scientist by the name of Dr. Tsian Kanchen, has produced genetic manipulations which have created new species of electronically-crossed plant and animal organisms. Kanchen developed an electronic system whereby he can pick up the bioenergetic field produced by the DNA of living organisms and transfer it electronically to other living organisms. By these means he has created incredible new breeds of ducks/chickens, with physical characteristics of both species; goats/rabbits, and new breeds of plants such as corn/wheat, peanut/sunflower seeds and cucumber/watermelons. These are produced by linking the genetic data of different living organisms contained in their bioenergetic fields by means of ultra-high frequencies biological linking. If the Russians have created this technology, then without doubt the United States and other powers have done so as well. Therefore, it is quite possible that the "Chupacabras" or ABEs could have been developed by humans.

Martin goes on to report that a chupacabra has been killed and blood tests have been done on the creature. The genetic analysis so far has revealed that the blood is in no way compatible with human blood nor with any animal species known to science. The traces ratio of magnesium, phosphorous, calcium and potassium are incompatible with those of normal human blood, they are much too high. The albumen/glouline [RG ratio] was also incompatible. The ratios found do not allow the results of the analysis to be compatible with those of any known animal species.

According to Martin, at present, we can't place the sample with any earthly organism. Therefore it could well be the product of a highly sophisticated genetic manipulation, an organism alien to our own environment or perhaps extraterrestrial. On the other hand, he cautions, the sightings may not be all that accurate, the "mutilations" not all that strange, and the evidence for these bodies, autopsies and blood tests remains little more than speculation[28].

## EL CHUPACABRA MOVES CLOSER

The following news story was released by writer Bucky Mahon.

*Goatsucker Sighted, Details to Follow - Strange beast plunders Puerto Rico, Florida, Mexico. Livestock drained of blood, entrails. Citizens ignore authorities' appeal for calm*

By Bucky McMahon

CANØVANAS, PUERTO RICO--An unwelcome anniversary is being celebrated here, one that elicits not joy from the citizens of this and neighboring towns, but anxiety. It was a year ago this month that the residents of Guaynabo, a suburb of San Juan, awoke to a troubling scene: Strewn about in the yards of several homes were the still bodies of two rabbits, two guinea fowls, and a dozen chickens.

---

[28] http://www.skepdic.com

Their necks were neatly perforated by double-fang bites, and their corpses had been drained of blood.

**Figure 8: This is said to be a Mayan carving showing a man fighting a Chupacabra.**

Two days later, in Canüvanas, a small city of 37,000 people located 30 miles east of San Juan, Michael Negron, 25, discovered an agile, erect, two-legged creature hopping animatedly in the dirt outside his house. "It was about three or four feet tall, with skin like that of a dinosaur," he said. "It had eyes the size of hens' eggs, long fangs, and multicolored spikes down its head and back."

These two incidents, the first in a pattern of unusual events that have swept across Puerto Rico and much of the rest of the Western Hemisphere over the last 12 months, seemed to warrant further investigation. A few days spent not long ago questioning the citizenry of this rainforest hamlet produced the following details.

The creature seen by Mr. Negron did not display friendly behavior. The morning after the sighting, Mr. Negron's brother, Angel, 27, observed the same beast crouched over the family goat, Suerte. Attempts by Mr. Negron to roust the mysterious creature succeeded, and it retreated hastily into the jungle.

Mr. Negron then turned his attentions to Suerte, lying dead in the yard. The goat had been neatly slit open and disemboweled, its warm viscera glistening in the morning sun. Gazing upon the scene, Mr. Negron later admitted to being struck by the surgical care that had been exercised upon his goat. It was his opinion that the unfamiliar predator had been browsing expertly through the goat's entrails, looking for something.

In the months following these encounters, other sightings were reported in the vicinity of Canüvanas, a densely populated city of ramshackle shacks and pastel cement homes perched on steep, lush hillsides. At least 15 people witnessed the creature. One Canüvanas townsperson found his cow lying dead in a field with two punctures in its neck. Another man, who maintained a small chicken aviary on the roof of his home--guarded by the family dog, Too--found the aviary plundered and the fowl dead. Later, the dog was located behind the house, trembling "in a state of fear," according to the farmer.

On another occasion, the creature paused on the sidewalk outside the home of Madelyne Tolentino, studying her as she hung her laundry out to dry. Mrs. Tolentino, 31, joined her husband and a neighbor in a hurried attempt to tackle the animal--which she described as both alien-looking and kangaroolike, with powerful hind legs and a strong sulfurous odor--but the beast managed to escape.

Disturbed by these developments, residents asked Canüvanas mayor Josè Soto Rivera to mount a campaign against the animal, which had acquired the name el chupacabras, the goatsucker. Mr. Soto, 52, agreed. "Whatever it is, this creature is highly intelligent," he later explained to the viewing audience of Cristina!, a Spanish-language talk show taped in Miami. "Today it is attacking animals, but tomorrow it may attack people."

## Midnight Jungle Searches

Given Mr. Soto's personal involvement with the goatsucker, his perspective seems necessary when examining how a community is affected by the invasion of a vampiric, possibly otherworldly predator. Happily, Mr. Soto agreed to sit for a lengthy interview, reclining in a leather chair at his mayoral headquarters, which occupies a prominent location on the town's shaded square.

Known locally as Chemo, a nickname from his days as a standout boxer, Mr. Soto is a quiet, ruggedly handsome man with a thin, dapper mustache. Before becoming mayor, he also pursued careers as a soldier, a mailman, and a police detective.

Mr. Soto said that on October 29, the Sunday before Halloween, he led an evening expedition of 200 Civil Defense employees and other volunteers into the dense jungle surrounding Canúvanas. They dressed in camouflage and armed themselves with torches, nets, spearguns, pistols, and other weapons. Seeking to capture a live goatsucker, they erected large, metal traps, baiting them with goats and small cattle.

"We're close," Mr. Soto recalled saying, referring to his prey. "I can smell him."

Unfortunately, the goatsucker eluded the posse that evening, and it continued to do so on subsequent weekly hunts. "We've never seen him," Mr. Soto acknowledged, speaking between occasional interruptions from his cellular phone. "We can't catch him or beat him."

## Rabbits Slain on Long Island

But even as Mr. Soto redoubled his efforts, the goatsucker's range grew, on a northwesterly track, with a flurry of sightings in south Florida, Texas, California, Mexico, Costa Rica, and the Dominican Republic. Reports detailing the goatsucker's movements arrived daily. Fears of imminent human casualties-- the driving force behind Mr. Soto's campaigns against the creature--were realized on April 15 of this year, with the first goatsucker assault on a human. Juana Tizoc, 21, received multiple bites and lacerations after being attacked by a goatsucker while strolling the fields near her family's farm in the town of Alfonso Calderon, in northern Sinaloa, Mexico. Ms. Tizoc described being set upon by the creature after it descended from the sky on "weblike" appendages--a detail confirming the hypothesis that several species of the creature exist, both winged and nonwinged.

On May 10, a rooster fell victim in Mendota, California, and the Fresno County Department of Agriculture subsequently logged ten complaints of goatsucker activity, prompting worried parents to cancel their children's prom outings. According to the St. Petersburg Times, 69 animals were attacked and killed on May 14 in the Miami neighborhood known as Sweetwater. The victims included geese, goats, chickens, and ducks. By May 17, half of Mexico's 32 states had registered attacks involving the creature.

These escalating reports led some communities in the United States to make light of the situation, an all too common reaction to unexplained phenomena. At the annual Puerto Rico Day festival in New York City, scores of paraders fashioned goatsucker costumes in an attempt to find levity in the tragedies befalling their homeland. On May 19, several pranksters in Cambridge, Massachusetts, claimed to have observed the creature, a sighting that was later determined to be specious. "I knew it was headed our way," Cambridge Chamber of Commerce staff member Alison Dowd later mused in the Boston Herald. "But I had no idea it was already here."

And yet that same week, out on Long Island, New York, an actual goatsucker struck the Bayshore home of Miguel Lopez, 42, dispatching a dozen chickens and seven rabbits with its classic double-fanged bite.

In the fearful months since the attack on Mr. Lopez's animals--and continuing up to and presumably after Outside's press date--goatsuckers have drained, killed, and mutilated hundreds of domestic livestock throughout the hemisphere, and, operating in increasingly brazen fashion, have effected scores of thus far nonlethal attacks on humans.

## DNA Results Inconclusive

Seekers of the goatsucker typically turn to Mr. Soto for assistance and advice. recently he entertained a group of 13 members of beyond boundaries, a UFO phenomena research group led by Jorge Marten, publisher of the periodical Evidencia Ovni. Mr. Soto introduced the visiting scholars to one of his constituents, a woman who had located a goatsucker nesting site. The woman had earlier brought samples of the creature's "oddly shaped" dung and hair--with minute traces of goatsucker flesh attached--to the mayor, who promptly sent them for DNA testing. (the results proved inconclusive).

Despite this laboratory setback, Mr. Soto perseveres, methodically stalking his prey using all techniques available to him. He maintains a thick file devoted to his adversary, with depositions from witnesses and experts, photos of the dead livestock and of the baited traps, and his own notes on the case.

The victims on Mr. Soto's conscience are many--some 200 innocent animals, several of which he was personally acquainted with, including horses, cattle, sheep, rabbits, peacocks, parakeets, a Doberman pinscher, and a Rottweiler.

Mr. Soto notes that some theorists have speculated that the creature may be the product of a gene-splicing lab, the abnormal result of industrial pollution, or part of a Central Intelligence Agency plan to destabilize the region.

Mr. Soto himself believes that the goatsucker is extraterrestrial, drawn to Puerto Rico by the Arecibo Observatory, the world's largest radio telescope, which nightly receives data from the planets beyond. "In my thoughts I know this is something from another world," he said.

Recently, the mayor shared his thoughts with an American television program, *Unsolved Mysteries*, and its host, Hollywood actor Robert Stack.

Eyewitness observations, the mayor noted, have provided a profile of the creature that is highly detailed: a cock's crest atop a simian head; large, red eyes; a long, lipless mouth with a flickering reptilian tongue; small, attenuated arms that are webbed for flight and that terminate in three curved claws; and dorsal spines of iridescent beauty that are capable of changing colors, depending on the goatsucker's prevailing mood.

At the mayor's request, Dr. Carlo Soto (no relation) performed autopsies on the dead livestock, and his report tells of deep, precisely inflicted puncture wounds "inconsistent" with any known animal.

The goatsucker apparently has highly specialized teeth of the length and diameter of a common drinking straw, with the same efficient liquid-sucking qualities.

Dr. Soto observed that the goatsucker's victims show an odd resistance to rigor mortis, and what little blood remains at the crime scenes resists the ordinary tendency to coagulate, thus remaining eminently drinkable.

## Observed at Close Range

Ismael Aquayo, Canüvanas's Chief of Civil Defense, is a slight-framed, bespectacled public servant who now spends most of his working days pursuing the creature. On a recent muggy afternoon, he agreed to lead this reporter on a round of goatsucker-related investigations. Mr. Aquayo climbed into one of his department's large utility trucks and set out for the fern-shrouded rainforest.

Known locally as El Yunque, the rainforest is the last remaining expanse of wilderness in this densely populated commonwealth of four million people. Among the practitioners of the island's many Afro-Caribbean religions, such as Santeria and Obeah, El Yunque remains a place of mystical power. Not infrequently, foresters discover small altars alongside the rivers, speckled with blood and ceremonial wax. Sacrificed chickens, their throats slit, can be seen floating down the forest's many streams, surprising tourists and picnickers from the city of San Juan.

Arriving at Campo Rico, a barrio of 3,000 people, Mr. Aquayo turned onto a side street and parked beside a tin-roofed garage, where he spoke for a moment with Miguel Tolentino, 35, an automobile mechanic and the husband of Madelyne Tolentino, the woman who spied the creature while hanging out her laundry.

Early on the morning in question, Mr. Tolentino had just begun repairs on a truck when, opening the hood, he flushed a goatsucker from its resting place beneath the vehicle. He saw it only for a second before it leaped away. Mr. Tolentino described the goatsucker as bounding, with little apparent effort, high over the trees--a leap that was later measured at approximately 40 feet.

Later that same day the goatsucker returned to the Tolentinos' neighborhood. It paced down the street, walking upright like a man, but slightly crouched. It stopped to stare at Madelyne Tolentino with its ovoid eyes. Mrs. Tolentino boldly stared back. Because this remains the longest close-proximity sighting of the goatsucker yet recorded, proper import should be given Mrs. Tolentino's observation.

The goatsucker appeared to be about three feet tall. It was brownish to black in color and seemed to have no hair on its abdomen. Its eyes were large and jellylike, with no apparent pupils.

It was at this point that the Tolentinos rushed the animal and the goatsucker bounded away.

Mrs. Tolentino saw the goatsucker one more time--a rare second sighting--on January 2 of this year. She was driving home and smelled the distinct, sulfurous indicator of goatsucker activity. Then, gazing up into the sky above her, Mrs. Tolentino spotted it--the goatsucker, floating in the air, rising and dipping almost gracefully. "Like a butterfly," she said.

**No End in Sight**

The Tolentinos' encounter is only one of the many entries in Mr. Soto's growing dossier on the goatsucker, which on the morning after this reporter's excursion with Mr. Aquayo, was laid open across the mayor's large polished desk. Sightings and tales of the goatsucker increase daily with--to Mr. Soto's visible discomfort--no end in sight.

"As a farming community," he said, "we can't relax knowing that this goatsucker is out there killing our animals. He could take out a child, a woman, a defenseless man."

Mr. Soto is up for reelection this November and plans to frame the upcoming campaign around an "anti-chupacabras ticket." In the meantime, he still hopes to capture a live specimen.

"Something very strange is going on in our town," he said at the close of the interview, "and the world simply does not want to accept it." Mr. Soto then laid his hand on the goatsucker file. "This thing is not a joke."

*Bucky McMahon is chief of this magazine's San Juan bureau*[29].

## CHUPACABRAS IN EL PASO

The following article was found on the Internet, published by a researcher who was tracking this mysterious creature. I reproduce it here four our edifications.

A recent report of sheep taken from a Midland County ranch makes me wonder if the ever-popular Chupacabra has made its way to West Texas.

For some of you who are unfamiliar with the legendary Chupacabra (pronounced chew-pah-khab-rah), it's a scaled, winged and fanged alien/beast that reportedly sucks the blood out of livestock.

Its name translated in English means, "the goat sucker." Its origin has been traced to South American farmers, who blame the creature for sabotaging their livestock. The lore made its way to Puerto Rico, Florida and even the Rio Grande Valley.

---

[29] http://www.outside.away.com/magazine

I figured it'd only be a matter of time before this nuisance followed me to Midland.

When I was in South Texas, the Chupacabra would make his way into the police reports at least once a month. The scenario always involved a rural farmer who'd call authorities after finding dead animals on his property - all of which sustained two puncture wounds to the neck.

Then, the complainant would come to our newspaper with Polaroid pictures of his decaying animals. My assignment would come soon after: I'd have to ask a serious lawman to explain how the alien killed an entire herd of cows and if charges were to be filed. I could just see the docket: Case No. 0001, the People vs. Goat sucker; charges: criminal mischief, cruelty to animals and unlawful flight to avoid prosecution.

Instead of making him laugh, the officer would throw me out of his office, telling me that I wasted his time with such absurd tales.

Here in the basin, the closest thing I've seen to the goat sucker is a news reporter who did a live shot from a pet cemetery in west Odessa. At prime time, this person poked at bloated animal carcasses with a branch , warning citizens not to make other people's property a final resting place for Barky or Fluffy.

However, I doubt the beast is lingering in this neck of the woods (or desert for that matter). The creature's not as dumb as we think he is. Obviously, he likes to roam the tropical climate, but probably made a detour to the southern United States to stir up a little scandal - or get a prescription for Viagra.

Or, El Niño's wrath could have scared the little guy over here. The impenetrable haze wafting from zillion-acre fires in Mexico could have forced Chupacabra to seek refuge in Midland, where he makes his home near a prairie dog town or at Wadley-Barron Park.

Either way, he won't be here long. There's way too little livestock for him to survive here. I'd imagine that he could move to Hawaii or the Virgin Islands, but maybe he hasn't acquired enough frequent flyer miles to make that voyage.

If I could meet him, I'd chide him for eluding me for appearances on the "X-Files," National Enquirer and "Unsolved Mysteries." Heck, I even looked for him at the Chupacabras Festival in Zapata, Texas, but all I found there was a 25-foot papier mâché replica.

At this point, I'd be happy if he could bring a little vigor into my life again, but I'm not counting on it. The smoky haze has probably chased him away to greener pastures, where there probably lives more goats fearing his arrival[30].

---

[30](Source: Midland Reporter-Telegram (Texas) / by Rick Lopez - June 13 1998)

## ZOMBIE DOGS IN TEXAS?

The following story supports the premise that there are creatures running around in Texas that are a mystery to everyone. Could this be one of the dreaded Chupacabras?

"Zombie Dog" Puzzles Experts
By Lynn Winthrop

Associated Press 10/12/2004

LUFKIN, Texas -- Local animal experts are having a hard time identifying a strange looking animal killed in Angelina County on Friday -- an animal that looks eerily similar to the as yet unidentified "Elmendorf Beast" killed near San Antonio earlier this year.

"What is that?" are the first words out of anyone's mouth when shown photos of the animal, according to Stacy Womack. Womack -- who has more than 20 years experience working at Ellen Trout Zoo and for a local veterinarian -- said she's seen and handled a lot of different animals, but that she's never seen anything like this one.

"It's not a dog," she said. "I'd bet my lottery ticket on that."

The animal's blue-grey skin is almost hairless and appears to be covered with mange. A closer look at the animal's jaw line reveals a serious overbite and four huge canine teeth, and a long, rat-like tail curls behind the animal's emaciated frame.

**Figure 9: A dead Zombie Dog.**

The animal was shot and killed shortly before noon Friday after crawling under her mother's house in Pollok. Womack said large dogs in the yard "went nuts" and alerted the family, but would only whine and wouldn't go under the house with the animal. Her brother shot the animal, tied a rope around it and dragged it out from under the house for a closer look, she said. Womack was called to take a photograph of the animal, and possibly help identify it, as well. A live animal, just like the one in the picture, darted across the road in front of her car while she was driving to the scene. When she arrived with her camera and expertise in tow, Womack said she almost couldn't believe what she was looking at.

"It was so necrotic, its tissue was just rotted," Womack said. "It had no hair, a severe overbite and its claws were entirely too long for a dog."

She said the animal's front legs were much smaller than it's hind legs, and that despite it's overall ghoulish appearance, it's extremely long canine teeth were in excellent condition. Also, despite having been shot, there was virtually no blood seeping from the animal's carcass. The animal's ear also "broke like a cookie" when it's head was held up for a photograph, she said

"It's body looked like something that has been dead for a month or so," Womack said. "Like I said, I've worked in the veterinary field for more than 20 years and I've never seen anything that bad."

The animal was male and weighed between 15 and 20 pounds, she said. The identical animal that sprinted across the road ran with it's head down and it's tail between it's legs, according to Womack, but wasn't tall enough to be a coyote or a wolf. She said the live animal is probably the dead one's mate.

"I would just like to see somebody go out there and try to trap the other one," Womack said. "Because it's in misery, too, and what if it gets into the population?"

Womack showed pictures of the animal to a Texas Parks and Wildlife game warden, who "totally freaked out" and called for a department biologist, she said. The biologist told her it was likely a coyote with mange, but wasn't able to match the animal's skull shape -- and overbite -- with pictures of coyotes in reference books, according to Womack. Pictures were also dropped off at the Texas Animal Health Commission, where the veterinarian was out of the office and hadn't contacted Womack as of Tuesday afternoon. She said a biologist was on the way to Pollok to collect a tissue sample of the animal, for DNA testing.

"I just want people to be aware that things like this happen," Womack said. "If it's not the mange, it's something that doesn't need to be in the environment."

C.R. Shilling, of the West Loop Animal Clinic in Lufkin said that after seeing pictures of the animal -- and stressing that his determination is "pure speculation" -- he believes the animal is probably a coyote. The animal likely suffers from demodex mange, he said, and possibly a secondary skin infection or even a congenital skin defect, as well.

"That's just a congenital defect," Shilling said when asked about the animal's unusual jaw configuration. "We'll even get dogs like that in here."

Shilling said that without seeing the animal itself, it's hard to make an exact determination of what the animal might be. The possibility of it being a dog/coyote mix would be "unusual, but possible," he said.

"It appears to be an extremely undernourished dog," Ellen Trout Zoo Director Gordon Henley said after being e-mailed several photos of the animal[31].

---

[31] I would point out that most Ivory Tower scientists make such identifications using second hand information or pictures rather than going out to look at the creature in question. This is very similar to the famous quote made by a mainstream scientist regarding meteors. "*It is impossible for rocks to fall from the sky because there are no rocks in the sky.*" Of course no one told the meteors that their existence is impossible.

"Wild animals don't typically wind up like that, but undernourished, neglected, domestic animals do."

After enlarging one of the photos and conferring with the zoo's veterinarian, Henley said he feels the animal's mangy, crusty skin could be a result of either neglect or living in the wild. Undernourishment or a congenital deformity could have caused the animal's gross overbite, he said.

"I think what we've got here is a poor, suffering, undernourished and possibly abused canine," Henley said. "Possibly a coyote, but more likely a dog."

WOAI-TV in San Antonio has aired several stories on the so-called "Elmendorf Beast" since a nearby rancher shot and killed one earlier this year. The animal depicted on the station's Web site, at www.woai.com, looks eerily similar to the one discovered in Pollok. The rancher from Elmendorf, located southeast of San Antonio, killed the animal after 35 of his chickens disappeared in one day. The animal was also almost hairless,

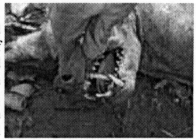

Figure 10: What big teeth you have.

with blue-grey coloring and four large "fangs." The station reported that tissue from the animal has been sent for DNA testing, and that it will be several more weeks before the tests are completed.

Speculation in the area as to what type of the animal the rancher killed has varied from simple to mystical. Some say it's a wild Mexican hairless dog, and other than the skin condition and jaw, pictures of the breed do bear a resemblance. Others believe it's the mythical chupacabra -- or "goat sucker" -- an animal Mexican folklorists say stalks rural areas killing livestock. One area hunting guide even believed the animal might be a muntjac, a small antelope-type animal imported into the state by ranchers, according to the station's online reports. Muntjac are herbivores, but do have upper canine teeth that are elongated into "tusks" that curve outward from the lips. Muntjac are also called "barking deer" for a sound they'll emit to warn others of predators. Like most deer, however, the Muntjac have split hoofs instead of paws, and certainly don't have long, rat-like tails.

A San Antonio Zoo mammal expert told WOAI-TV the animal is clearly a member of the canine family, and could possibly be a mix between a dog and a coyote. The expert also said the animal was clearly suffering from some sort of skin ailment, and may also have a congenital deformity of some sort. Sightings of similar animals have been reported across the country, from California to Maryland[32].

---

[32] This story was from the Associated Press 10/12/2004.

The following story had been posted on the Internet regarding the sighting of a mysterious creature in El Paso. Could it have been the mysterious Chupacabra?

by Elias S.

I live in New York but am originally from El Paso, Texas. It is Father's Day and I just got off the phone with my father. I asked him how things were going and about his dog, Blue Eyes. This is the story I received:

A few nights before, he and a friend and stayed up late into the night drinking and talking. Around 4 a.m. he realized the time and told his friend he was calling it quits and going home for the night. The friend went to sleep and my father walked to his home and passed out. He said soon after he was awoken in the middle of the night by his dog yelping loudly in the backyard. He said it was like no sound he ever heard the dog produce and that it sounded like the dog was being killed. He grabbed his gun, which he always kept loaded (a very common thing in West Texas), and went out to his backyard porch to investigate.

The dog, at the end of the yard (the dog always slept by the door) was pinned on his back in that submissive posture a dog will make when overpowered by a stronger animal (the dog is a large pit bull) and was screaming wildly as it squirmed on its back. My father then said, as the sun was not out yet, that he squinted to see what was wrong with the dog. He said he saw a large black shape on top of the dog and, thinking it was a man, warned him to get off the dog, but the man didn't listen. My father shot at the black shape and it was startled enough to let go of the dog, which split the scene as fast as it could. The creature then stood on its two legs and stared at my father.

He said it had an animal's eyes that seemed to glow, or like an animal, reflect the light of what's around. My father then shot another round at it and it didn't move. He shot one more and he said that it spread out its wings that it had tucked behind its back, which he said practically spanned the length of his backyard gates, which are 14 feet, and flew off. The dog trembled through the rest of the night.

The next morning he went back and found no footprints, no blood from the shots at the animal. But he went toward the sheet metal wall behind the scenario and noticed by the dents in the metal that he missed the first shot completely. The second bullet seemed to have gone through the animal and lightly dented the metal (a bullet loosing much force when it tears through an object, and the third bullet is completely unaccounted for. He says it either went into the air or was a direct hit that lodged within the animal, its souvenir from its trip to West Texas. I asked him why the beast didn't kill the dog, seeing that it could have if it wanted to, and he said that it seemed as if the beast were trying to pick the animal up and fly away with it.

I write this to you because the last thing he said before he hung up the phone was to go on the Internet and see if I could find anything about Chupacabras sightings in El Paso and Juarez, which I did. Another thing, as he himself said, these things are definitely physical and can be killed, seeing how it was stunned by the sound of the first shot and fled at the third shot which might have hit it. And if it did hit him, surely it must have blood and vital organs, then can we expect a strange corpse to end up somewhere in the Southwest? I don't know if I believe in these things, but I believe my father. He's a drinker, but he's been a drinker his whole life but he has never, within city limits, taken a loaded pistol and fired in a backyard before.

Another thing of interest to the story:   The area he lives in has many dogs, one in every yard, that bark at the slightest noise. No time during the whole episode did these obnoxious dogs bark once, not when the dog was yelping for help, not when my father was screaming at the top of his lungs, nor when the three bullets rang out. It's as if the dogs knew that their silence might save their lives. They were facing a natural predator. Its a crazy story, I know, but worth re-telling. Another question he brought up: Is there a migratory passage these animals follow regularly? If we began to view them as animals that have patterns of repetition, then we can advance further than attributing them to the supernatural or to aliens or to government cover-ups. Its fun to think that way but reality is always stranger than fiction[33].

## ANOTHER MYSTERIOUS SIGHTING

The Chupacabras Curse

by Maria

I live in the Pacific northwest. Since I was a child I have had to deal with what I saw at my window during an Indian summer in 1964. There are nights even now that I shut tight the shades on my windows because I know its close. My story is this:

I was about four and helping my mother in the bedroom with the laundry, done earlier at the laundry mat. Being four, I really wasn't much help, but my mother was trying to keep me busy as my older brother and sisters were preparing to take their baths when the knocking started.

It started at the front of the room, which faced outside to the street (the curtains were drawn on the big window as it was dark outside); it was coming from outside. I asked my mother what the knocking was and she told me it was

---

[33]http://paranormal.about.com/library/blstory_july03_08.htm

just the wind, and with that picked up folded clothes that were to go into the dressers in my brothers' room. When she left, the knocking got louder and more insistent. It had moved from the front of the house to the side of the house where there was a smaller window also with its curtain drawn. The knocking became more of a pounding and was shaking the curtain of the small window. I was alone in this room when I decided to look. It almost seemed like the curtain jumped into my hand when I reached for it and drew it back.

There on the other side of the window was this face (if you can call it a face). It had huge red eyes, a snout like a dog, very large pointed ears on either side of its head, bristly hair on its skin like a pig, the skin seemed like scales, then the teeth. This thing smiled at me and showed me two rows of razor sharp teeth with incisors that crossed over the bottom and top of very thin lips which were curled at the end with its smile. One hand rested on the pane of the window, which had three fingers with long claw-like nails, and it looked at its hand as it seemed to be testing the strength of the glass then raised its other hand and motioned to me to come out (the finger crook/beckoning). I screamed once, let go of the curtain and ran out of the room into my mothers arms and passed out. My father and mother would never tell me if they believed it or not, but it was also at this time we started to pray The Rosary every night until I was 9. My parents divorced not far after we stopped.

I have learned since this incident from other family members that there is supposed to be a demon that is bound to our family and the bloodline through a curse placed on one of my ancestors by a priest. Those who are part of the bloodline will see it twice in their life, the story goes, once while they are young and once again before they die. The first time is that you know it's there (and if given the opportunity, the demon will take a child as part of its payment to be bound by the curse); the last to try to steal the soul before it leaves to heaven.

There are many in my family that have seen this thing and many more that will not talk about it. My family is Mexican American and it is more than a myth or legend to try to scare children. I was only until I heard the stories of the Chupacabras and the description that I realized there were more than just my family and the story of the curse. I believe now that it watches and passes by to "smell" the blood of my family to check if its time to appear again and take advantage. Before I told any of my children of my own experience, three out of my four had already seen it. Now two of my grandchildren have. It always seems to know when to come, when you are alone and small. I don't fear my death, I fear being alone when it happens.

## MORE MYSTERIOUS HAPPENINGS IN EL PASO

This next event was reported by someone who gave their name as Leslie, from El Paso on January 6, 2003.

Subject: UFO Sighting/ Paranormal Experience - Location - El Paso, Texas -

County: El Paso - Zip Code: 79936  Date: September 7, 2002 - Time: 10:00 to 10:30 PM - Witnesses: 1 - Objects Shape: Light - Number of objects: 1 - Object had lights -Object emitted beams of light - There was interference associated with the object Other: See explanation below.

## Event Description:

I was walking out of the kitchen, where I have plain view of the sky out of the living room windows high up, almost on the ceiling
There are two windows across from one another, in a corner. At first I felt a large vibration, like a rumble and thought someone had crashed (our street is accident prone), but then I turned out the light to see and I was overwhelmed by a bright light.
It was as if someone had a flashlight right up to the window! It was very still, and so was I! I rationalized it as a plane or copter, but there was only bright, white light, and it didn't move. Copters and planes here have visible red and blue lights and they're constantly on the move with a soft humming sound, this was a scary light.
I turned the light back on and saw the clock, it was only 10:00 PM.  I stood there waiting for it to move, for sirens, anything, and when I looked at the clock again it was 10:30 PM.
Suddenly, it began to fall really fast, just a straight drop. I fell to the floor, afraid that if it was a plane or an attack we were in for it with this thing so close, but nothing ever came of it, and I haven't seen anything like it sense.
What I thought strange was my watch had stopped on 10:00 PM.  The clock in the kitchen too, and the TV went static.  It made me queasy.

## ANOTHER UNEXPLAINED EVENT

This next event was reported by some who gave their name as Jacob V. - El Paso, Texas - September 1, 2001 at 18:43:26

Subject: Unexplained Event - Location: El Paso, Texas - Date: 9/1/01 - Time: Approx. 3:00 AM Zip Code: 79930 - County sighting took place: El Paso - Witnesses: none - Additional Info: Home

## Event Description:
On September 1, 2001, I had an experience that has left me questioning all "logical" explanations and only leaves me thinking more. At around 3:00 AM on this day, I had just got home and got ready for bed and had this weird feeling, almost like there was someone there with me. Although my dad and his girlfriend were there but in separate rooms.

62\Spirits of the Border, Volume III

So I laid down and this feeling worsened, to the point that it was making me feel ill. All of a sudden as I was drifting into sleep, I heard a very unusual almost non-human voice call my name. I freaked out! But as I tried to get up, this force paralyzed me. I couldn't move or scream which made it twice as frightening. Then from within me this deep and long almost gurgling sound came. I could feel every little vibration it sent out. At the same time in my mind I could see these things. Demonic looking things, voices, and images. I would've thought it was a dream but I could feel this thing in the room. A stillness of a sort. Which is weird because my dad usually goes in there and makes small talk, but he didn't this time.

Anyway, although this might be graphic, these sudden urges to hurt myself..... These were images I could see in my mind as I very much inexplicably desired. I started to suddenly pray out loud and it left me for a couple of seconds, then returned and left within seconds. I then got up and quickly left the room. I felt a mixture of scared and confused, with a sort of comfort that God does listen.

I have a feeling things were adding up to this incident like, lights and ceiling fans turning on when they were obviously off, hearing knockings and walking, hearing keys drop when no one else was home, a sudden depression overcoming me, and besides the fact that I know that there is something extremely strange going on and has been going on for some time; years actually.

The reason that I am submitting this is because I am looking for help. An explanation at the least. Only because I have seen doctors, psychiatrists, and psychologists; and still no one can explain all they do is give me medications and useless coping devices. I would go to seek spiritual advice but I feel so spiritually lost that I don't know what to believe in.

I would really appreciate it if there is anything that could be done or advise on how to deal with this.

THANK YOU!!!!!

Now this event brings up an interesting point. Is it possible that some people that we call schizophrenic and lock up because they claim that they hear voices in their heads are merely being targeted for mental harassment by entities that we refuse to admit exist. There have been hundreds of cases of such mental contact down through the ages. I would point to the Miracle of Fatima and the exploits of Joan of Arc as two instances when the mysterious voices that spoke to the "contactees" were believed to be from God. Suppose that they were from some other entity. In the minds of the authorities of many countries over the centuries, if such voices are real they must come form either God or the Devil.

## OTHER LIGHTS IN THE SKY

Almost everyone has heard of the Marfa Lights that bounce around the countryside, eluding all attempts to catch or explain them. Ivory Tower scientists who can't be bothered to come see the mysterious lights have ascribed them to car headlights. However, this does not explain how or why Indians saw the lights many centuries before the automobile was ever invented. I would guess that these same Ivory Tower scientists that ascribe the lights to the headlights of automobiles would claim that the early Indians must have just imagined that they saw the Marfa lights. After all, there can't be any lights in the sky because there are no lights in the sky!

Surprisingly, the El Paso region has its own Marfa Lights, through they get little publicity as can be seen in the next story.

## Hueco Tanks Park

Phoenix and the Southwest have a long history of unexplained lights. The Marfa Lights of east Texas regularly play hide and seek with viewers. When I visited the historic Hueco Tanks Park near El Paso, Texas, several of the employees there told me that they had seen strange lights in the sky on a regular basis just above the rock formations. In those rock formations are what look like huge water storage tanks cut out of solid rock. The whole area was considered sacred by Native Americans.

## UNSOLVED MYSTERIES

In addition to the Chupacabra and mysterious lights in the sky, there have been a number of other little publicized mysteries unearthed in the El Paso area. For example, early in the last century, a 30 + year old male skeleton was unearthed in a mining area of the El Paso area. The Skull had two small horns protruding from the forehead area. Witness of this unusual event was a Texas Ranger investigating another murder case.

There was never any explanation about what happened to the owner of this unusual skull. It would seem to be that if in fact this skull was of recent origin, then surely someone would have noticed a man or woman wondering around with two horns growing out of their forehead. Of course, perhaps the skull was much older than it seemed and belonged to an ancient resident of the El Paso area.

Added to skulls with horns, which remind me of the horns allegedly embedded in the forehead of the devil, there also seems to be a real life Big Bird wondering around the landscape as we shall see in the next story. It appears that Sesame Street is not the only place that has huge birds.

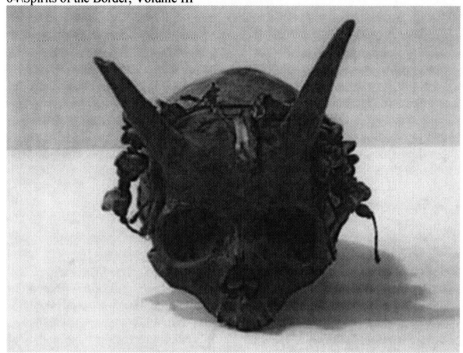

**Figure 11: The Horned Skull Unearthed Near El Paso.**

## BIG BIRD LIVES

There is hardly a child who has not seen the famous Big Bird on the educational television show, Sesame Street. However, it now appears that Big Bird does not just exist on television and in the active imagaintion of children.

The following story was printed in the Fort Bliss, Texas Monitor. Though it was designed to be one of the so called silly Halloween stories, it does illustrate a point that I have been trying to make. That point is that this is a strange world in which we live.

**Feathered Friend? -- For some, legend of Big Bird remains a mystery**
October 31, 2004

Alma Walzer
*The Monitor*
McALLEN — For decades, bird lovers have flocked to the Rio Grande Valley to see a large variety of their feathered friends. But in 1976, hunters scoured the area trying to win a reward for the capture of a creature which became known to residents here as Big Bird. For about two months in the mid-1970s, Big Bird — not the friendly tall, yellow bird that loves children on Sesame Street — terrorized Valley residents.

The 5-foot-tall bird was described as "horrible-looking," according to The Monitor's archives. Its wings were large enough to be folded over its body and it had large, dark red eyes attached to a gray, gorilla-like face. Its head was bald and it made a loud, shrill sound through its 6-inch-long beak.

Tom Waldon claimed to have found its tracks on Jan. 2, 1976, near his home in Harlingen. The three-toed tracks measured 8 inches across and pressed an inch and a half into the ground.

Three teachers from San Antonio claimed to have seen Big Bird in that city as well, on Feb. 24, 1976. The trio later pointed to a picture in a book of a pteranodon, an extinct giant flying reptile, as being most like what they had seen. Some bird experts told area residents that the bird was a lost condor or a jabiru, a large Central American stork which can boast a 10-foot wing span, big tracks and a featherless head. The jabiru has a breeding ground about 250 miles south of McAllen, near Tampico, Mexico, experts pointed out. But just as mysteriously as it arrived, Big Bird seemed to disappear overnight. But for some Valley residents, what exactly the Big Bird was is still a mystery.

## THE FIRST SIGHTINGS

The Big Bird sighting thought to be the first was Jan 1, 1976, when Tracey Lawson, then age 11, and her cousin Jackie Davies, then 14, were playing in Lawson's back yard near Harlingen.

The two girls say they saw the bird standing about 100 yards away on an irrigation canal, according to the Atlas of the Mysterious in North America. Lawson went inside to get her binoculars, and when she returned, she saw the bird staring back at her. Big Bird was more than 5 feet tall, she said, and when she and Davies ran inside to tell her parents, the adults did not believe them.

On Jan. 8, 1976, The Brownsville Herald and the Valley Morning Star ran a piece that told the story of Alverico Guajardo and a strange "birdlike" creature which he claimed to have seen outside his home one day earlier.

"I was scared," Guajardo said at the time. "It's got wings like a bird, but it's not a bird. That animal is not of this world."

Guajardo said Big Bird had large wings but it never flew while in his presence. Its eyes were as big as silver dollars and its long, skinny beak was three or four feet long, he said.

It made a terrible noise, and although the sounds seemed to come from the creature's throat, which pulsated as it made the noise and its beak never moved, Guajardo said.

The Brownsville Herald article indicated that reports of the large bird began shortly after a number of cattle mutilations made the news in Cameron County, but there was no proof that the bird had caused the strange mutilations.

## GROWING LEGEND, GROWING FEAR

As more sightings of Big Bird were reported, its legend grew. One Valley radio station offered a reward of $1,000 for the capture of the bird, archives show.

Johnny Carson even joked about Big Bird on The Tonight Show. The West German newspaper, Die Bild Zeitung, ran a story about the bird on its front page on Jan. 15, 1976.

Tejano artists Raul Ruiz and Wally "The Taco Kid " Gonzalez recorded songs about Big Bird.

It was official: Trying to spot Big Bird became more popular here than searching for UFOs.

The almost daily reports of Big Bird sightings and the frenzy of Valley hunters to trap the bird in an effort to claim the cash prize prompted the Texas Parks and Wildlife Commission to issue a warning.

"We have a number of species of birds that do exist in South Texas in the Valley area," said commission officer Ed Dutch at the time. "Many of them have wingspans up to perhaps 10 feet or in excess of 10 feet, and some of them are on the rare endangered species list."

The punishment for catching a protected bird could cost a hunter $5,000, Dutch said.

The sightings of Big Bird were reported from every type of person, including two San Benito police officers.

Patrolmen Arturo Padilla and Homero Galvan, traveling in separate police cars, reported seeing a huge bird with a 15-foot wing span gliding through the air.

"It's more or less like a stork or pelican-type of bird," Padilla said. "I've done a lot of hunting, but I've never seen anything like it."

Padilla said the bird had a wingspan of about 15 feet. He said he was willing to shoot it if he saw it again.

"It's a true story that happened in Starr County in the early 1980s ... There were reports of the bird killing cattle because the ranchers were finding cattle mutilated and drained of their blood." — Javier, 27 eyewitness. Big Bird was sighted along the river near Laredo as well, by Arturo Rodriguez and his nephew Ricardo, as they were fishing on the banks of the Rio Grande, newspaper archives show.

Television footage showing three-toed footprints, measuring 9 inches by 12 inches, and believed to have been left by Big Bird, fed the fear felt by area residents.

When one eyewitness said he believed the bird was large enough to easily scoop up a small child off the ground, parents began to keep their children indoors, instead of allowing them to venture outside to play.

Fear took a tighter grip on the Valley after Jan. 15, 1976, when a Raymondville man told police officers he was attacked by the bird.

"I felt some wind and looked up and this big bird attacked me," said Raymondville resident Armando Grimaldo, who was 26 years old at the time.

Grimaldo's neighbors found him in his back yard shaking and screaming, and reported that his shirt and jacket were torn. A man from Eagle Pass said he was attacked as well, archives show.

Francisco Magallanez's claim that he was attacked was given some credibility by law enforcement officials, who said Magallanez had marks on his shoulders. His physician, Dr. Arturo Bates, told police the marks were made by some type of animal or bird.

The Monitor reported that Magallanez, who was 21 years old at the time, admitted he was drinking at the time of the attack.

## EXPERT'S EXPLANATION

On Feb. 1, 1976, Texas A & M ornithologist Keith Arnold said he believed Big Bird was a large Central American stork, which at times has been observed as far north as Oklahoma, according to The Monitor's archives[34].

The stork, also known as a jabiru, had a 10-foot wing span, leaves large tracks and has a featherless head, Arnold said.

Arnold said he had examined a jabiru in 1973 when it was found in a weakened state near Houston.

## URBAN LEGEND

Big Bird became larger than life when the tales about it were told over and over.

Some of the stories can be found in the Special Collections Department in the library of the University of Texas-Pan American.

For years, UTPA students have been asked to write down what they know about local legends, and Big Bird has always been a favorite. Because the students never intended for their stories to be published, The Monitor will not print their full names.

Javier, 27, of Rio Grande City recalled the story which connected Big Bird to the mysterious cattle mutilations.

"It's a true story that happened in Starr County in the early 1980s," Javier wrote. "There were reports of the bird killing cattle because the ranchers were finding cattle mutilated and drained of their blood.

"There was no explanation and people were shocked because the cattle were supposedly mutilated using surgical instruments and there were no tire tracks or foot prints near the dead cattle," Javier wrote. "After the bird disappeared, there were no more reports of mutilated cattle."

---

[34] Of course there are no reports that Keith Arnold bothered to come to El Paso to make an on the scene identification. That is not how Ivory Tower scientists conduct business.

A 49-year-old man from Olmito, who withheld his name from the report given to a UTPA student named Yadira, said he had proof the bird attacked him.

"He left a bar a little late and was about to get in his car when he was attacked by a giant bird," Yadira wrote. "It cut him up, so when he got home his wife bandaged him up.

"He told her the story but she didn't believe him," Yadira wrote. "The next day the wife used his car and found bird feathers on the seat and the floorboard."

Another UTPA student, Esequiel, said he was in sixth grade at a Pharr elementary when he saw the bird for himself. His story is also in the library collection.

"We were at recess and saw a huge bird-like object in the sky," Esequiel wrote.

"My friend and I were the only ones who saw it, even though there were a lot of students playing outside.

"We told a teacher about it and she said it was probably an unexplained event like a UFO or something," Esequiel wrote.

## LEGEND DIES

On Feb. 11, 1976, the legend of the magnificent winged bird died. Some farm workers saw Big Bird in a fruit orchard about two miles south of Alamo, and within an hour, about 50 people had gathered to see the bird for themselves.

The bird stood quietly and watched the group of people walk around, including a television reporter who filmed the bird. The film showing a 4-foot tall silvery-blue bird was broadcast around the state on Feb. 12 and Feb. 13, 1976, and the bird was identified as a great blue heron by Don Farst, a curator at the Gladys Porter Zoo in Brownsville.

Farst said the great blue heron was not uncommon in the Valley.

"They usually stay near the bay or in arroyos, feeding on small snakes and lizards," Farst said at the time.

## COINCIDENCE?

Just when we thought it was safe to go back outside, another big bird made headlines.

On Feb. 17, 1976, The Brownsville Herald ran a story about a big bird that died after it became entangled in a barbed wire fence in Logan, Ind.

The bird, named Boomer by his owner William Brasier, had been lost for four days before it was found dead in the fence line.

The 6-foot, 2-inch tall ostrich-like creature was a South American bird that can run up to 40 miles an hour, but cannot fly, Brasier said at the time.

Brasier believed Boomer got caught in the barbed wire while trying to jump the four-foot fence to freedom.

---

So does a real life Big Bird still roam the desert in the still of the night? There is no question that there is much that takes place about which we known nothing. Some of these reports are not unlike the winged creature that has terrorized the northeast for decades. Perhaps Charles Fort was correct after all.

As if matters are not scary enough, a report of a UFO abduction in the El Paso area was brought to my attention. Do we really know what moves across the land after the sun goes down?

## ABDUCTIONS

This report was made to the website to which I was directed on March 9, 2004. Rather than try to explain the situation, I think the author of the report said things in the best possible manner.

Received: March 29, 2004

Dear Mr. Vike,

My son sent me a link to the website http://www.rense.com/general38/scoop.htm regarding scars that are "scoop marks" and asked me to tell you my story.

I actually have two scars on my thighs. My skin is extremely white unless I have been in the sun, so the one on the left thigh is nearly invisible and the one on the right nearly so. The scar on the left thigh is oval shaped, about the size of a thumbprint, and full of tiny pinpricks. It is located high up near my groin and originally was on the inside of my thigh. Over the years (and as I gained weight), the scar migrated toward the front of my thigh.

I have a strange memory about receiving this scar. I remember that I was less than six years old. I was in a doctor's office and he gave me what I remembered as a "vaccination". I was lying on a table screaming as he did the procedure, and something or someone was holding me down. I could see my mother behind the doctor. She was standing still, almost frozen, staring at us and not reacting at all - which was extremely strange since she normally was overly reactive and could not stand to even see me get an injection. Years later I mentioned the incident to her and she denied it ever happened, even when I showed her the scar.

The scar on my right thigh is triangular and featureless, about a quarter inch in length. I have attached a photo of this scar. I have no memory of receiving this scar, although I can remember what caused every other scar I have. My son wrote you and told you about the day we talked about our scars (erroneously stating that mine was on the right thigh). What I find very odd is that he cannot remember that his sister was there when we discussed our scars. My daughter also showed us a scar on her thigh that was identical to ours. None of us remember getting these scars, nor can I remember any injuries my children might have received that would have resulted in this kind of scarring.

When I lived in El Paso, Texas, I often watched the desert sky at night hoping to see shooting stars. I don't recall ever seeing anything that might have been considered a UFO - at least not at night, but I do remember one incident very vividly - and it happened in broad daylight. I was driving on what used to be called War Road in Northeast El Paso in the summer of 1977.

We frequently drove this road to and from our house. My children were both in the car with me on this occasion. An extension of the University of Texas at El Paso had recently been built nearby, but at the time, this road was not as busy as it has become now that houses have been built all along it and it has become a major freeway called Gateway North/South.

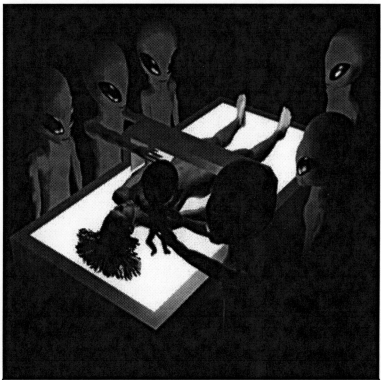

I had turned onto War Road from Hondo Pass and as I neared the college I saw a small circular object in the sky. It looked like an oversized Frisbee at first. As it came closer, I slowed my vehicle to get a better look at it. I remember yelling to the children to look at the object, but they couldn't

Figure 12: Do mysterious aliens actually kidnap earthlings?

see it from the back seat. The object was traveling slowly across the road, like it was hovering, and it was spinning as it went. Small markings around the edge resembled windows. It appeared to be about three foot across and less than a foot deep at the center axis. I had the vivid impression that there was nothing alive within it, more like it was a remote control device. Suddenly, as though whatever was controlling it became aware of my presence, it shot down at an angle into the desert between me and the college buildings. I stopped the car, intending to go look at it more closely. Just before I got out of the car, however, I glanced in the rearview mirror and saw several cars coming toward me. There was no place to park as there was no shoulder on the road and I had to drive on to avoid being hit.

The area where this occurred was near several military bases, including Fort Bliss and MacGregor Range. When I mentioned the incident to friends, several warned me that I shouldn't tell too many people about it because it might have been a test flight by the military of something created using alien technology. I have no idea what it really was.

My son told you about his dreams and wanted me to tell you of similar ones I had most of my life. I had dreams many times that were always the same. I was in a place that was formed of metal walls. In my dreams I always thought of it as "home" although it never resembled any place I ever lived. I would decide to go somewhere and instead of walking I would bend at the waist, lift my feet and float. I would propel myself by pushing on the walls or grabbing projections and pull myself onward. These dreams occurred when I was a child long before the first space flights and before I ever read any science fiction stories. They continued until my mid-30's.

My son also wanted me to mention that the extensive medical records of my son, my daughter and myself were "lost" from the military hospital in El Paso - Beaumont - within two years of my husband's retirement.

Mr. Vike, I would prefer that you didn't use my full name if you decide to have my story posted on the website. Other than that, you are free to use this information as you wish. I hope you find this useful.

Sincerely,

I have presented a number of stories about odd and mysterious happenings in the El Paso area. I will leave it up to the reader to determine which to believe and which not to believe. However, as near as I can determine, all of the stories that I have presented are true.

While still on the subject of monsters and other unexplained happenings in El Paso I also present the following chapter regarding the possibility of Big Foot also being seen in this area.

# CHAPTER FIVE

# DOES BIG FOOT LIVE IN TEXAS?

I have heard stories about something called a desert ape being seen around El Paso. As near as I can determine from my reading, there is no such thing as a desert ape, at least in the United States. So what is it that people are [35]seeing? These sightins certainly require some investiation as I have never heard of a desert ape before. Could these so called desert apes actually be the illusive Big Foot? Please consider the following information that was given to me from what appears to have been a longer article.

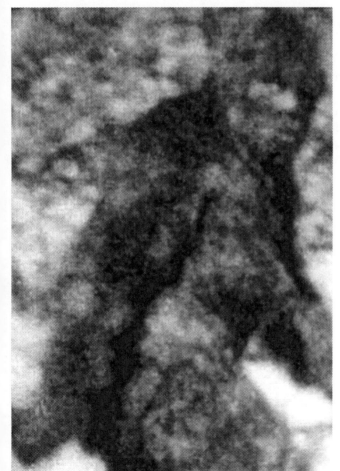

*"What are the most common aspects in Bigfoot sightings? Typically they are spotted in wooded areas, on or near mountains, near cave systems (underworld entrances), near water sources (for drinking... or other???), and*

**Figure 13: This is a copy of the most famous Bigfoot photo ever taken.**

*many times a calling out of some kind is heard (being anywhere from happy to sad to crying to moaning to yelling to warning of danger or a warning for you or another nearby creature) and stinky smells (typically a very horrible stench) often occur. It is because of the lack of the woods in the "desert apes" sightings near El Paso, TX that caused me to believe that something else might be happening in this area. Footprints are another dead giveaway towards geological changes... in the microcosm or the symbolic aspect of leaving behind a track or tracks that are photographical, measurable, that indicates an impression and change in the earth itself, causes our eyes to look downward toward this earth to look for clues, etc... well it all shows signs in and of the physical world and that perhaps more clues will be found there in that realm. All of these aspects of bigfoot sightings (footprints, water, caves, roaming on the earth, smells, screams, etc.) all point to the lower realms of earth, the underworld, but with highly significant middle urth overtones and spiritual implications which show more meaning behind it all than previously recognized.*

*Thanks to Don Blackmon who was with a few other men (covered in my Desert Apes article) back in the 1970's in the Horizon City area (east of El Paso) where they saw footprints that appeared to be from a bigfoot, I was able to find out more information that not only triggered some extensive research into the geological aspects of bigfoot sightings, but it brought out more meaning in a dream I had last year, and the implications of my son/nephew's sighting back in November of 2001 just north of El Paso, above Las Cruces, NM.*

*Don Blackmon said:*

*"There are caves in the surrounding mountains but as to specifically in the Hueco mountains, I don't know. I do know that the Franklins have caves and multiple natural springs, as well as the Organs. Beasley cave near Pyramid peak (at the N end of Anthony Gap) was a cave which at one time had stalactites and stalagmites. If that was possible in the area then I suppose the Huecos could have the same. There are also numerous rock caves and mines in the area as well. My particular theory is that Bigfoot sightings are most often near geologic fault lines. A fault line lies under El Paso and runs through the SW to California. El Paso has had tremors throughout the years while I lived there but most hardly registered on any scale. The desert to the West of El Paso in New Mexico has frequent tremors as anyone can tell you that has camped out overnight near the volcanoes."*

*I took Don's personal research and did some of my own, mostly because I knew for a fact that small tremors did happen in El Paso, as well as there being numerous friends of mine who have been in the caves in the Huecos (near where I live) as well as what my brother describes as "the wettest cave I've ever been in" concerning a cave at Anthony Gap on the north side of the Franklin mountains. That doesn't even include the cave(s) that have been spoken of around the Horizon City area SE of El Paso which at least 2 primary (and separate/unrelated) sources know about, but no one else has been able to prove yet.*

*Several weeks later, in early July, more sightings were reported in New Mexico. From Albuquerque to Roswell to Carlsbad. Some sightings were reported in Texas -- Marfa and Sierra Blanca. El Paso and Juarez residents also saw strange apparitions. The objects flew directly above the El Paso International Airport on the east side of town. They circled over Juarez to the south and skirted the mountain there -- then flew over the Franklin Mountain due north to the Organ Mountain range sixty miles away. The objects then angled over Alamogordo and headed straight to the Hueco Mountains to the east of El Paso. When they returned, they hovered over the El Paso International Airport once again.*

*The mysterious craft had completed this maneuver in less than two minutes ... at times they were out of sight over the horizon ... returning silently without incident. No airplanes were dispatched to intercept these objects. But the radar had them in full view at all times, on display monitors at the airport. On screens at the Air Defense Center at Biggs Field, and on various radar screens at Fort Bliss, White Sands Missile Range and Alamogordo.*

*Again, the local press made no mention of these events. The government information offices for the military bases had no comment. Even the Mexican newspapers printed nothing. The new sightings were almost a duplicate of the Deming, Las Cruces and Alamogordo events. Marfa citizens saw the lights at sunset, as they glistened in the orange sunset. The lights circled the city for several minutes from 7:45 to 8:00 PM then moved to the west. The lights moved in formation, in smooth spirals and then in straight lines. They moved very high in the sky -- then would swoop low almost touching the ground. Then they were gone.*

*Five minutes later, at 8:05 PM, the objects appeared over Sierra Blanca, more than 80 miles to the northwest. The sky was still glowing from the setting sun and the objects appeared to float in the air, then moved about in the unusual spirals and straight line trajectories Observed over Marfa. The display was unusual because it lasted until 8:45 PM when the darkness had closed in. The lights were observed in the dry air over Sierra Blanca -- moving across a sky lit with thousands of brilliant stars. The display was more spectacular than any meteor shower ever seen before ... except that it was terrifying. The crowds in Sierra Blanca gathered outside their homes to watch the lights ... wondering whether they were super secret planes in maneuvers or whether they were what everyone assumed -- visitors from another realm.*

*The objects were observed by many. Highway patrolmen on Interstate 20 and Interstate 10. Police and sheriff personnel in many towns and counties throughout the area, which covered thousands of square miles. Personnel at the Sierra Blanca check point for the Immigration and Naturalization Service. Many more saw the eerie sight ... as they stopped their vehicles on the desert roads.*

*Travelers on the dusty highway to El Paso and Fort Stockton. Truckers pulled their rigs off the roads to see the unusual aerial displays.*

*The only thing all noticed was the fact that the lights did not flicker or flash like the airliners that usually streak across the sky. They did not see the familiar strobe lights that the modern airliners also have. The shapes overhead did not have the usual cross shape of fuselage and wings they expected. And the lights seemed to pulsate, to glow bright ... then dim in unusual ways. And there was no sound whatsoever as they passed overhead. That was the most unusual thing of all."*

## WAS THE HORIZON CITY MONSTER A BIGFOOT?

The following story was in the El Paso Times on Thursday, July 31, 2003[36].

**Neighborhoods** Thursday, July 31, 2003

## Some residents believe in Horizon City's monster[37]
*Adriana M. Chávez*
*El Paso Times*

More than two years ago, Cecelia Montañez saw the creature for the first time: more than 7 feet tall, with faded dark brown fur, and standing in the desert near Eastlake Boulevard and Darrington Road.

"I saw a big gorilla-like thing walking toward the desert," Montañez said.

Montañez says she and other Horizon City residents have witnessed a large, bigfoot-type creature lurking in the desert, usually near Eastlake, and near Lake El Paso. While others, including law-enforcement officials, believe the sightings are part of a hoax, Montañez said what she and other people have witnessed is true.

The legend of the monster goes back to the early 1970s, but no actual evidence has been found, according to many longtime Horizon City residents.

Montañez, a retired secretary, moved from East El Paso to Horizon City three years ago. She said she has seen the creature on two occasions, the last sighting taking place near her home last October.

---

[36] Chavez, Adriana, *Some Residents Believe In Horison City's Monster*, El Paso Times, July 31, 2003.

Montañez said that after the first sighting, she remembered an article that ran in the Sept. 20, 1975, edition of the El Paso Times. The article reported that three teenagers saw a gorilla-like creature near the Horizon City golf course. Bill Rutherford, a former deputy with the El Paso County Sheriff's Department, said in the article that he did see a track, but that it "appeared to have been dug."

"Someone had to have made those tracks," Rutherford said in a recent phone interview. "There's a lot of people that were very upset, but it never bothered me. I didn't think it was for real."

Rutherford was a deputy until 1979, and in 1988 became Horizon City's first police chief. He retired after 10 years, and remembers that although he didn't believe the teens' stories, he felt obligated to investigate.

"I was a deputy sheriff, so I was regulated to do something," Rutherford said. "I never saw it. I thought it was a hoax.

Horizon City Police Chief Tony Aguilar has been the town's chief for about two years, and said he doesn't recall any reports of bigfoot sightings.

"We've had reports before of meteorites landing in the desert, but nothing about bigfoots," Aguilar said.

Aguilar remembered hearing about a hermit who may have lived in the mountains near Horizon City in the early 1970's.

"He had long hair and he was unshaven," Aguilar recalled. "A lot of hunters at one point found a little cave, and found old cans, and like he had been living off the land."

Although Montañez maintains the creatures live in caverns that exist underneath Horizon City, Phil Goodell, a geology professor at the University of Texas at El Paso, said no such caverns exist.

---

[37] For more information, I also highly recommend the following website: http://www.unifiedworlds.com.

[38] As usual an Ivory Tower Scientist quoted, Phil Goodell, a geology professor at the University of Texas at El Paso had no evidence when he said there are no caverns underneath the town. Naturally he spoke from the air conditioned comfort of his office and did not go into the field to check whether or not caverns exist beneath Horizon City. I have also been told that there are no caverns beneath El Paso, so I guess the massive cavern found by a City Work crew was just their imagination.

"Large desert expanses can't have caverns," Goodell said. "You have to have limestone rock, like Carlsbad Caverns does."

Montañez said she got some of her information on the creature from at least one law-enforcement official who has investigated the creature sightings and developed a profile.

"He said the mothers go out to find food, and that they nurse their young just like we do," she said.

Aguilar said if anyone reported seeing the creature to police, "we would look into it and take it seriously, with whatever information we had to work on."

Montañez described the creatures as having red glowing eyes, "like cats," she said, and as being vegetarians. Since El Paso is mostly desert with no vegetation, Montañez said, the creatures suck the blood out of small animals and eat their organs.

Irene Scanlon, 57, said she heard about sightings of the creatures a while ago, but has never seen them.

"It sounds like they're trying to make it seem like a chupacabra," Scanlon said. "I don't believe it at all. I think it's just someone trying to get publicity."

But Montañez said she's not trying to seek publicity, and would like to see Horizon City become a tourist attraction like Roswell, which is known for being the supposed site of a UFO crash in 1947.

"My daughter didn't believe it either, but when she saw it, she changed her story," Montañez said. "They really exist."

Montañez has told of her experiences to friends and family, including two Socorro High School varsity baseball players.

"I've been looking for them around the desert," said George De La Fuente, 16, a junior at Socorro High, who has been watching for the creature along with his friend, Anthony Paez, 15, a sophomore at Socorro. "I just want to see them. I have to see one to believe it."

*Adriana M. Chávez may be reached at* _achavez@elpasotimes.com_

The columns shown on the next three pages accompanied the story shown above. However, there are some errors in the information given here that I will show.

Illustration by Nacho Garcia Jr. / El Paso Times

Victor Calzada / El Paso Times
**The legend of the Horizon City monster** dates back more than 30 years near Lake El Paso, though there is no tangible evidence that it exists.

## A closer look

- **Witnesses of** the Horizon City creature claim it is between 7 and 8 feet tall with very broad shoulders and an elongated head.

- **Cecelia** Montañez, who claims to have seen the creature twice, says the creatures "have very short hair and are a faded brownish-maroon color."

- **Montañez** said the creatures also have red glowing eyes and a mouth that resembles that of a bulldog.

- **Many witnesses** say the

creatures can be seen near Lake El Paso late at night drinking water.

This article about the creature was on the front page of the El Paso Times in 1975.

- **Others say** they have heard the creatures humming as they drive through Eastlake Boulevard, or know the creatures are around because of their strong odor.

- **Montañez** said the creatures live in caverns underneath Horizon City, but Phil Goodell, a geology professor at the University of Texas at El Paso, said there are no caverns underneath the town[38].

## Big foot tidbits

- **For more than** 400 years, people have reported seeing large, hair-covered, man-like animals in the wilderness areas of North America.

- **Sightings** of these animals continue today. Real or not, these reports are often made by people of unimpeachable character.

- **For more than** 70 years, people have been finding, photographing and casting sets of very large human-shaped tracks. Most are discovered by chance in remote areas. Tracks Remote areas. Trackscontinue to be found.

- **The cultural histories** of many Native American and First Nation peoples include stories and beliefs about non-human "peoples" of the wild. Many of these descriptions bear a striking resemblance to the hairy man-like creatures reported today.

- **This information** suggests the presence of an animal, probably a primate, that exists today in very low-populated densities. If true, this species, having likely evolved alongside humans, became astonishingly

adept at avoiding human contact through a process of natural selection.
• **To others,** this information points to a cultural phenomenon kept alive today through a combination of the misidentification of known animals, wishful thinking and the deliberate fabrication of evidence.

*Source: The Bigfoot Field Researchers Organization; www.bfro.net*

**THE ORIGINAL 1975 ARTICLE**

His Face Is Pushed In And His Ears 'Point'
**By Bill Moore, September 20, 1975[39]**

Many residents of Horizon City cast a leery eye towards the surrounding desert these days. Some say there is a strange creature lurking about.
During the past week, numerous teenagers have reported seeing the creature on the Horizon City golf course and the area south of there. Footprints have reportedly been found, shots have been fired and one youngster says he got a good look at the face.
"His face was all pushed in and flat like a bulldog's. And he had this big nose that stuck out," Bill York, 15 of 16010 Mohested, who said he got a good look at the creature on the golf course driving range. "His eyes were sunk in deep and his jaw jutted out."
Other descriptions given by the creature by various teens report it as being about 8 feet tall, 3 1/2 feet wide and leaving footprints 14 inches long 8 inches wide.
Some say it is hairy and has pointed ears.
One boy reportedly got close enough to shoot at the creature with a rifle. He says he hit it at least six times at close range. No blood was ever found.
The creature was reportedly first cites last Saturday when Billy Fuller, 14, of 19008 Bremerton, and Kathy Ellis, 15, of 18010 Carson thought they saw something walking on the golf course.
Officer Bill Rutherford of the sheriff's department came driving by. The youngsters flagged him down. He reportedly flashed a light in the direction of the movement and reported he saw nothing. The teens, though, said it was the first time they saw the creature.
It ducked down to the ground and just took off," said Miss Ellis. "We know we saw it, but Mr. Rutherford says he never did. I think he said that just so people would not start getting scared."
An adult has yet to be found who can support a claim of sighting the creature.

---

[39] Moore, Bill, *His Face Is Pushed In and His Ears Point*, El Paso Times, September 20, 1975.

"We think some adults have seen it, too. But we don't have their names," said one of the teens. "In fact, there was a lady who nearly hit it with her car. But I don't know who she was."

All the creature's tracks have also reportedly been destroyed by vehicles and persons out searching for it.

Rutherford, who reported to Sheriff Mike Sullivan that he saw a strange track, said it appeared to have been dug. the two tracks he reported seeing led away from the golf course in the southerly direction and were about 20 feet apart. They were the only tracks to be found in the soft, desert sand in the area.

Creature hunters from throughout the El Paso area convened on Horizon City Thursday night and combed the nearby desert for nearly five hours without results.

"Those guys were out there in the dark shooting at anything that moved," said one teen-aged girl. "I'm more afraid of them than I am of the creature."

Rutherford also reported that two anthropologist from the University of Souther California showed up to study the situation. But after they were told of the prints and description, Rutherford said they went back and got on the first plane back to California.

"I don't know a lot of the people around here don't believe we saw anything," said Miss Ellis "But there really was something out there. And it really scared us bad."

© *The El Paso Times*

## FOOTPRINTS FOUND IN 1975

### 1975 Bigfoot Footprints Found

Source: BFRO/TBRC

On Mon Dec 29 15:02:11 2003, The following information was submitted:

**Name**: (withheld)

**Gender**: M

**Age**: 49

**Street Address**: (withheld)

**Country**: USA

**Date**: 09/12/75

**Time**: approx 1600 hrs

**Weather:** dry, warm

**City**: Horizon City

**County**: El Paso

**State**: TX

**Location hwy**: Horizon Blvd and Horizon CC golf course, West approx. .5 mile

**Location water**: drainage ditch next to the golf course

What happened : Found approx. a quarter mile of footprints along a sand dune in the creosote bushes. Backtracked to the NE until lost upon hard ground. Lost to the SW at a hard arroyo and could not pick up the trail again. Photographs were taken and the prints were 17 inches long and 7 inches wide. The remarkable thing about the prints were that all five toes were not evident in all the prints... indicating the creature that made the prints had flexible toes (not like a fake foot) where the little toe and the one next to it had lifted occasionally when the prints were made. Another remarkable thing about the prints were that they led often through the middle of 4-foot creosote bushes, crushing the main branches, indicating to me that the prints were not faked because a human would never have done this and risked physical injury. The search was started due to a number of sightings in 1975 which the El Paso Times reported and named the creature the "Horizon City Prince." It all started after 9-1-75 when a 17-year-old reported a face-to-face while dove hunting on or about 9-1-75 near the golf course. A number of reporters also had a visual encounter during a moonlit night and reportedly saw a dark, large, bipedal figure striding down a large sand dune. I happened to be out at night with a friend of mine named Sam B. in his Jeep when I noticed something wrong with a creosote bush as we passed. We circled back and discovered the crushed bush and the large footprints. We took a dune buggy back the next day and searched for the same bush by following the tracks from the night before. That's when David N., Frank H., and I tracked the prints and photographed them. David N. has the photos and I haven't been able to locate him for some years. I now believe he lives in Leesville, LA. but as yet I haven't found him. Frank and Sam still live in El Paso.

**No physical evidence**: see above...and I will send them if I can find Dave N. terrain :

**Other (Describe Below) other**: sand and desert with yucca, creosote (greasewood),

**Activities**: driving in off-road vehicles...a common recreation in El Paso

**Prior sight**: I left the area in 1981 and don't know about subsequent incidents but several sightings occurred during that September

**Prior sound**: It's the desert and strange things/sounds occur all the time

**Farm**: The developers of Horizon City had attempted to install a recreational lake about 3 or 4 miles East of this location and held water at this time

## SIGHTINGS FROM 1973

**Here are a couple of other older El Paso area sightings**
Source: BFRO/TBRC
1973 Bigfoot Sighting

The first time was when I was 12 years old I heard what I thought was a women screaming near a river. I felt so helpless it was in the late night and could not wake up my sisterthe screaming was that of blood curding that even now I can still remember and Istill get very spook by just thinking of it. I am now 47 years of age. Would you believethis took place in El Paso just outside a small district of Ysleta Texas.

The second time was when I was 17 It was a crisp cool evening about twilight in the valley of Socorro Texas a few miles from Ysleta this time I was walking with my cousin in the distance of an ambdon cotton field I saw what was about 8 or (9) feet high at first I didn't believe what was happening it was walking towards us it was greyish brown in color the back ground was a small canal

I told my cousin to be quiet and my instincts said to ran I began to run my cousin followed then passed me. it had entered our house that evening threw the back door what made this so scary was it had pulled the door right off its hinges and walked into my bedroom where my mother and aunt where sleeping

I had given up my bed for my aunt that night she had had a fight with her husband and so I slept with my other aunts house about a block away it was the first day of school and we had to get up early because my other cousin would be giving us a ride when the next day I stopped in to pick up my school supplies my mothers face was white and told me about what had happen the night my brothers heard my mother scream and it left a few days before that however I could feel something weird around the house we were renting I would sometimes leave the side door open for my big brother because we never knew when he'd be coming home one night before all this happened.

I heard what I thought was my brother I called out his name Trinidad is that you it was after midnight there was a uncomfortable uneasiness because I had heard this spoons rattle. I then heard something come through the living room I covered my head with the covers and felt something scaring at me I was alone that night

I believe this creatures do exist I also believe that they migrate into Mexico I know that the Indians of New Mexico marcirated into Mexico the Navajo Geranimo.

The third time was when I was about 16 I was with my boyfriend we were on the Rio Grande making out in the back seat it was late at night and I heard something that put chills down my back I said to Mike what was that he said it was nothing maybe an owl or something I was really spooked and didn't want to be there any more so I lost interest in making out reaaaal quick and made him take me home. All this incdents happened near the Rio Grande There is as folklore would have it said to be the crying lady who comes out at night looking for her children she had drown in the river God had punished her by never giving her peace she would be forever crying out along the river for her dead children.

This is the legend I grew up with it is a old Mexican wives tale I know better We tend to protect our subconscious with the Easter bunny and Santa Claus not what were really afraid to accept the fact the the boogie man is real and living among us . Also Noticed Nothing expect I could have messed myself!

**Conditions around** 7:00 dark twilight it was cold
**Other Witnesses** about 5

**Other Stories** no we moved soon after
**Landscape** gas station near corner of the road and on Moon City rd.

**Year** 1973
**Season** Fall
**Month** September
**Day of Month** 03
**State** TX
**Directions to Location** not a problem
**Nearest Town** El Paso
**Nearest Road**


## CURRENT SIGHTINGS

So that the reader does not think that Big Foot has gone away, let us look at a sighting from 2004.

**New Sighting Report 2/13/04**
Additional Source: http://texasbigfoot.com/ElPaso2.html
**"Tailless Monkey" Seen in El Paso Desert**
**Witness:** Male
**Name:** Brooks D.
**Age:** 22
**Date of sighting:** Tuesday 7/29/03
**Location:** East of El Paso, TX (El Paso county)
**Time of incident:** approx 7am (1 hr after sunrise)
**Weather Conditions:** summer morning
**Closest Highway:** North of Montana St (east of El Paso city limits) in the desert with scattered houses around the desert.

**Closest Water Source:** A pond is nearby that fills with water when it rains.
**What was seen, heard, observed, encountered, or found:**

This report is being sent in by TBRC West Regional Leader, Sharon Eby, based on eye-witness interview today. The witness told me the following:

Early in the morning, about an hour after sunrise I stopped to go to urinate because I had to go so bad. I stood by a bush and noticed a large tree trunk about the distance from me to that "water tank" (please note that witness pointed to a tank that sat about 125 feet away) up in front of me. Then I thought to myself, "What the heck is a tree trunk doing here in the desert!" I had not ever seen it there before and it appeared to be about 4 feet high or so and was dark colored. Suddenly I saw the "tree trunk" stand up! I then noticed that it looked like a monkey... but with no tail. Then I started to freak out really bad because I was actually looking at a large monkey right there in front of me! His shoulders were really broad, his color was dark, like blackish with some red, and his face was just like a monkey.

Witness showed the height of the creature at approx 8 feet tall when standing upright (fully upright like a human) with longer arms than a human, but lots of hair, noticing that the hair hanging down from under the arms was approx. 4-5 inches long, dark but reddish in color.

Witness continued: I saw him stand up, turn to glance at me for a second and then looked away from me and started walking away from me like I wasn't even there, or like he didn't care that I was there. I watched him walk away into the desert. I didn't tell too many people at first because I figured they would laugh at me, but then 2 days later that article came out in the El Paso Times newspaperabout the bigfoot that was seen south of there in Horizon City so then Istarted talking more about seeing the bigfoot. I spoke with one lady and she was really interested in hearing my story because she said she had a small dog and that a large creature like that reached down in her yard to steal the dog, but when she yelled it quickly leaped over the wall in one single jump.

**If animal(s) were seen can you describe:** Just the bigfoot standing up after I thought it was camouflaged as a large tree trunk. His shoulders were broad, arms long, he stood like a man but looked like a tailless monkey with dark reddish hair that was long hanging off the arms. He was so big and wide!
**Sketch:** yes

Photos Taken: no

**Footprints or other physical evidence:** I spoke with the witness' father Wayne and he said that Brooks did not tell him about the bigfoot sighting until a week after it happened because Brooks was afraid he (and others) would just laugh at him and not believe him. Wayne offered to take Brooks out to the sighting location to look for footprints but by a week later they would be long gone.

**Terrain:** Desert terrain, mequite mounds, greasewood, cacti.

**Activities of witness prior to occurrence:** Going through the desert on his usual route and stopped to go to the bathroom because it was urgent and he could not wait.

**Any other incidences prior or since this occurrence:** Witness was unaware of any other bigfoot sightings in the area until he saw the article in the El Paso Times, and then started speaking with others.

**No sounds heard**

**No odors smelled**

**Any farms or agricultural facilities in the area:** Ranches and homes. A military base not far away that is mostly all desert[40].

So there you have several detailed sightings of unknown creatures. Are these some of the world famous Big Foot sightings or is something else wandering through the desert around Horizon City?

---

[40] Report written by TBRC Field Investigator Sharon Eby 2/13/04

# PART III

## HAUNTED EL PASO

In my first book, I wrote that El Paso is one of the most haunted cities in the country and I discussed a number of locations in El Paso that were said to be haunted. However, in my research, I discovered that there are so many haunted locations in El Paso that no one book can do justice to this rich supernatural history. I have also discovered more information on some of the locations that I discussed in the previous book that I believe deserves to be made a part of this record.

It has also come to light that while El Paso is one of the most haunted places in the country, the area around El Paso is every bit as strange as we shall see. Therefore, I am now going to discuss some more haunted locations within, and without the boundaries of our city. There is no question that in many locations ghosts walk the night, waiting for the unfortunate human who comes their way.

# CHAPTER SIX
# THE MAGOFFIN HOME
### 1120 Magoffin Avenue
### El Paso, Texas 79901

**Figure 14: The front entrance to the Magoffin House.**

When the subject of ghosts and hauntings comes up, the first thing mentioned by someone in the group will be the Magoffin House, location at 1120 Magoffin Avenue. In spite of the fact that it is not the most haunted location in El Paso, it is certainly the best known. Probably two thirds of those that have seen this series for the first time ask if the Magoffin Home is in the book.

Now operated by the Texas Parks and Wildlife Department, the Magoffin House has been a landmark in El Paso since 1870. This venerable old home remained the Magoffin Family Home until 1976 when it was jointly purchased by the City of El Paso and the State of Texas. Any building that has been the home to a single family for so long can't help but have absorbed the personality of this wild, driven bloodline and so it appears that the majority of the spirits that still occupy this symbol of yesteryear are related in some way to the Magoffin family.

## James Wiley Magoffin

**Figure 15: James Wiley Magoffin**

Born in 1799 in Harrodsburg, Kentucky, James Wiley Magoffin ventured to Mexico in the early 1820s seeking adventure and opportunity. Though still in his 20's, James began a transporting and trading business. He began to sell books, cloths, medications, printing presses, lumber and wagons along the Santa Fe-Chihuahua Trail[41]. In 1825, his close friend U.S. Secretary of State, Henry Clay, recognizing the growing influence that Magoffin enjoyed among the Mexican people and appointed Magoffin as Consul to Chihuahua and Saltillo, Mexico, a position he filled until 1832. During this time period, James Magoffin met and socialized with many wealthy Mexican families. It was during this time period that he met and married his first wife, the socially prominent Maria Gertrudis Valdez de Veramendi in 1830[42].

The happy coupled settled in Chihuahua and raised five children, but there was an ever present cloud on the horizon. Tensions between the ruling body in Mexico City and the United States were growing. By 1844 James and Maria sensed that war was inevitable because of the strained relations between Texas

---

[41] The route he traveled ran from Independence Missouri, through Santa Fe, New Mexico, El Paso, Texas and into Mexico until it ended in Chihuahua,
[42] His second wife was Maria's sister.

and Mexico. They decided that they and their five children would move to Independence, Missouri, to be safe from tension. It was also a good business move because James would be at the head of the Santa Trail. The many business connections gained through his marriage coupled with his own business sense and respect for Mexican culture won him standing as a trusted trader and merchant on the Santa Fe and Chihuahua Trails.

James and the children arrived in Missouri in 1845, but sadly Maria died along the way. James decided to work even harder now that he had five motherless children to care for. The Magoffins bought a farm and lived in Missouri until 1849 when they moved to El Paso, the mid-point of his business route.

Though he no longer lived in Chihuahua, Mexico, Magoffin's influence still extended into both U.S. and Mexican politics. So it was only natural that in 1846, President James K. Polk asked Magoffin to join the military force commanded by General Stephen W. Kearny on the march to Santa Fe. It was directly as a result of Magoffin's actions while with Kearny that the New Mexico territory was surrendered to the American forces without a shot being fired[43]. His actions shortened the war and saved countless lives on both sides of the action.

Hoping to be able to stop the war completely, Magoffin went directly to Chihuahua to see influential friends. He believed that with the help of his many friends in Chihuahua, the government in Mexico City could be convinced to stop the war. Unfortunately, when he arrived in Chihuahua, he was arrested as a spy and imprisoned in Durango for several months. Upon his released, he went back to Washington DC where he was paid $30,000.00 for his efforts.

When the Mexican War ended in 1848, Magoffin hoped to restart his trading business along the Santa Fe- Chihuahua rail. However, he found that high Mexican duties on trade goods made a profit almost impossible. So in 1849, James Magoffin settled opposite El Paso del Norte. He purchased 100,000 acres of land between Ponce de Leon's estate and Concordia, the property belonging to Hugh Stephenson. Magoffin called the territory he owned Magoffinsville. This grant of land initially encompassed all of present-day downtown El Paso and more. Magoffinsville was a small town complete with a general store, livery stable and a spacious residence for his family. Further away, a half mile from the Rio Grande, he built a plaza with adobe buildings surrounding it. Missing female companionship, and wanting a mother for his children, Magoffin returned to Chihuahua and courted Dolores Valdez, his late wife's sister. They were married in 1850.

As Magoffinsville grew, it was only natural that both the wealth and the political influence of James Magoffin would grow as well. A few years after the founding of Magoffinsville the local military post, which had been established

[43] Jones, Harriot Howze, El Paso, A Centennial Portrait, El Paso County Historical Society, Superior Printing, El Paso, Texas. 1972.

earlier to protect and defend residents against attacks by Mescalero Apaches and fierce Comanches, relocated to Magoffinsville. Because of the structure and location of the adobe buildings, they were chosen for the military post which became Fort Bliss. James Magoffin was given the very lucrative military contract to feed and supply the troops.

Unfortunately, again the threat of war loomed darkly on the horizon. The American Civil War was fast approaching. Just as the country was divided, so to, El Paso was divided. James Magoffin was solidly on the side of the South and worked hard to ensure that El Paso voted for succession. For his efforts he was appointed a Commissioner for the Southern Cause for West Texas[44]. In fact, when BG Twiggs surrendered the Military Department that included El Paso to the Southern cause, Magoffin accepted the surrender of Fort Bliss.

After the Confederate debacle in New Mexico, the remnants of the Confederate Army withdrew to El Paso. However, with the advance of the Union Forces, the garrison of El Paso withdrew downriver. The land of many formerly prominent residents of El Paso who had supported the southern cause was confiscated and auctioned off to the highest bidder. Being one of the most prominent Southern officials in the area, James Magoffin lost his beloved Magoffinsville.

After the Civil War ended, through his own efforts and those of his friends, James Magoffin worked hard to reestablish title to his former holdings. Returning El Paso, he began to once again build his fortunes. Upon his return, he found that what the war and squatters had not destroyed of his beautiful Magoffinsville, the flooding of the Rio Grande in 1867 had washed away. He was forced to literally start over from scratch.

Even though this area was his home, James continued to travel from Missouri to Chihuahua and take care of his businesses. When the San Antonio El Paso road opened up, he frequently visited his daughter in San Antonio, where he died in 1868[45].

## Joseph Magoffin

Born in Chihuahua, Mexico on January 7, 1837, Joseph was educated in private schools in Lexington, Kentucky and Missouri. Joseph Magoffin joined his father in Magoffinsville in 1856. The worthy son of a very astute father, Joseph helped extend the family interests throughout what is now the state of Texas. During his travels Joseph made many friends and business associations which served him well when he assumed his father's position.

Loyal to the Southern cause like his father, Joseph joined the Confederate Army in 1862 to oppose the Union invaders. It was while he was

---

[44] Ibid
[45] Ibid

serving in the Confederate Army that he met and married Octavia MacGreal of Victoria, Texas in 1864.

Following the Civil War, the couple returned in El Paso in 1868. While Octavia's life centered on their children, James and Josephine, Joseph's attention turned to the construction of their residence and the growing community. One of the incorporators of El Paso in 1873, his active civic and political life included four terms as mayor, and the establishment of city utilities, the first hospital and the first public schools. His business interests were equally extensive and ranged from banking and real estate to transportation.

**Figure 16: Joseph Magoffin**

During his 1882 administration as Mayor, mule-drawn trolley cars became an accepted form of transportation in El Paso. A pair of mules traveled the two routes. One route went down San Antonio Street and returned on present-day Magoffin Avenue. The other route ran from El Paso Street to Seventh Street, to Stanton and cross an international bridge into Juarez. The trolleys later evolved into the better known street cars.

Joseph Magoffin also organized the El Paso Water Company which changed the left of the average citizen of El Paso drastically. No longer did people have to carry water from the Rio Grande, wait for the mud to settle before being able to drink the water. El Paso's volunteer fire department also took shape during his administration.

Mayor Magoffin, who liked sports, responded to a public demand and started two baseball teams. They played against each other every Sunday afternoon, thus providing entertainment for the people in El Paso.

Besides serving as a mayor, Joseph Magoffin contributed significantly to El Paso in other ways. He helped organize the State National Bank, holding the position of vice-president for many years. In addition, Magoffin served as Justice of the Peace, Collector of Customs, and District Judge in his lifetime.

## THE MAGOFFIN HOME

In 1873, Joseph recovered his father's property, which federal officials seized after the Civil War, and began construction of the family's home. What began as a small, three-room house grew to twenty rooms between 1875 and 1901. The house is a prime example of Territorial style architecture. This style took the native material of the Southwest, abobe and embellished it with Victorian touches, inside and out. Built in phases, the single story structure has three wings arranged around an open patio. The exterior was plastered and scored to give the appearance of large stone blocks.

Historical photographs of the home's interiors taken between 1887 and 1910 reveal typical late-Victorian decorations, furnishings and arrangements.

Carpets, wall paper and painted or papered ceilings reflected the home of a locally prominent family of the time.

In the late 1920's the home's interiors were remodeled and modernized in the Mission Revival style. Gas heat was installed and the utilities were updated. It was home to four generations of Magoffins, spanning 110 years. Many of the original 1880s Eastlake style furnishings remain in the home today.

## THE LAST RESIDENTS:  THE GLASGOWS

Among the later residents of the Magoffin home were Joseph and Octavia's daughter, Josephine, and her husband, army officer William Jefferson Glasgow, whom she had married in 1896. Although the couple and their five children moved often during Glasgow's military career, they returned to El Paso and settled in the Magoffin house in 1927. After their deaths in the 1960s and the home's purchase by Texas Parks and Wildlife Department and the City of El Paso, daughter Octavia Glasgow continued to live in the house until she died in 1986.

## THE GHOSTS

It is certainly not unusual for rumors of hauntings to spring up regarding an old house and the Magoffin House is certainly one of the oldest in the area.

However, the stories that have come from the Magoffin House seem to be much more believable that the average ghost story, as the spirits have been seen far more than is normal in a supposed haunted house.

There are many in El Paso that maintain that Octavia Magoffin is often seen tending her beloved flower garden outside the rear of the house, while others swear that Uncle Charlie Richardson still sits in his rocker, passing the time inside their family home. However, both of these well known individuals have been deceased for more than 75 years. Those working at the Magoffin House have been heard to say that they prefer to say that the Magoffin family members still occupy the home only now in more ethereal manner.

Mary Kay Shannon is the current Manager of the Magoffin Home State Historic Site. Even though the historic home is rich in history, the management of the facility fears that the presence of spirits overshadows the real purpose for which the home is open to the public. Word spreads about the spirits of the Magoffin House faster than the unique history, so people will come because they've heard it might be haunted rather than because of the historic aspects. Unfortunately, this somewhat narrow minded attitude causes the management to downplay a portion of the actual history that could result in many more people coming to see this fine old house in the hope of seeing a spirit. What does it matter why someone comes to see the Magoffin House as long as they learn something about the history of the house and the area?

Connie Wang was partners with Joanne Shaw in a company that gave ghost tours and told me of some of the events that they experienced at the Magoffin House. It was during one of these tours in 1998 that the little girl was seen sitting in the window of the front room of the Magoffin House as if she was waiting for someone. The room in question was the formal parlor and it was later found that no one was in the room as the group approached the front door and no little girl was in the house at all at the time[46].

The individual who had seen the little girl sitting in the window was Julie Evans, someone who was taking the tour and a friend of Connie's[47]. According to

**Figure 17: The window where Julie Evans saw the spirit of Rose.**

Connie, Julie went back for several visits to the house in order to further investigate the spirits. She felt that the girl she had seen in the window was young and loved red roses. Because of this love for roses associated with the young girl, she has been named Rose by those who feel her presence. Julie also had the feeling that James Magoffin, whose picture hangs in the room, was not very happy with the tremendous amount of activity taking place in the home.

---

[46] This story came from Connie Wang.

[47] Another record of Julie Evan's contacts with the spirits of the Magoffin House can be found in Magoffin Home: A House Where Spirits Dwell by Clinton "Bud" Dehrkoop., Casa Magoffin Companeros. 2000.

On a later visit, Julie and Connie came together in order to try and get more detailed impressions of the little girl[48]. Both women sat on the window ledge in the formal parlor and tried to contact the girl. It was believed that she was eight years old and very sickly. Julie believed that the girl's name was Rose and she also found that there were three other spirits in the formal parlor that she believed were adult.

Julie and Connie found that the spirit of Josephine Magoffin Glasgow was one of the adult spirits in the parlor. She was wearing a long dress with a light colored collar and she was reading a book. One of the people present agreed that Josephine had gone to the finest schools of the day and was a very well educated woman.

During this time in the parlor, Julie tried to communicate with the spirits in the room. She felt that the little girl, who name was found to actually be Rose was supposed to have died in the early 1890s of what Connie believes based on information supplied by Josephine's spirit, of Lou Gehrig's disease.

In addition to the spirit of Josephine Glasgow and Rose, whose last name is believed to be White, other spirits seen or felt within the front parlor of this historic old home include Octavia Magoffin, Joseph Magoffin's wife and Charles C. "Uncle Charlie" Richardson.

One of the best known manifestations of the presence of spirits within the Magoffin Home is Uncle Charlie's rocking chair which sat in the family parlor near the fireplace. This is where he was known to sit and take his afternoon naps. In fact, it is said that he died in this rocker during one of his naps and no one knew that he was dead until the family members were unable to rouse him from his nap.

The old rocker has in later years been moved into the Great Hall that runs through the middle of the house. Though it now sits silently, its owner gone on to the great beyond, a number of people have maintained that they have seen the chair begin to rock without anyone touching it or any breeze that could account for the movement. Does Uncle Charlie come back to enjoy his rocker? There are a number who believe that he does indeed enjoy the occasional rock.

Other guests have made mention of the fact that they have felt someone tap them on the shoulder when there has been no one around them. It would not be the first time that a spirit tried physical touch to gain the attention of the living.

Another manifestation that still has not been explained concerns Josephine Magoffin, the daughter of Joseph Magoffin. She married her husband, Lieutenant William Jefferson Glasgow, in 1896 and the wedding reception was held in the Magoffin Home. In 1996, there were plans to reenact the event and arrangements were underway. One afternoon, a staff member saw a lady in a long white dress standing in the Great Hall. When he went out to see who the lady was that he had seen, the Great Hall was empty. He later saw a picture of

---

[48] These memories were from a tape recording made for me by Connie Wang.

Josephine Magoffin in a long white dress and swore that this was the lady he had seen in the Great Hall that afternoon[49].

**Figure 18: The wedding reception of Josephine Magoffin.**

## MY OWN ADVENTURES IN THE MAGOFFIN HOUSE

I first met Connie Wang when I took a ghost tour on Halloween 2001. One of the stops on the tour had been the Magoffin House. We had first stopped at the International Art Museum on Montana and I had witnessed a supposed haunting that had turned out to be a sighting staged by the staff of the Museum in order to support the tour. So when we arrived at the Magoffin House, I was not particularly expecting to see anything other than perhaps another staged event.

When we entered the Great Hall, both a docent working at the Magoffin House as well as Joanne Shaw and Connie Wang began to relate the events that

---

[49] This was told to me during a ghost tour that I took of the Magoffin House, but much more detail was found in Magoffin Home: A House Where Spirits Dwell by Clinton "Bud" Dehrkoop., Casa Magoffin Companeros. 2000.

had taken place in the historic old home. I was standing just inside the rear door with my arms folded listening attentively to the history of the home. I was certainly not expecting anything to happen out of the ordinary.

At one point in the presentation, someone tapped my arm gently and a very lovely young woman in a period dress asked me to please allow her to pass by where I was standing. She could have easily have walked around me, but I was trying to be polite by moving out of her way. She then walked slowly and gracefully across the Great Hall and entered the room leading to Josephine's bedroom.

After she passed by, I moved back to my position near the rear door which allowed me to see into the room leading to Josephine's bedroom where the very pretty young lady had gone. I was a little surprised that I did not see her, but I thought very little about it. I idly assumed that there was a photo shoot taking place which would account for the dress the young lady was wearing. Imagine my surprise when I discovered that there was not a photo shoot taking place that day and that no one else remembered the young lady that had brushed past me.

This incident would have been enough to give one pause for thought, but this was not to be my only brush with the unusual during this particular visit to the Magoffin Home. The tour next went into Josephine's bedroom room. We entered this bedroom through the room that connected it to the Great Hall. There are two rooms adjoining Josephine's bedroom which can only be entered either from this bedroom or from the outside of the building. The floor plan is relatively simple, so afterwards this only added to my puzzlement.

As we entered Josephine's bedroom, the room to our left was Uncle Charlie's and was also probably used by General Glasgow. It definitely has a male presence that can be readily felt. However, the other room, known as the children's room was where my next puzzling event happened. I was standing near the foot of Josephine's bed listening to the tour guide explain the various items of furniture in the room and the various uses to which he family had put the room over the years and from where I was standing, I could see into the children's room. There was a bed just inside and to the left of the entrance to the children's room from Josephine's bedroom. From my position I could see that someone wearing what looked like jeans and boots was lying stretched our on the bed. The booted ankles were crossed and the person was obviously at ease. At the time, I gave this individual lying on the bed little thought.

After the discussion of Josephine's room was completed, the tour first went into Uncle Charlie's room and we were given a ten minute talk about the history of the room and its various occupants. Then we crossed Josephine's bedroom once again and entered the children's room. As I passed the bed I had seen someone lying on I could see a slight indentation, but in spite of this indentation, the bed was very neatly made. I made some comment on how neat the bed was after being used so recently and was overheard by the docent[50] who asked me what I was talking about.

I explained what I had seen and was adamantly assured that no one, at any time, was allowed to lie on the beds in the Magoffin House. Frankly I had assumed that the figure I had seen was someone planted by the ghost tour to cause a scare or an employee of the Magoffin House resting for a few minutes. These mistaken beliefs were quickly dispelled by the somewhat irate docent who appeared horrified that someone would have the audacity to touch let alone lie down upon one of the Magoffin House beds. I was just as adamant in asserting that I had most definitely seen someone laying on the bed in the children's room just a short time before. As I mentioned, I naturally, assumed that it was someone helping create some spooky sightings for the tour group, but to this day, Connie Wang continues to assure me that they had nothing to do with anyone lying on the bed or any other piece of furniture at the Magoffin House.

At the time of this occurrence, I had not been aware that one night in 1999, after the house was closed for the day and the alarms activated, someone or something had sat on the beds, walked on them and generally caused havoc with the very neatly made beds throughout the house. I was told by the person that had first discovered the disruption that the pillows on the bed in Josephine's bedroom looked as if someone had rested their head on them for a long period of time[51]. Even the bed in Uncle Charlie's room upon which were laid two of General Glasgow's uniforms was depressed around the uniforms as if someone had punched or sat on the bed. No explanation was ever found for these events.

## CAUGHT ON CAMERA

Now that I have written two very successful books about the ghosts of the El Paso area, many people are now bringing me stories of hauntings. One of these stories also concerns the Magoffin House and what are believed to be some of the tricks played by Uncle Charlie.

El Paso is a city with a long rich history. Television Station KCOS, the El Paso Public Television Station prepared a film version of the life of Henry Flipper[52], the first black graduate of West Point. During the filming of this historical documentary, Uncle Charlie's room was selected as the location in which to film some scenes to be made a part of this show.

---

[50] A docent is an unpaid volunteer that helps give tours and take care of the property.

[51] This tale was related by both Connie Wang and also written about in <u>Magoffin Home: A House Where Spirits Dwell</u> by Clinton "Bud" Dehrkoop., Casa Magoffin Companeros. 2000.

[52] This production was entitled *Held In Trust* and documented the life and times of this remarkable man.

According to all reports, in one scene that was shot in Uncle Charlie's room, the lead actor was supposed to be packing a bag of clothing by the light of a very right floor lamp. As soon as the cameras starting rolling, the light was snapped off. The filming was stopped while the actor cut the lamp back on and then the cameras began to roll again. A second time, the light was cut off, but no living person was near the lamp other than the actor. Finally the lamp was removed and the scene was successfully shot.

I am also told that between takes, items on the set would be moved about so that before filming could start again, every single item had to be checked in order to make sure that it was returned to its proper place. Finally, I am told by an individual at KCOS who asks to remain nameless that during editing, one scene contained a mirror which, in one frame, reflected a face that no one could identify. Did Uncle Charlie want to be part of the movie[53]?

If spirits do linger on after death, then is it so odd to think that they may not want to be part of the activity that is now taking place in the home that they loved?

---

[53] I have had three different people tell me about the eerie happening during the filming of the movie, but I would also point those who wish to read more about this and other events to <u>Magoffin Home: A House Where Spirits Dwell</u> by Clinton "Bud" Dehrkoop., Casa Magoffin Companeros. 2000.

## CHAPTER SEVEN
### Home at the Corner of Magoffin Street and
### El Paso, Texas

**Figure 19: This was the home of Joseph Magoffin's Mistress.**

In the almost reverent worship that some of the current generation have demonstrated for historical figures such as Joseph Magoffin, it is very easy to forget that he was a man just like any man living today. He also had the same needs as any man as well as the same temptations. It may come as a great shock to many, but Joseph Magoffin had a mistress that he cared for just as much as he did for his wife.

Though Joseph Magoffin had a very lovely wife at home, she either could not or would not endulge in the type of activities that Joseph desired. The moral structure of the day was such that ladies indulged in sexual conduct only to carry on the family name and produce an heir. Sex was not something that one did for pleasure. However, according to many of rumors that circulated at the time, Joseph was a man with a very high sex drive. His wife, I am sure indulged him, but not with the enthusiasm and abandon that he seemed to desire. As a result, enter the "other woman."

According to my information, after suffering the embarassment of becoming stuck in the bath tub at one of the local houses of pleasure, Joseph Magoffin decided that not even his reputation could with stand the scandal that being caught enjoyjng the services of a prostitute. Being both an intelligent as well as a wealthy man, Joeph Magoffin came up with a very novel idea to solve the problem.

Of all of the women that Joseph Magoffin enoyed associating with, there was one who seemed to be the perfect paramour for a man of his stature. Over time, this lovely young lady became what was known as the other woman. Of course a divorce was out of the question for someone in the political arena and the "other womnan" was content to live in the shadows, seeing him whever it was convenient.

To both reward her for being so understanding and to have her close by so that he could see her whenever it was covnenient, Joseph Magoffin built the house pictured above for the "other woman". Since he was a married man and a prominent political figure in El Paso, he had to very careful when and where he was seen with his lady friend. She loved to dance, so he had a small ballroom constructed on the second floor of this house where the two of them would spend hours dancing to the music that they both loved. So well did she live the role he asigned her that even today, very little is known of this loving woman. However, through she is gone physically, clearly she has not forgotten the house where she spent many enjoyable hours dancing with the man she loved but could have for her own.

Over the last few years, the owners of this proeprty have tried to lease out the rooms in order to supplment their income. Additionally, in the rear of thehouse, some apartments were built to expand the number of rooms that could be rented out. Unfortunately, this was another case of even the best laid plans going awry. As fast as renters would move into this lovely old home, they would move right back out again. According to the few that would talk about the situation, they would hear footsteps and voices coming from empty rooms. Some evenings they would hear fait music coming from the part of the second floor that had been originally designed as a ballroom. One of two people swore that they could hear the rythmic footsteps of a couple dancing.

So after a number of renters rotated throug the house, the owners boarded it up, hoping to at least rent out the apartments built in the backyard. As can be seen from the pictutre, the old house is being allowed to fall down. These days, no one goes inside to disturb Joseph and the "other woman." Perhaps in death, she possesses the full attention of the man should could not openly have in life.

# CHAPTER EIGHT
## EL PASO CONVENTION AND VISITORS BUREAU
### One Civic Center Plaza
### El Paso, TX 79901

**Figure 20: El Paso Convention and Visitors Bureau**

The El Paso Convention and Visitors Bureau is a circular building located adjacant to the Convention Center, though few seem to know where it is located. Few of those who occupy the building during the day remain much after closing time. But one evening, one of the employees remained late, wanting to get a project finished.

The worker glanced at the clock sometime later and was surprised to see that it was rather late in the evening. He decided to go to the breakroom in order to stretch his legs and see what snacks were available from the vending machines.

Believing that he was alone in the building, the worker was shocked to come upon a man who was wearing what was later described as turn of the century clothing. The worker froze at the sight of the intruder. The oddly dressed man walked up to him as if it were the most ordinary thing in the world for him to be in the building and politely asked if the worker could give him directions to a good restaurant. Before the startled worker could utter a word, the oddly dressed gentleman faded from view[54].

---

[54] Metz, Leon, *EL Paso Ghost Sightings Aren't Unusual,* El Paso Times, August 9, 1999.

# CHAPTER NINE
## CATHEDRAL HIGH SCHOOL
### 1300 Block of North Stanton
### El Paso, Texas

**Figure 21: The entrance to Cathedral High School.**

Cathedral High School is not the oldest high school in El Paso[55], but it is one of the oldest as it was officially dedicated in September of 1925[56]. This formal dedication also marked the official arrival of the Christian Brothers, the first Catholic educators to teach in the school. It might also be noted that the Christian Brothers was a very old religious order, founded in 1680 in Rheims, France, and had a well earned reputation as superb educators and stern disciplinarians. Cathedral High was specifically formed by the Diocese of El Paso to be the diocesan boys' high school.

The facility that had become known as Cathedral High School also once served as the home of the El Paso Community Center, St. Patrick's School and the Catholic Youth Organization. There was tremendous public support for this new high school. In fact, this was made very clear during the Depression era,

---

[55] El Paso High School has that distinction being opened in 1916.
[56] Author unknown, *EP Catholic Education Began in 1879*, El Paso Times, July 4, 1976.

when the school received financial help from a local Catholic Men's organization called "A dollar-a-month Club".

For many years after its formal dedication, that bilding that contained Cathedral High actually contained two schools and a separate community center, with the Christian Brothers operating the High School in the south wing and the Sisters of Loretto operating St. Patrick's Elementary School in the north wing of the building. It was not until the early 1940s that the Community Center closed and St. Patrick's moved to its present location next to St. Patrick's Cathedral[57].

Today, this venerable old school is alive and well in downtown El Paso. Occupying almost an entire block on Stanton Street, the area is alive with the comings and going of students. It would be interesting to see how many of them are aware of the school's "other" history.

This school's most haunted place is the third floor of the building, which is also the floor containing the freshmen lockers and most of the freshmen classrooms. I have heard reports of a large number of sightings of a "thing" that slams lockers and runs down the hall to vanish suddenly.

There was an incident involving an unsuspecting freshmen who went to get something from his locker that was located on the third floor. As he retrieved what he had come after from his own locker, he glaced toward the end of the hall and noticed that the door to one of the lockers in that section was standing open. He started walking down the hall to see whose locker was left open when the locker door was slammed close and a white figure started running away from the freshman. The puzzled student gave chase wanting to see what was going on, but when the figure rounded the corner, it simply disappeared. The freshman was only a few steps behind the fleeing figure when it turned the corner and there was not place that it could have hidden. However, when the freshman turned the corner, thinking he was only a few lengths behind his quary, the hallway was empty.

Another part of Cathedral that is haunted is a staircase that leads up into a separate classroom that is attached to the third floor. I have had many former students tell me that once you walk into this classroom you can feel an eerie presence in the room. The hairs start standing up on the back of your neck and you get the feeling as if someone is either watching you or is standing right behind you. However, no matter how much you search around the room you can find no trace of anything either living or once living.

---

[57] Author unknown, *Cathedral Passes 50th As 'Community Center'*, El Paso Times, September 7, 1976.

# CHAPTER TEN
# JESUIT HIGH SCHOOL

**Figure 22: Jesuit High School**

Jesuit High School has had a tremendous impact on an entire generation of EL Pasoans even though the school only oeprated a little over twelve years. The building that house Jesuit High School was originally built by members of the Jesuit Order in 1926 and served as a refuge for Jesuits escaping from Mexico during the anti-Church movement. until it was closed in 1950.

Then in 1958, members of the Jesuit Order returned to reopen the facility as Jesuit High School which operated from 1960 until 1972 when it closed once again. In 1975, the Ysleta Independent School District heard that the buildings were to be torn down and the land sold and made a successful offer for the 48 acre complex. Shortly thereafter, the former Jesuit High School became Hillcrest Junior High School.

According to the book *Up River* by Professor Richard Aguilar, the old building in which Jesuit High School was opened consisted of four floors counting the basement, set on a sandy mound overlooking most of the valley. The floors, classrooms, corridors, stairs, doorframes, desks, lockers, papers, pencils and pens were constantly coated with a fine dust that crunched underfoot and stuck to the heel of your hand when you tried to write. In keeping with the

Jesuit tradition, the place was absolutely austere, not a single picture on any of the walls, everything designed for some functional and practical purpose.

The Jesuit Brothers who administered the school even painted all the furniture the same color, an odd tone, something like a Sunday hangover, as if they'd mixed together whatever was left over in a lot of different paint buckets, the general belief was that the drab paint was a gift from some hardware store.

The building was built in the shape of an M. The right leg of the M and part of the upper angle held classrooms and offices. The cloister was on the other side. A chapel stood in the center, with the cafeteria in the basement. A coat of arms was set in the floor just outside the chapel, beneath the letters AMDG (Ad Majore Dei Gloriam) BVMH (Beata Virgine María Honorem) were a two-headed eagle, byzantine-style with no crowns, and a brown and white striped shield, the symbol of the San Ildefonso School. The schoolyard was unattractive too, with only a couple of listless bay trees and some scraggly grass.

From all reports, discipline was strict at this Jesuit school. The first regulation to be learned by those students living in Juárez and the chicanos who by some miracle had survived the U. S. school system without forgetting their Spanish was that it was forbidden to speak that language in school. This certainly made it difficult for those who had no formal training in reading and writing in English. The Jesuit idea of discipline has traditionally been very strict, so naturally it was believed that punishment could teach a student to speak English insteaf of Spanish. This punishment normally consisted of being forced to stay after school and do laps around the recreation field.

A student that committed some type of infraction would receive a demerit. Each demerit, three were given for speaking Spanish, cost the offending student three laps around the field and each lap took about 10 minutes. So when a student piled up a lot of demerits, not only did he get a good workout, but it would get dark before he finished the dreaded laps.

Students being punished weren't allowed to speak during their disciplinary laps. Of course for those students who lived in Juarez, these laps caused additional problems. Since the school was so far from Juarez, about 15 miles from home, the parents formed a carpool with the idea of saving on gasoline and sharing the ordeal of driving 30 miles round trip. These trips also meant waiting in long lines at the international bridges and putting up with a carload of nosy adolescents.

Unfortunately if one of the students from Juarez was given demerits and as a result punishment laps, all of the students in the carpool were actually punished since they were all required to wait for the one being punished to finish his laps. The culprit was finally received by the carpool with icy silence and more punishment awaited him at home. The offender knew that he was in for a constant barrage of *"why are you late, you're incorrigible, you don't study, you're lazy, you'll never make anything of yourself, we're spending our hard-*

*earned money to send you to a good school and all you do there is eat your lunch, we're really not surprised because you've always been irresponsible, don't think for a minute you're going to borrow the car because if that's how you act in school, how can we expect you to behave yourself when nobody's watching you."* As with most religions, guilt and peer pressure were potent weapons used by the members of the Jesuit Order to regulate the behavior of their charges.

As someone once observed, everything must end, even the worst of hells. So it was that for a number of reasons, eventually, Jesuit High School was closed. After a few years as Hillcrest Junior High School, a new building was built nearby for the students and the old building was used as storage. However, even though it was no longer used, security patrols walked through the old building on a regular schedule.

## THE GHOSTS

The original building that had been used as Jesuit High School burned down in the early 1990s, but according to all reports, it was a building where spirits were unusually active. Though the massive old building had been deserted for sometime, I have heard a number of stories of security personnel entering the restrooms and be greated with all of the faucets suddenly turning on or all of the toilets flushing in unison. As if this was not enough, I have been made aware that several security and maintenance personnel would hear the sounds of footsteps in the deserted hallways and a sound like thje jungling of the key rings that some of the Jesuit Brithers worse hainging from their belts.

I would suspect that if anyone could remain long after the death of the physcial body it would be a member of the Jesuit Order. Their training seemed to insure that members of their order were of unusual intelligence, and possesed a singlemindedness of purpose granted only to those maiden aunts that we all rememebr as children.

I had occasion to talk to Bob Omspaugh, who is currently security coordinator at Eastwood High School, 2430 McRae Boulevard. Prior to moving to Eastwood High School, he had previously worked security at both the original Hillcrest Junior High School, the name given to this well known facility when it was taken over by Ysleta School System on December 9, 1975 as well as the new building built nearby.

He was one of those periodically greated by the faucets turning on by themselves and he also periodically heard the sounds of footsteps in empty halls. I had the opportunity to talk with him at great length about his time as security in this old building. Though by the time he joined the security staff at Hillcerst Junior High School, the students had all moved to the new building, the security of the old building was still a major concern.

**Figure 23: Bob Omspaugh.**

As with most old buildings that sit empty and that have seen better days, the old Jesuit High School Building generated its share of ghost stories. As young boys will, they dared each other to go into the hautned building. Many took the dares and crawled through conventiently opened windows or doors left open by thoughtless workers. More than a few came running out with new stories or horrible creatures and ghosts that roamed the empty dimly lit halls of this once bustling building.

He also talked about the many times that either guards, workers or passersby would smell smoke inside the building or the many reports made to them of fires burning on the grounds of the old school. Even when actual flames were spotted from a distance, by the time they reached the site of the fire, it would be gone, no smell and no sign of any embers. Is it coincidence that it was fire that finally destroyed this monument to an earlier time?

# CHAPTER ELEVEN
## JAXONS RESTAURANT
### 4799 Mesa
### El Paso, Texas

**Figure 24: Jaxon's at 4799 Mesa.**

This information is from a new article that I discovered about Jaxon's.

Jaxon's restaurants, a 27-year-old El Paso institution and one of the few successful, large-scale independents, is being sold to a man who waited tables there nearly 20 years ago.

"We have a purchase agreement. It's not closed. Due diligence is under way. I hope it will close by the end of the month," said owner and founder Jack Maxon.

"It's a tough business and I'm tired. I found the right guy. He's young, enthusiastic. He's going to carry Jaxon's forward. He may be able to grow the business – make it better," Maxon said.

**Figure 25: The Original Jaxon's.**

The purchaser is El Pasoan Gary Helsten, who has been managing Chili's franchises in El Paso, New Mexico and Arkansas for several years.

"I plan to keep the same names, the same staff, the same menu. Jack has built up an incredible business and if it ain't broke I'm not going to try to fix it," said Helsten, reached by phone in Farmington, N.M. Helsten was in Farmington to open a new Chili's franchise – one of the last projects for his Chili's franchises.

An El Paso mainstay, Jaxon's opened in 1973 at 508 N. Stanton. A decade later the restaurant moved to 4799 N. Mesa. In 1986 Maxon opened another location at 1135 Airway.

The restaurants employ about 150 people and serve an average of some 4,000 customers a week each. Terms of the purchase were not disclosed.

Helsten graduated from Coronado High School in 1980. He worked at Jaxon's on North Mesa in the early 1980's while he pursued a degree in business and marketing at UT-El Paso.

After graduation he worked at Studebaker's with Jim Paul and the late Orville Story, and then with Cisco Foods before moving on to Chili's about 10 years ago.

Did he ever dream of owning Jaxon's while he was waiting tables there?

"No. I certainly never thought I could be the owner," Helsten said

Maxon said one of the things that made Helsten attractive as a buyer was that he seemed likely to continue operations in much the same way.

"He's a terrific guy and I understand he doesn't plan to make any changes," Maxon said.

Helsten confirmed that.

"Jaxon's has been what I consider a landmark. It is something that is unique to El Paso and I plan to keep it just the way it is for a long time to come. I'm not going to change a thing," Helsten said.

"I bought Jaxon's because of Jaxon's. It's what I like and why I made this commitment. I believe in what Jaxon's does as a local restaurant and what Jack did as a local restaurant operator," he added.

So what changes would he make?

"I've got a lot of experience in the restaurant industry, so I hope to bring some operational advancements. But the staff, the menu, the services, none of that is going to change," he said.

So how's business at the time of the sale?

"Business is good," said Maxon. "But it's time for me to move on. Twenty-seven years is enough. I'm ready for a change — for something else. I'm not sure what that will be yet. I do have some opportunities to become involved in other things."

Whatever they are, it won't be another restaurant.

Maxon said he will be signing a non-compete contract at the close of sale. He does, however, plan to remain in El Paso.

To some extent, the restaurant business has been affected by the same kinds of mergers and consolidations seen in other industries, making it more difficult for independent operators such as Jaxon's to compete.

Maxon said Jaxon's has managed to survive and grow because, "We're more agile. We can change faster. But I have to give credit to my managers. We've had great management teams that have gone the extra step to take care of our customers." Christine Martin is the general manager at the Mesa store; Airways is run by Rick Melendez.

## THE GHOSTS

What he didn't know when Gary Helsten bought Jaxon's was that he also purchased the rights to a ghost that periodically haunts the building at 4799 Mesa after the customers leave for the night. I had heard from some former employees that when they stayed late at night after closing, they would sometimes hear what sounded like someone coming in the front door, even though they would have locked the front door after the last customer had left. Footsteps would be heard coming from the front door to the entrance of the dining room. Each time, a search would be conducted, but no one was ever found.

Other times, some of the cleaning crew would be in the kitchen area

**Figure 26: The bar area of The Original Jaxon's.**

working and hear what sounded like someone moving bottles of alcohol and shifting glasses, as if they were making themselves a drink in the bar area. On one occasion, one of the cleaning crew saw a dark figure standing just inside the dining area. This particular worker felt that the figure was watching her and she naturally assumed that it was the manager. But when she approached to see who had entered, the figure faded away.

On another occasion a figure was seen standing behind the bar as if looking or a particular drink. When the kitchen worker got up enough nerve to enter the bar to determine the identity of the unknown figure, the bar area of empty. To date, no one has been able to determine the identity of the figure, so tehre is no way to pin it down to a particular time frame.

The building at 4799 N. Mesa is an old one. A restaurant called The Terrirtorial House was a restaurant that occupied this building before the Original Jaxon's was ever thought of, so perhaps the ghost that haunts the building now is left over from this prior restaurant, I have not been able to find out and so we shall never know.

# CHAPTER TWELVE
## CRISTO REY CATHOLIC CHURCH
### 8011 Williamette Avenue
### El Paso, Texas 79907

What is now known as the Cristo Rey Parish and the Cristo Rey Catholic Church was dedicated in 1972, but the church named Cristo Rey Catholic Church was originally a much older mission chapel known as Our Lady of the Valley Church. This church, which is part of a cloistered convent, is only open to the public during Holy Week.

Many visitors have spoken of seeing what appeared to be a kindly older nun dressed in traditional habit of the order. Some talk of having seen her enter from the side of the chapel, but most maintain that she is usually seen praying at the altar's communion rail. The majority of those who enter a church and see a Nun praying at the communion rail take great pains not to make any noise so as to not disturb the devotions. However, if someone does approach the praying Nun, she is said to slowly fade away.

## CHAPTER THIRTEEN
## CROCKETT ELEMENTARY
### 3200 Wheeling Ave.
### El Paso, Texas 79930

**Figure 27: The sign in front of Crockett Elementary[58].**

By the year 1915 school enrollment in El Paso had reached 9,696. While by today's standards this is not a significant number of students, it was beginning to strain the capability of the city to handle the growing enrollment with existing facilities. Compounding the problem was the continuing growth of new houses in the northeast part of the city. To deal with this new growth, the city of El Paso created a new addition that was called Manhattan Heights[59].

New housing areas meant new students to add to an already overcrowded school system, therefore, on March 31, 1916, the School Board approved the

---

[58] This photo is from the author's collection.
[59] McCloughan, Mercedes, The History of Crockett School, privately printed in El Paso, Texas in 1995.

purchase of a block of land in the Manhattan Addition upon which to build a new school. On May 1, 1916, the Board voted unanimously to purchase block 12, Manhattan Addition. Though the land was acquired by the School Board in 1916, the architects, Beutell and Hardie, were not designated until December 16, 1919. However, once the plans were accepted, things moved quickly, with the firm of R.E. McKee being designated as General Contractor. So it was that the newly built school, originally called Manhattan Heights School, opened its doors to the first students on November 29, 1920, though many of the twenty-two rooms contained within this school building were not yet completely finished.

It had been believed that the new school would allow the School Board to be able to deal with the increasing number of students for some time however, at a Meeting of the Board dated March 21, 1922, a motion was passed to build an addition to the newly opened school. Things moved rapidly at this point, as the students returning to school in September of 1922 found that a new auditorium and eight new classrooms had been completed over the summer. The name Manhattan Heights School had also been changed to Crockett.

There were also fewer students attending the newly expanded school as the responsibility for teaching the seventh and eighth grade had been transferred to the newly opened Austin Junior High School, leaving only six grades being taught at Crockett.

## THE ARCHITECTURE

The architecture of Crockett is also somewhat different from the other schools built in El Paso. The new auditorium and the eight new classrooms added in 1922 were built around a courtyard. The courtyard was planned to be an oasis of greenery for the students to enjoy when they had breaks from their studies. English ivy was planted and encouraged to grow up the walls, evergreen trees and shrubbery were planted to enhance the feeling of sitting in a restful backyard. As the years passed, graduating classes donated stone benches to increase the seating areas and a merry flowing bird bath was added. It was in this hidden spot that the School PTAs held teas and school art classes spent hours sketching this garden spot[60].

The front entrance of the school, which is shown on the next page, is very striking in design, decorated with five terra cotta shields. It was anticipated that these five shields would symbolize the good qualities and ideals that every Crockett student should strive to achieve. The emblems embossed upon the terra cotta shields were specifically chosen to represent the ideals.

The shield at the left of the main entrance contains a Roman battleaxe and staves. These symbols were chosen to represent courage. The Roman influence was chosen because they were known throughout history as being the bravest of soldiers. In fact, the Roman armies were such fierce warriors that they

---

[60] Ibid.

conquered the known world. Crockett students were urged to show courage by standing up for what is right and being willing to play fair even when they were losing. The ideals embodied in the teachings at Crockett are some that many of our elected officials could certainly emulate in the way that they carry out their duties as our representatives[61].

The second shield from the left as you enter the building contains sun

**Figure 28: The shields over the front entrance of Crockett School[62].**

rising over an open book. This symbol represents enlightenment. This symbol was also to remind the students of Crockett how fortunate they were to be able to get a decent education as it was not too long in the past that only the children of the wealth were able to attend good schools and be taught by capable teachers. This shield also symbolized the concept that learning is to the mind what sunlight is to the body, giving strength and enjoyment[63].

The center shield, containing a fleur de lis on a checkered background was selected to represent the virtue of loyalty. The selection of the fleur de lis, also called the lily of France and the symbol of French Royalty for centuries, was based the idea that life is a game and one is expected to show loyalty in the game of life. First there is loyalty to one's self and then loyalty to school, parents, God

---

[61] Ibid.
[62] This photo is from the author's collection.
[63] Ibid.

and country. Certainly, the three selections so far are virtues that we should all possess but unfortunately, many do not[64].

The fourth shield contains the symbol of a cog wheel, symbolizing industry. Our society functions based upon work done by mechanical devices and this work is indispensable if society is to survive. It was envisioned that this symbol would illustrate that industry was the opposite of idleness and the student that is industrious in the classroom and at home is one that will succeed in growing just as society in general grows based upon hard work[65].

The fifth and final shield above the doorway of this historic school contains a single star and a diagonal stripe. These symbols stand for the endeavor of high ideals. Just as a star is high in the heavens, so to should our aim in life be high. Each student should strive to be generous, kind, clean and honest.

Most people know about the five shields, though they may not have any

**Figure 29: The sixth shield can be seen above the arched doorway[66].**

idea what the shields represent. However, most do not know that there is actually a sixth shield which can be found above the side and rear entrances of the building. This sixth shield contains a football, which represents physical training and the Greek lamp which represents learning. This combination, it was felt would result in a well rounded student that is physically healthy, demonstrates good sportsmanship and is very knowledgeable.

---

[64] Ibid.
[65] Ibid.
[66] This photo is from the author's collection.

## THE HIDDEN MEMORIAL

There is much about this historic building that is known only to those that have had the good fortune to either have attended the school or have a need to visit someone at Crockett. Crockett School has had long running ties with Fort Bliss and the U.S. Military in general. Within this building on Wheeling is one of the most beautiful memorials to those who have served this country that it has ever been my privilege to gaze upon.

In memory of the gallant men and women who were once students at Crockett that served in the Armed Forces of the United States, a most unusual memorial window was placed around the front door for all that passed through to remark upon.

This truly beautiful memorial window is made up of twenty-five

**Figure 30: The memorial window around the front entrance of Crockett School[67].**

sections. Inside of each section is the full color representation of a medallion upon which is drawn either the insignia of one of the branches of service or a picture depicting men and women who answered the call of their country to take up arms. The center medallion contains the inscription *"We live in the lives of those we love; we do not die."*[68]

---

[67] This photo is from the author's collection.
[68] Ibid.

This truly unique work of art was conceived by Miss Alice Swann, principal of Crockett from 1923 until her retirement in the spring of 1948[69]. Ralph Baker of Baker Glass Co. helped design and construct this one of a kind stained glass window. The cost of this one of a kind memorial window was paid

**Figure 31: The upper portion of the memorial window showing the center medallion[70].**

from Library fees, proceeds from programs presented at the school, cafeteria surplus money and a donation by R.E. McKee. Miss Swann had envisioned the memorial and began saving money immediately after the bombing of Pearl Harbor in December of 1941[71]. The El Paso Herald Post covered the dedication of this unique memorial on May 8, 1945.

Also unique are some of the decorations adorning the walls of the auditorium. Rather than paintings or the school emblem, along both walls are plaster casts that are 48 inches wide and 62 inches long. In 1926, two new ones were added, one representing the "*Spirit of 1917*" and the other, representing the "*Spirit of 1776*". In this day and age of growing opposition to the ideals and martial spirit that made this country what it is today, it was very refreshing to enter a building where the patriotism of those who administer the school is very evident and the teachers that I talked to were not shy in voicing their belief in the school and our country.

---

[69] Ibid.
[70] This photo is from the author's collection.
[71] Ibid.

I left this school sorry about only one thing, that everyone in El Paso could not see the unbelievable work of art that surrounds the entrance to this school. If nothing else, it would demonstrate to everyone that once, this country was united in its support of our military and in its belief in the high ideals espoused in the Declaration of Independence.

**Figure 32: The window as seen from the stairs leading down to the exit[72].**

## A TIME CAPSULE IS FOUND

Many old buildings in El Paso hide secrets and thebuilding that houses Crockett is no exception. When air conditioning was installed at Crockett, it meant opening many walls that had been sealed since the original construction was completed in order to install the duct work. In the wall of one of the science rooms on the third floor, a veritable time capsule from the 1930s was found[73]. Included in this uncovered treasure trove were papers, pictures, drawings and a number of items used in the daily instruction.

## HIDDEN ENTRANCES AND SPIRITS THAT WALK THE HALLS

The building is aged back to the 1920's and supposedly served as a hospital to war veterans. There is no question that there has been a long

---

[72] This photo is from the author's collection.
[73] Ibid.

connection between the school and the military from Fort Bliss. In fact, when a school hjad to be chosen for the education of the children of the former Nazi scientists now working for the U.S. Government, it was Crockett that was selected. However, there is evidence that this relationship with the military may go even deeper than many suppose.

It's said that on the second floor of this old building a child, not knowing the history the building, had witnessed a man walking down the hall with a bloody gauze bandage wrapped around his head and an amputated arm. She was puzzled by the appearance of the man, but he appeared as real as you or I. However, when the young student reported what she has seen, the ensuing search revealed that there was no such man in the building. Others have told me that there are many stories about such wounded individuals being seen walking about the building. Perhaps it is true, especially if the stories of the building having been used as a hospital are true.

I inquired at the school office regarding any sightings of ghosts and almost in unison, the four people in the office replied that the only spirit in the building was the Holy Spirit. The unfortunate fact is that the preconceived notions of the staff that there are no ghosts makes it very difficult to get to the truth.

I also asked the staff members that I met during my visit about the stories that I had heard that some of the hidden tunnels beneath El Paso may have an exit at the school. As I expected, all of them denied having heard any such stories and was I was adamently told that such stories were just myth. Faced with such total denial, I decided to abandon my quest for information with the school.

However, in the course of my research I actually met a young man who played in the tunnels as a child in the 1960s. As confirmed by many others of his generation who had played in the tunnels, my informant and his friends entered the tunnels through an entrance in the railroad yards. He related many stories to me of the games he and his friends played beneath this city.

According to this young man, during one jaunt into the tunnels with some of his friends, they decided to play a trick on him by running off and leaving him in the darkness. His friends did not know that he had a small inexpensive flashlight in his pocket, so he was not left completely lost.

Rather than taking the sensible couse of action of returning to the surface, he continued forward trying to follow his friends by the dim light of his cheap flishlight.However, the dim light caused him to become disoriented and he missed a turn. Rather than catching up with his friends, he came to a point where a second tunnel branched from the first one. He said that it appeared to him that the new tunnel ran toward the river. He decided to stay in the main tunnel which eventually brought him to a point where he believed he could exit the tunnel system.

To his surprise he came out of the tunnel to find himself inside a building. After roaming around by the aid of his dim flashlight, he realized that he was "inside" Crockett School.. Like any young boy that finds himelf in a place he shouldn't be, he explored a good portion of the building before going back into the tunnel system and making his way home.

How many other secrets does this old school hide from the world?

## CHAPTER FOURTEEN
## DEL VALLE HIGH SCHOOL
### 950 Bordeaux
### El Paso, Texas

The academic history of Del Valle High School has long been one of the most distinguished of El Paso schools,. However, a number of people have told me that at one time Del Valle had a dark side. This may be true, but I have not been able to find any independent verifications, so I can't confirm the stories one way of the other.

According to the local legends, it's been long known that in this school three young guys went on a rampage and whether intentionally or not, killed some members of the Del Valle High School Band. A number of people have told me this story, but so far, no one has been able to show me any proof such as a newspaper story confirming the murders.

There are many who now maintain that late at night, you can hear the screaming of the killed band members as they run for their lives from their killers.

## CHAPTER FIFTEEN
## DESERT VIEW MIDDLE SCHOOL
### 1641 Billie Marie Drive
### El Paso, Texas

This is another story that I have been unable to confirm. According to several people, one night one of the coaches came to this school and heard what sounded like someone punching some of the lockers with their fist. A search revealed that there was no one else in the building.

According to another long time resident of El Paso, one morning one of the Lunch Room workers arrived at the school early to begin her duties and had occasion to go down thehallway that led to the gymnasium of the school. To the surprise of the worker, a white figure dashed down the hall and through the locked doors into the empty gym. As far as the worker was aware, there were no students in the building as of yet.

## CHAPTER SIXTEEN
## THE TOYS R' US CHAIN

This next hautning is a little unusual in that it is not confined to just one store in the chain of toystores. In fact, this is the first time that I have heard of a number of stores in a chain being haunted. However, research has revealed that several of the stores of the Toys R' Us chain have resident spooks. I think it necessary to talk about all that I have been able to confirm in order to give the complete picture of what goes on in these stores. Naturally, I will begin with the two stores in El Paso.

## TOYS R' US
**801 Mesa Hills Dr.**
**El Paso, Texas 79912**

**Figure 33: The Toys R' US Store at 801 Mesa Hills Drive**

There are some buildings that gain a reputation as a result of some event that happens in or around the structure such as the famous gunfight in front of the Paso Del Norte Hotel. Though the gunfight had nothing to do with the well known historic hotel, people still remember the event in connection with what is now the Camino Real Hotel. So too people remember this particular Toys R' Us store as a result of the tense hostage drama that played itself out within the confines of this store dedicated to the fun and enjoyment of children of all ages.

# HELD HOSTAGE

This particular event began with a man by the name of George Rivas, a career criminal and his gang of followers known as the Texas 7. According to the records that I can find regarding this man and the crime spree that he cut through the stores of El Paso, George Rivas became a career criminal in his early 20s. He was described by almost everyone that knew him as being highly intelligent with a larger than life ego. In hindsight, there should not have been any surprise that he plotted the Connally Unit breakout and appointed himself ringleader of the infamous Texas 7. He is, without a doubt, a perfect example of a wasted life. He had intelligence, leadership ability and talent, all of which he used to plot his various crimes.

George Rivas was born in El Paso, Texas, on May 6, 1970. He was described as a six foot tall, 231 pound brown-haired, brown-eyed criminal with rugged good looks and a soft-spoken voice. Friends say that he could have been just about anything he wanted to make of himself had it not been for his lust for cash.

Rivas, described by a former classmate as a "Beavis and Butthead kind of guy," had aspirations of becoming a policeman before he turned to a life of crime, and spoke of his dream often. Unfortunately for both himself as well as the citizens of El Paso, he would never become a police officer. Raised by his grandmother and grandfather after his parents divorced when he was 6, Rivas cruised through high school without attracting a lot of attention. Having a fascination with guns, he named his two dogs Ruger and Baretta, and began to plot how to raise some quick, easy money without the annoyance of having to work for it like everyone else.

Rivas did not get into trouble with the law until shortly after graduating from Ysleta High School in 1988 where, according to a high school spokesman, he was looked at as a quiet guy, something of a loner, who did not participate in any school activities. After graduation, he was faced with having to earn a living and was unable to find a job that suited him. So in 1989, he committed his first robbery and burglary; unfortunately for him, he was caught. However, as he had no prior criminal record he was sentenced to probation for 10 years.

It was while he was on probation that Rivas enrolled at the University of Texas at El Paso embarking on a program of general studies in the fall of 1992. After three semesters of curbing his greed and criminal bent and in need of some ready cash, he dropped out in the spring of 1993 and embarked on a short-lived criminal career that would land him in prison.

Based on his modus operandi, there is no doubt that he not only planned and orchestrated the breakout of the Texas 7 from the Connally Unit, but it is almost certain that he planned the robbery of the Radio Shack in Pearland, as well as to a string of at least a dozen holdups in Texas, New Mexico, and Arizona.

One of the robberies he was suspected of committing occurred on October 3, 1992, at a Radio Shack in El Paso. According to a police report, he was suspected of handcuffing a salesman and then robbing the store of cash, two-way radios, as well as other merchandise.

Less than three weeks later, on October 23, he was alleged to have entered a Checker Auto Parts store under the guise of buying a car battery and pulled a gun on a salesman. He was then alleged to have forced the salesman to remove his uniform shirt, after which he handcuffed him and forced him into the restroom. Rivas then put on the uniform shirt and forced the store's assistant manager to open the safe, of which he cleaned out all the cash on hand.

Barely two weeks after the auto parts store robbery and still continuing his assault on the businesses of El Paso Rivas then walked into an Oshman's Sporting Goods store near closing time under the guise of looking at ski boots. He went so far as to ask the assistant manager to keep the store open a bit longer so that he could purchase a pair of the boots, and explained that he was waiting for a friend to bring his wallet to him. When he was satisfied that he had the assistant manager's cooperation, he pulled out a gun and ordered him to call all of the employees together.

As the puzzled employees arrived one by one, Rivas told the employees that he was with store security. After he had gathered everyone together, he pulled out his gun and announced that this was a robbery He then called an accomplice on a two-way radio, took a uniform shirt from an employee and put it on so that he wouldn't unduly stand out just in case someone unexpectedly came in, such as the police. Next he and his accomplice handcuffed all of the employees except one to a heavy ski grinding machine in the rear of the store. Afterward, Rivas forced the store's manager to empty the safe for him. He took all of the cash, $5095, as well as 58 guns. Not wanting to leave any finger prints that might identify him, Rivas didn't touch anything during the robbery, but instead forced the employee to pick up and pack the items that he wanted to steal.

"I've written down all of your license plate numbers and can find out where you live if anyone tries to identify us," Rivas said as he and his accomplice left the store. He also said that he would return and kill them if anyone called the police.

The employees waited about twenty minutes after Rivas and his accomplice left the store. They then dragged the ski grinding machine to a phone and called the police, after which they dragged the machine back to its original location out of fear that Rivas might return and find out what they had done.

Rivas's next known robbery occurred on May 12, 1993, when Rivas, donning a blond wig and brandishing a gun, went inside a Furr's grocery store in

El Paso and forced all of the employees into a back room. He took all of the cash that he could locate.

Then on May 25, 1993, Rivas and an accomplice disguised themselves as security guards and walked into the Toys 'R' Us store at 801 Mesa Hills Drive. After rounding up eight employees, Rivas and his accomplice robbed the store. Although his previous robberies had been carried out with military-like precision, in this case he somehow missed one of the employees who escaped and called the police. When the police arrived, Rivas and his accomplice held them at bay for more than three hours by using the employees as hostages. However, a SWAT team was called in when the police officers realized that they weren't going to get anywhere. The SWAT team stormed the store and found Rivas, wearing a blond wig, hiding in an air conditioning duct. They also recovered some of the guns that had been stolen from the Oshman's sporting goods store robbery earlier. Although his arrest ended the string of local robberies, he was still suspected of committing the numerous robberies in other parts of Texas, Arizona and New Mexico.

With such a history, is it any wonder that perhaps something lingered after the conclusion of the horrific events set in motion by George Rivas? There does seem to be something indefinable taking place within this store.

## The Ghosts

I approached the manager of the Mesa store and asked if there were any stories about hauntings in his store. To my surprise, he took my question very seriously and openly discussed some of the events that have taken place there.

According to the manager, one evening after closing, some of the3 employees that were stocking the shelves saw a figure in a black shirt disappear down one of the aisles. Thoiugh they called out, the figure failed to answer them. Since only members of management wear black shirts, it was naturally assumed that the manager had returned to the store. The employees that had seen the figure searched the building, but found no one.

Another young man told me that each evening, the staff makes sure that all of the toys are proeprly shelved and that the aisles aer clean. However, many mornings, they will find toys on the floor as if children have been playing with them. Occassionally, they will hear low giggling as if there are young children hidding in the store, but no matter how they diligently they search, no one is ever found.

The layout of the store leaves a number of areas that can't be easily seen due to the high shelves. So each evening at closing, the staff makes the rounds of the aisles making sure that no one is hiding in the store before the doors are locked. In spite of the nightly searches, former employees have told me that they have heard what sounds like heavy breathing and the foootsteps of a heavy man come from the stock room and walk down the aisles. The worker would stop what they were doing to go see who was in the store, but they would never find anyone.

One worker told me of being in the store late at night and hearing someone get a soda from the machine in the Employee's breakroom. However, when the worker cautiously looked into the breakroom, it was empty.

## TOYS R' US
### 9801 Gateway West
### El Paso, Texas 79928

It is said that at this store, that sometimes figures aer seen moving about the store late at night and on more than one occasion, when employees have entered the musical toy aisle, all of the toys have began to play.

## OTHER HAUNTED TOYS R' US STORES

So both of the Toys R' Us stores in El Paso have resident ghosts. This is unusual enough to cause some concern, but then, as I have said, El Paso is one of the most haunted cities in the country. However, there are stores in this chain in many cities.

So would it surprise you to find out that the Toys R' Us store in Las Cruces, New Mexico is also haunted? That's right, the Las Cruces store also has a resident ghost, however, you will have to wait for book four in this series to read about the ghosts of New Mexico.

This makes three stores in the same chain with ghosts, does this raise yor eyebrows? Surely there can't be any more haunted stores in this one chain, or can there? How about a haunted toy store right in the middle of Silicon Valley, California. That's right, another haunted store and this one has gained national attention (every place but in El Paso).

## SUNNYVALE, CALIFORNIA TOYS R' US

According to a writer for the publication Adweek, a ghost has been terroriizing the Sunnyvale, California Toys 'R' Us store. For more information, read on. (American Pulse).

Koeppel, Dan
Adweek's Marketing Week.

June 10 1991, v32, n24, p17(1) in Academic Index (database on UTCAT PLUS

*A 'ghost' tramps the aisles seeking his lost love*
*The children have left, and the din has subsided. Another hard day's shopping is history at the Sunnyvale, Calif. Branch of Toys 'R' Us. Yet there might be activity inside the vast, silent emporium this midnight, none of which has to do with the straightforward business of retailing.*

*Inside, it is said, toys topple from the their shelves. A skateboard rolls down an aisle, clanking aimlessly into a wall. But nobody is in this Toys 'R' Us this midnight. Or anyway, nobody alive.*

*In the tony heart of high-tech Silicon Valley, could there really be such a thing as a haunted retail outlet?*

*"I'm a skeptical person," says Toys 'R' Us assistant store director Jeff Linden. "But something's definitely happening here."*

*In the past few years, store management has tried to get to the bottom of several curious developments. Linden recounts stories of objects flying 20 feet through the air and hitting employees. Shelves left neat in a locked store have been found in disarray the next morning. And then there was the talking doll that cried "mama" over and over-but would only do so when put in a locked box.*

*If nothing else, it's attracting curiosity-seekers. "My daughter insisted we visit when she came here from Hawaii," said a woman (who declined to identify herself) at the local Chamber of Commerce.*

*But that doesn't mean that store workers laugh off the matter. "Some of our employees are spooked," Linden says. "They won't go into certain parts of the store alone." He hastens to add that the "ghost" hasn't affected day-to-day store operations in any tangible way. Yet the incidents were taken seriously enough that management let a local psychic visit the store.*

*"I thought they were seeing things," says 'private psychic counselor' Sylvia Brown. I usually find ghosts in old houses. Not in a modern-day retail store." But Brown changed her mind when she walked into the store. "I felt something," she says. "Especially in the last aisle on the left."*

*It was in that supernatural aisle that Brown got permission to conduct a séance, a summoning of spirits. Brown says the whole problem comes down to one scenario, namely that "Johnny is waiting for Beth." The ghost, she says, is one John Johnson, a circuit preacher who set up his tent in verdant Sunnyvale at the turn of the century. In those days, apples grew on the current site of the store. "Beth" is Elizabeth Yuba Murphy Tafee, daughter of a prominent rancher. But his love went unrequited. So poor Johnson-or "Yonny," as the employees have dubbed him-is doomed to tramp the aisles of the orchard qua toy store. He is reduced to bewailing his plight, searching for his lost love and occasionally beaning employees with a package of rubber ducks.*

*Of course, many observers consider the ghost about as real as a Ninja Turtle.*

*"My response is 'Skeptics 'R' Me,'" says James Randi, a prominent debunker of psychic phenomena. "There are lots of silly people who make all kinds of declarations."*

*But Brown can produce a photograph (see above) from the I that she claims includes old Johnson. He is looming in the misty background, leaning against a store shelf. Brown says there was nobody in her group standing anywhere near that location during the séance.*

*Such "proof" doesn't cut much ice with Randi. And some of Brown's claims don't stand up too well when checked.*

*Brown says police are "constantly" responding to alarms at the store. Lieutenant Andy Pate, of the Sunnyvale Department of Public Safety, says the store has "no more alarms than any other large retailer." But the stories persist. Local papers and TV have looked into the lovelorn spook.*

*"That's part of the hype," Randi says. "Why don't they install a video camera? Why don't they put the place under surveillance? Call me, and I'll get rid of the ghost in three days," says Randi. "Of course, I don't think they'd like that."*

That may be the point. "Sales go up after reports of the ghost," says Linden. "A lot of people think this is a great thing."

So maybe nobody's in any great hurry to smoke out Old Yonny Johnson.

A reader of the web page sent me this note:

## Other Comments on the Sunnyvale Hauntings

The public airing of the story regarding the haunting of the Sunnyvale, CA Toys R' Us store has resulted in an out puring of emails to various websites by customers, former employees and others who have seen what they think are ghosts at this store. I am taking the liberty of including a few of the most interestingg.

Date: Sun, 02 Feb 1997 11:01:59 -0800

From: "C. Coffman" (turnkey@themall.net)
To: obiwan@netcom.com

Subject: "Haunted" Sunnyvale Toys'R'Us
Hi there,
Just read about the Sunnyvale "haunting" on your Paranormal page...I have some stuff to add to that, for your consideration. Remember that old show w/Jack Pallance, Ripley's Believe it or Not? They had an episode about that Toys'R'Us. In it, their "psychic" said the ghost (whom she also named "Johnny") was a local farmboy who died while chopping wood on the farm which used to

stand in that locality. Her version goes that he cut his leg with the axe, bound it in a handkerchief, and attempted to continue chopping the rest of the wood. He died from loss of blood. The reason she gives for him still hanging around is: since he didn't realize the wound was fatal (by just ignoring it and continuing his chore), he doesn't realize he is dead. She thought he was trying to communicate with people.

Anyway, I seem to recall ol' Jack Pallance setting up a infra-red camera in the store after-hours, which picked up something weird just as an inflated rubber ball fell off a store shelf.

Believe it or not. (As they say...;)
turnkey@themall.net

Another reader sent this in:
From: "Tom & Ellen" (scooter@sgi.net)
To: obiwan@ghosts.org

Subject: Toys R Us

Date: Wed, 10 Sep 1997 02:34:41 -0400

Ghosts at Toys "R" Us is nothing new to the employees at the Greensburg, PA store Either. After reading the current story of the California store it struck me as very, very familiar. I have worked the over-night stock shift at the Greensburg store for almost a year now and have seen many similar occurences. Boxes in our back stock room have mysteriously fallen off of shelves, perfectly neat and straight isles of merchandise are messed by the time morning crews arrive. Some employees, I among them, have seen an apportion moving about the store. Usually its just a black form that you catch out the corner of your eye as it goes past an isle your working in. "Homer" as we have lovingly named him , (We all feel this is a male entity) is usually just mischiefious , not harmful. Of course, at about 4 AM you can get kind of tired playing with Homer, but we find if we just ignore his antics he moves to a different part of the store. Many employees refuse to work night shift because of Homer. One stock person worked one night building extra bikes for the summer rush. He obviously peaked Homers interest because none of us had problems that night except him. He kept complaining that he would lay a tool down one place and find it in another, or that he felt like he was constantly being watched. He claimed to have felt a very cold place by his construction area but no where else in the stock room. This stock person will not work overnight anymore.

Homer, rumor has it, is a victim of a car crash behind the store before the building was built. There is a cliff that has a hotel on it directly behind the store and somehow, we assume suicide, the man drove off the cliff to his demise.

As for me I just deal with Homer when I have to and leave him be. He hasn't hurt anyone, just frightened a few people. If I feel particularly disturbed in one area of the store I do something else and go back later.

**Figure 34: The Sunnyvale, CA Toys R' Us Store.**

There are still more emails.

From: Anonymous
To: obiwan@ghosts.org

Subject: Toys R Us story
Date: Monday, February 09, 2004 7:26 PM

Hi,
I have a story on the Toys R Us that confirms the encounters that people have described. I worked at the store in 1983 during the holiday season. My section of the story was the last two aisles, referred to as the infant and pre-school aisles. I was also a cashier. Many times while using the restroom, the

water faucet would turn itself on after I would turn it off. I just thought the bathroom was in serious need of a remodel.

As was store policy, we would be required to restock the shelves after the store would close at midnight so we would usually continue to work until one or two in the morning. One Saturday evening we finished restocking and then put everything away — it was a rule that nothing could be left on the floors. Then we all left at the same time and would wait for the manager to turn on the alarm and lock the doors. This was mostly for our safety in walking to our cars so late at night. Sunday morning I had to work the opening shift and was there a little early so I had to wait for the manager to arrive and open the door. As we walked in we saw that all the little riding toys (big wheels, tricycles, etc.) we scattered all down the aisle. I was upset because I thought I would get in trouble since this was my section and my responsibility to clean up the evening before, but my manager just said "looks like the ghost was busy last night" and continued to open the store. Another afternoon while it was quite, I was on a short ladder restocking a peg wall and I felt someone touch my hair and tap me on the shoulder. I thought it was a customer but no one was there. It gave me quite a chill. After that I just tried not to be all alone if possible!
Stacy

From: "john daudel" (jadaudel@hotmail.com)
To: obiwan@ghosts.org

Subject: toys r us Sunnyvale

Date: Monday, December 08, 2003 9:45 AM

Hello, I grew up in Sunnyvale as well, I would like to point out that TOYS R US went up in the WHITE FRONT parking lot behind the WHITE FRONT gas station- in the first part of the 1970's, as a child I can remember no matter where I looked, trees, trees, and more trees,( there were even huge red woods in front of Fremont high at one time) and stories about farmer's with rock salt shot guns, but never knew anyone shot, it was a great time to be a kid there, like growing up in the woods only the trees are shorter, by 1975 most of the tree's were history (very sad) any how back to TOY R US, the"ghost" is said to be that of a labor worker for a one Mr. Murphy land owner (owned a great deal of land) and that Mr.M hacked off this guys arm/hand, it has also been said that it is Mr.M's ghost, I really can't say who it is, and the sad part of this story is I feel there are ghost in our world and ever one at TOYS R US but in all the years I grew up in Sunnyvale, even worked at said store for a short time, I myself never saw anything or knew any one who had, please feel free to e-mail me

From: "mike D." (mikedawg9412@hotmail.com)

To: obiwan@ghosts.org

Subject: haunted toys r us

Date: Sunday, September 21, 2003 2:26 PM

I worked at Toys R Us about 2 years ago and I was working there for about three months. It was mainly for holiday work to make a little bit of money. Anyway there was really only one time I saw something that freaked me out. One time another employee helped me carry a ladder to get a product down for a customer. We carried the ladder over to the aisle were we need it we were starting to open up the ladder, and a little toy just fell from no where. It was strange because just as we were opening the ladder it just fell and there is no way it could have fallen off of the shelf. Just a little story to let u know about.
Former employee,

Mike

From: Robertodellh@aol.com
To: obiwan@ghosts.org

Subject: Toys-r-us.

Date: Friday, June 21, 2002 10:56 AM

I grew up in Sunnyvale from '51 to 73. The orchard behind Toys-r-Us was always considered spooky, before a Whitefront department store was built there in the sixties, the building that Toys-r-Us now occupies. As kids, we rode our bikes over there, hid them in the wild blackberry bushes, and ventured into the orchards, where we knew a man with a rock-salt loaded shotgun would be stalking us. We were brave enough to go into the bing cherry trees and gorge ourselves, but the border between the cherry trees and the plums was where we balked. It was definitely weird beyond that. Rumors of ghosts, and a ramshackle village from another time figured prominently. For several years friend and I shared the same recurring dreams of this muddy village, perhaps from the 1890's, or possibly as late as the 1920's. Robbers and prostitutes, before we were aware of what those types were, figured in these dreams. Also vicious dogs and dirty, mean mules and horses. I believe that the ghost of the man who chopped his arm off at a well there and died, is the main ghost in Toys, but others are involved. The area we were most concerned about was between Wolfe road, and closer to, Laurence Expressway, about a quarter mile south of el Camino, unless I'm confused, 20 years down the line. We also used to sneak onto the grounds of the Winchester Mystery House when we got a little older. There was a ghost of a Doberman pincher there. This was before they built the Century 21 domed

cinemas, or whatever that was called, on her orchard there. Also, has anyone heard of a house in Saratoga that belonged to the violinist Yehudi Menuhin, which had once been a Nunnery in which 2 nuns were gassed accidentally? In the late sixties we visited the tenant there who performed what we considered a very good parlor trick, where all the windows would be locked by us, and we would take a short walk around the grounds, and return to find all the windows flung wide, supposedly by the asphyxiated nuns. Ever hear about that place? I live in London now, and love to explore the zillions of haunted places all over this country. Thanx for your rapt attention!
Robert Hawkins.

Date: Thu, 14 Oct 1999 17:31:16 -0700

From: Alejandra Gonzales (alejandra@santa.com)
To: obiwan@ghosts.org, alejandra@santa.com

Subject: Toys 4 us ghost
Hello,
         I 'm a past resident from Sunnyvale, California. I lived there till I was 12 and I'm 20 now, living in San Jose. I don't believe in ufo's and I don't believe that Elvis is alive either. But I can account to what happened to me when I visited Toys R US .. in Sunnyvale.
I used to go to the Toys T Us all the time, when I was a kid with my mother. One day after going to Burger King we went to Toys R Us. I loved looking at dolls and going through the aisles alone to find something I could persuade my mother into buying. Well, it wasn't busy that day, and I was roaming around all happy tryin' to find something. I started going to the aisle I wanted with Barbie's and all that. I look down each aisle just to see what is down there.. so I could stop and glare. Just as I pass an aisle, I look down it and there is a Frisbee in free flight.. just .. glidin'.. down... but there was NO ONE I MEAN NO ONE!! I didn't think anything of it...
I went to the aisle I wanted... I found a Barbie and started down the aisle to my mother as I turn around to get another outfit for my Barbie.. there are three Barbie doll boxes.. on top of each other... in the middle of the floor.. NO ONE was in the aisle and it was too quick for anyone to run get all of them and put them on top of each other and then run off. I was too young to think anything of it... again!!..
So.. afterI get home.. I told my sister what happened.. after she called me stupid and all that.. she told me how it was haunted.. I didn't believe her till I saw the show later.. years to come.. on .. Sightings.. I was freaked out.. my hair was standing on end...
so now I know .. what happened... I wasn't just a crazy kid ! LOL

From: "Wynter Mitchell" (suprgrrl@pacbell.net)
To: obiwan@ghosts.org

Subject: Ghost Stories

Date: Tue, 16 Mar 1999 15:44:31 -0800
Re: Toys R Us Sunnyvale
    I went there to do a story for my school paper and I felt something push me aside as I went to the back of the store, I was there for about 2 hours trying to get a sense of the whole atmosphere. Only that push confirmed it for me. It was not a strong push, but it was like someone was trying to get by, it wasn't hostile, it was similar to a polite "excuse me, you're in my way". I was content.

Date: Mon, 07 Jun 1999 12:03:28 -0700

To: obiwan@ghosts.org
From: Chris Garcia (garcia@computerhistory.org)

Subject: Haunted Toys R Us
    I just wanted to write in on the Haunted Toys R US story. My dad used to pal around with most of the Bay Area Parapsychology folk (and Sylvia Brown) and almost went on the over-night where the famous photo came from. He did visit around 1 am one night, a friend of his being a night watchman. What he saw was not a man, but a black fog-like mass which moved about the board game aisle. This would have been in early 85. I have heard and seen some strange things while shopping there, but nothing I can pinpoint (mostly just hearing things from aisles where there aren't any people, a few things out of the corner of my eye)
Just thought to drop a line
Chris

Date: Tue, 4 Jul 2000 23:45:14 -0700 (PDT)

To: stories@ghosts.org
yourname Steve

email broken@wt.net
    Well, I just noticed your website has a section on the Toys R Us haunting and I figured I'd add something to it's section. I worked at that Toys R Us for one Christmas season and I live in Santa Clara (city right next to Sunnyvale) so, I've been there plenty of times. I have to be honest in telling you that I didn't see many things happen in the aisles and most of the employees would probably agree that most of the weird activity tends to happen in the stocking areas. The store itself looks HUGE when you walk in and it almost seems like there's no

place where stock is kept but the actual store is surrounded by stocking areas (save for the front). The left side where you walk in is shipping and receiving (where my girlfriend worked at the time) and the back of the store is the biggest stock area (where most of the weird stuff happens). Ok, so here's the experiences.

On one of my first nights working I was being trained by another employee and we were going through all the boxes on the second floor of the stock room in the back of the store. He informed me that we should take an early break (heh) so, we pulled out one of the large boxes stacked up on other boxes, shifted it to the center of the floor and sat on a box between other boxes to sort of relax and hide from any possible managers. While we were sitting there we started to hear very heavy footsteps heading our way so we peeped over the top of one of the boxes towards where the footsteps were coming from and we were completely alone in the entire upstairs back area. I'm fairly down to earth so I chalked it up to sounds perhaps from the downstairs area (although they were quite apparent footsteps).

Now Christmas time is QUITE busy so usually there are people there restocking around the clock. However, one night we got finished very early and my current girlfriend at the time had finished up with one of the managers and they were the last two to close the store. They both incidentally had to be back there in another 6 hours so they rushed home to bed and then back to work. Upon opening the store together, they had found a monopoly board all set out as if someone was preparing to play it. The pieces were on the board but the cash wasn't scattered anywhere or anything. (Monopoly is a very old game btw). Also, several of the girl employees had claimed that they'd occasionally feel someone 'petting' the back of their hair in the back rooms although my ex g/f had never felt anything. **Shrug** That's about all I know of it. Didn't really feel any 'strange' feelings or hear 'SPOOKY' sounds. Just weird stuff that could have an explanation.

Date: Mon, 14 Aug 2000 00:15:27 -0700 (PDT)

To: stories@ghosts.org
yourname marian
email mbunchsolorio@yahoo.com
Hello all, I worked at the SUNNYVALE Toys r us for about three years. A lot of the stories I read on this website seemed a bit extreme. But don't get me wrong I don't doubt you all experienced something. I actually had a few frightening experiences when I was there. But nothing major. For example I was the money counter stuck early in the morning in a little room with only one window, so many times I saw someone out of the corner of my eyes watching me. But when I would turn to look no one was there. Yeah it could have been sleep deprivation. The store has now been remodeled but back in the day(1995-

1998) there was a lot of activity on aisle 15C (that would be where the Fisher Price items were. Legos were just down the aisle). People said they felt the cold chill I also did. Other associates said they could hear him on the roof (like he was walking back and forth kicking the stones), also the toys playing music by themselves and toys falling off the shelves. I personally never heard him. Never really saw him full on. We really did not talk about it at work unless it was mentioned on t.v. You all can imagine how many phone calls we would get "is this the haunted Toys r us?". Honestly I can't really say 100% either way. I am very scared of seeing something that shouldn't be there (A GHOST!). Maybe that is why I did not have a lot of encounters. Let me just say when the power would go out and it usually would at least two times a year I would be the first one out the front door.

There was a few things that I've read in various places that did make me quite upset: #1 I have never heard Toys R Us(big wigs) brag about the fact that there is a ghost at one of their stores. It's not like they chose to have a ghost there. #2 Regardless of what he is doing there he does not pray on or bother the females. He never hurt me and now when I go to that store I feel very at ease not frightened. HE IS NOT A BAD GHOST! Last but not least I am still with Toys R Us, although a different store I thought I finally got away from the "haunted" Toys R Us and then I come to find out that a few people who work at my store think it's haunted. I know I am very contradicting in this very long story. I am sorry I guess I do believe!

Marian ☺

ALWAYS A TOYS R US KID!

## The Toys 'R' Us Ghost?

**Figure 35: A photo of a ghost.**

This picture on the previous page was reportedly taken with infrared film during an investigation at the Sunnyvale, California, Toys 'R' Us store. Witnesses claimed the man leaning against the wall was not visible and did not appear in photos taken at the same time with normal film. A June 1991 *Adweek* article tells the tale:

*"The children have left, and the din has subsided. Another hard day's shopping is history at the Sunnyvale, California, branch of Toys 'R' Us. Yet there might be activity inside the vast, silent emporium this midnight, none of which has to do with the straightforward business of retailing.*

*"Inside, it is said, toys topple from the their shelves. A skateboard rolls down an aisle, clanking aimlessly into a wall. But nobody is in this Toys 'R' Us this midnight. Or anyway, nobody alive. In the heart of high-tech Silicon Valley, could there really be such a thing as a haunted retail outlet? 'I'm a skeptical person,' says Toys 'R' Us assistant store director Jeff Linden. 'But something's definitely happening here.'*

*"In the past few years, store management has tried to get to the bottom of several curious developments. Linden recounts stories of objects flying 20 feet through the air and hitting employees. Shelves left neat in a locked store have been found in disarray the next morning. And then there was the talking doll that cried 'mama' over and over—but would only do so when put in a locked box...But that doesn't mean that store workers laugh off the matter. 'Some of our employees are spooked,' Linden says. 'They won't go into certain parts of the store alone.' He hastens to add that the "ghost" hasn't affected day-to-day store operations in any tangible way. Yet the incidents were taken seriously enough that management let a local psychic [Sylvia Brown] visit the store."*

It was this 1978 investigation that yielded the infrared photograph and information about the identity of the ghost. According to Brown, the ghost told her he was named John (or Johan) Johnson. At the turn of the 20th century, he was a mentally handicapped worker on a ranch at the current site of the store. He was smitten with Elizabeth Yuba Murphy Tafee, daughter of the owner. His love was not returned and after his death from an accidental leg wound many years later, he remains tied to the site. To date, this information has been verified in the historic record.

**Legend:** The ghost of a disappointed lover haunts the Toys 'R' Us store in Sunnyvale, California.

**Origins:** If you like a good ghost story, this 1993 newspaper story is for you:

Enter the Play-Doh aisle at your own risk. Browse the children's books with caution. And don't even ask to go upstairs, where the toys are stacked.

The Toys 'R' Us in Sunnyvale is haunted by a man named Johnson, employees and psychics say.

"I don't believe in ghosts," said Putt-Putt O'Brien, who has spent 18 years stacking toys at the store. "But you feel a breeze behind you. Someone calls your name and there's nobody there. Funny things happen here that you can't explain."

Rag dolls and toy trucks leap off shelves. Balls bounce down the aisles. Children's books fall out of racks. Baby swings move on their own. The folks at Toys 'R' Us say they've tried to explain it logically but can't.

"Many people have experiences, not just one or two of us," O'Brien said. "He's like Casper. Nothing he does ever hurt anybody."

Others have taken notice, too. Newspapers have written about him.

The toy store has been featured on television's *That's Incredible* and other shows. A Hollywood script writer for the movie *Toys* spent two nights inside doing research. Psychic Sylvia Browne held a I there in 1978 and has been back a dozen times.

Browne said Johnson told her he was a preacher and ranch hand in the 1880s on the Murphy family farm, where the toy store sits today. He spoke with a mild Swedish accent, and his first name was John, Yon, or Johan. Ten of sixteen people assembled there for the I said they heard a "high buzzing noise" when Browne was supposedly listening to the ghost.

Browne said the ghost told her he had been in love with Murphy's daughter Elizabeth, who ran off with an East Coast lawyer. Old news clippings say Johnson accidentally hacked his leg with an ax while carelessly chopping down trees. Another story said Johnson was found dead in the orchard with an ax wound in his neck. Both stories say he bled to death.

O'Brien said she saw Johnson once: A young man in his 20s or 30s, wearing knickers, a white long-sleeved work shirt, and a gray tweed snap-brim cap, walked past her. Another time she heard the sound of galloping horses.

"Yohan used to exercise the horses, they say," O'Brien said.

Now he apparently gets his exercise playing with the staff. There was the time when men were waxing the floor, for instance, and a teddy bear kept appearing in each aisle as they moved their equipment through the store. There's the overwhelming sweet smell of garden flowers that haunts Aisle 15C, next to the Mickey Mouse dolls and the Batman toothbrush sets. So, now the obvious question: Is it all just a desperate sales gimmick?

"It's very good publicity for us," said store director Stephanie Lewis. "But I personally don't believe in it." But even if Lewis doesn't believe it, others do. "Last week we had to chase three or four teenagers away," she said. "They were sitting out front at 4 a.m. with a Ouija board, trying to conjure up the ghost. Once a week someone comes in here asking about it. Teenagers beg us to let them spend the night on the floor."

"I have employees who will not go into the women's bathroom alone," Lewis said. That's because Johnson follows them in there and turns on the water faucets, she said.

Longtime employees say Johnson has also pulled pranks on contractors who come to do short-term jobs. They see a toy leap from a shelf and refuse to come back.

O'Brien believes Johnson lives upstairs in a breezy, cool corner. The pranks he pulls upstairs are also harmless, she said, but it's spookier because one is usually alone. "When I go up there, I'll say, 'Johan, I'm only here to work,'" O'Brien said.

So if the place is haunted, why stick around?

"It's a good ghost," said Lisa, another employee, who didn't give her last name. "It's fun here."

Barbara "spirited" Mikkelson

**Last updated:** 29 October 1998[74]

## CHAPTER SEVENTEEN
## UNIVERSITY OF TEXAS AT EL PASO
## HAUNTED DORM
### 500 W. University
### El Paso, Texas

In the first volume of this series, I wrote about several haunted locations at the University of Texas at El Paso (UTEP)[75]. Since that book have been on the market, I have heard several new stories about different hauntings at this well known University. Most of the stories have to do with the buildings that house classrooms or offices, but I hve heard one or two stories about a haunting in one of the dorms. I could not track down the actual eye witness, but I was furnished the following e-mail regarding one such incident.

**Dorm Room Ghost**

By: Calf98@aol.com

My Name is Erika and I had an experience once at a dorm I was staying in over the weekend I was 17 or 18 I'm not too sure now. I'm from El Paso, TX. and I was staying at the University of Texas at El Paso. Now, I had never really heard about anything strange going on at these dorms we were staying at until my experience was shared.

I was coming to the end of a very long day. I had woken up early around 5 am. to get ready for the science fair. No, that isn't the reason

---

[74] http://www.snopes.com/horrors/ghosts/toysrus.htm

[75] Hudnall, Ken and Connie Wang, The Spirits of the Border: The History and Mystery of El Paso Del Norte, Omega Press, El Paso, Texas. 2003.

for going to the university but this is part of the story. I went to my science fair and was there almost all day. It ended around three in the afternoon. I was in a rush to finish because I was meeting my friends at UTEP to begin another season of the Young Leaders Conference (YLC). I was very excited to see all my friends but I was also very tired.

The conference went underway and it finished into the night as it always had every year. By the time we did room check I was extremly exhausted. I was a councelor at the time so we did room check and then all of us were going to hang out that night on the floor above to eat pizza and see how everyone was.

I was rooming with my best friend name Veronica. She came in, let me know where everyone was going to meet and if I was interested in pitching in for pizza. I told her that I was too exhausted to eat and that I just thought it best to go straight to bed. I told her that she should go without me and if she wouldn't mind being very quiet when she came in so she would not wake me. She was fine with that and said she would see me in the morning and asked me to wake her up when I got up the next day. I agreed and went to sleep.

I have to explain to you the way the dorm room looked. When you walked in the room the beds were against the wall on the same wall. They were parallel to the wall and the only thing between them was a sink. All the closests and cabinets were on the opposite side of the room. When I slept, I put my head towards the door and my feet towards the window. There was a window on the opposite side of the room from the door. I liked sleeping in that bed every year because I liked looking out the window. The whole room was dark and I was getting pretty sleepy. I guess I must have gotten to the point where I was finally asleep when things started to happen.

I remember that I heard that the cabinet door opened and slammed shut. I really didnt think much of it because I just figured that Veronica came in and the door of the cabinet must have slipped from her hands and slammed shut. I started to get to sleep when I heard the closet door open and shut again. I wasnt aggitated but I forgave her again for it. Finallly, the sink light came on. I knew she had to turn it on to brush her teeth so I was still okay with most of the noise. Then it got ugly. I heard the water in the sink on and then her bed light came on. As soon as that happend I heard the cabinet and closet doors opening and shutting quite fast. Then that lights for the entire room came on.

All this noise at once was just enough to drive me crazy. I finally got so fed up with it that I sat up and yelled towards the window, "Vero will you knock it off, I'm trying to get to sleep and I thought I asked you to please be quiet when you came in".

At that moment all the lights went off and the sink water stopped running. There was no way for all of those things to have turned off on their own all at once unless there was more than one person in the room. But the funny thing was, now that I realize it, there were no sounds of foot steps.

About half an hour later Veronica walked back in the room. I asked her if she had been in the room just a while back and her and another friend confirmed to me that they had just come back so they could go to bed. This other friend was just walking her back. I never told Vero what happend that night, I never really told anyone about it until I started hearing other people with their own stories. I know for a fact now that someone died in those dorms.

I don't know why or how but I do know that they don't house students in those dorms anymore. I still think about it to this day and wonder what that lonely student wanted. Was I in their room? Or did they just feel like causing some hell and annoying me? I guess I'll never know!

Did the ghost of a student that died in the dorm come back for a short visis?

# CHAPTER EIGHTEEN

## EL PASO COMMUNITY COLLEGE

## VALVERDE CAMPUS

**Figure 36: Hautned Photo Lab at EPCC.**

In the first volume of this series[76], I made mention of a haunting at El Paso Community College, but at the time that forst book was published, I had very litle information. Now, I have a little bit more information about at least one of the spirits that haunt the Community College.

According to the information I have been able to obtain, the most famous haunting at the El Paso Community College takes place on the second floor of the Valle Verde Campus' A-building. It is on the second floor where you can find EPCC's photo lab. This lab is said to be a place where something unusual and perhaps unearthly lurks, waiting on the unsuspected person who walks into the lab. Students and faculty have reported feeling this presence lurking in the back of the photo lab. The revolving door has opened by itsself and the curtain has opened as if someone is watching you.

---

[76] Hudnall, Ken and Connie Wang, Spirits of the Border: The History and Mystery of El Paso Del Note, Omega Press, El Paso, Texas. 2003

Some students have even reported that they felt someone touching their shoulder and breathing on the back of their necks.

According to those who have had occasion to become familiar with this haunting, there was an EPCC student nicknamed "Rambo," who spent much of time in the lab. One day, Rambo snapped and tried to kill himself, but just n the nick of time, others prevented Rambo from hurting himself. After a consultantion between EPCC administrators and Rambo's personal physician, it was decied to send him to Beaumont Army Medical Center. For treatment. However, Lab assistant Hector Fierro added, "He jumped out of a window while at the hospital and died. They say Rambo is here."

No one seems to have any idea what made Rambo suddenly snap and try to kill himself, though one of two people that I have met while researching these stories maintain that Rambo was in turn haunted by something that finally droe him off the deep end. Whatever may have been his reasons, many of the night cleaning crew and students who have had need to work in the Photo lab afer dark maintain that Rambo has returned to continue spending his time in the lab. In fact, some janitors will not go into the photo lab alone at night[77]. The school was built on top of the old Prices Dairy, and some believe a presence from the dairy has found a new home in the school photo lab.

---

[77] Saucedo, Erca, *El Paso Ghost Stories*, El Conquistador, El Paso Community College, El Paso, Texas. October 24, 2002.

# CHAPTER NINETEEN
# STEPHEN F. AUSTIN HIGH SCHOOL
**3500 Memphis**
**El Paso, Texas**

I mentioned a bit about the hauntings of Austin High School in the first volume of this series[78], but I did not have a great deal of information. Luckily, in the interim, I have had the opportunity to collect a number of new storiesa bout thie old school.

In 1929 the El Paso Board of Education decided to build a new high

**Figure 37: The building of Austin High School.**

school in east El Paso. The students, who were to come from Austin Jr. High, requested that the name Austin High School, their school colors, and their traditions be taken with them to the new campus. Stephen F. Austin High School opened its doors to students in September, 1930. The campus, designed to accommodate 1,000 students, had a first year enrollment of 1,130. Current enrollment is about 1,900 students.

R.E. McKee Construction Company built the school for $450,000. An old Spanish mission architectural style was used. The main building is constructed of light tan bricks and is fireproof. Sloping parts of the roof are covered in red Spanish tile. The structure is surmounted by a 103 foot tower built

---

[78] Hudnall, Ken and Connie Wang, Spirits of the Border: The History and Mystery of El Paso Del Note, Omega Press, El Paso, Texas. 2003.

at a cost of $4,000. The classrooms have marble floors and the hallways are floored with terrazzo. The stadium was built with funds from the federal government through the Public Works Administration. Funding for this structure was also aided by R. E. McKee, who donated $11,000. The stadium, named in Mr. McKee's honor, was completed on January 14, 1936.

The neighboring community has long been involved in the development of many traditions at Austin High School. Many ex-students have become community leaders in the fields of medicine, law, banking, and real estate. The Manhattan Heights addition, home of many of Austin's ex-students, is listed in the National Registry of Historical Sites. Many fine older homes can be found in this area. A portion of the student body is military dependents from Ft. Bliss, William Beaumount Hospital, and Biggs Field. These students help to give the student body a more diverse ethnic and cultural mixture. This is very positive asset for the school.

## THE GHOSTS

According to all reports from those at Austin High School who have experienced this particular haunting, one of the ghosts at this school is not politically correct. He seems almost to have gone to the William Jefferson Clinton School of Social Conduct. Female students, especially those who are consdiered very pretty, have been known to receive a firm slap on the behind or sometimes, if they are especially well endowed, it is said that they have their blouses blown up over their heads by Austin High's resident spirit.

Others speak of a tall, gray-haired man wearing a brown suit and white shirt, carrying a brief case who has apparently been spotted roaming the halls of the high school. It is said that this gentleman, whoever he may be (or was) is said to be "very friendly" to unsuspecting females.

Head custodian, Beto Sanchez said he has had three close encounters with the ghost. On one occasion, he heard footsteps and jingling keys going up to the second floor and opening the theater door. When Sanchez went into the theater to investigate, someone unseen shut the door.

On a second occasion, Sanchez saw the man through a window from the outside when he arrived at work early one morning. When he called the police, they informed him that motion sensors showed someone running back and forth in the second floor hallway. When both Sanchez and the police went into the building to investigate, they didn't find anyone. But, suddenly, the "man" threw a folding chair into the hallway. Unfortuantely, or perhaps fortunately, depending onyour point of view, they never found anyone in the building.

Many people have even spoken to this mysterious man in the brown suit without knowing that they were speaking to a ghost. Sanchez remembers a city police officer saying he spoke to a man in a brown suit. Immediately, Sanchez and the police officer went looking for him and but could not find anyone.

Clerks at Austin feel they have encountered the ghost while working late in the evenings. One night, clerks searched in vain for a lost memo throughout a desk in one paticular office. Before leaving, the clerks decided to enter the office and search one final time. Upon entering, they found that the document had suddenly appeared, sitting neatly on top of the desk[79].

Few know that just as is the case at El Paso High School, Austin High School has a maze of tunnels running underneath it. Some even maintain that the tunnels lead fmothe basement area of the school up toward the cavern that was found just off Murchison.

It has also been reported that an old assistant principal still walks the halls of the school that he so dearly loved, The ghost has been known to walk the second floor and has even thrown a metal folding chair into a hall[80]. I wonder if this particular ghost could actually be the mysterious man in the brown suit that has so successfully eluded capture?

## CHAPTER TWENTY
## SAN JACINTO ADULT LEARNING CENTER
### 1216 Olive Avenue
### El Paso, Texas

**Figure 38: Central School.**

The Central School, located on the corner of Myrtle and Campbell Streets, served its purpose for many years. As El Paso grew, the need for change became apparent.

In January 1905, 12 lots of the Magoffin Homestead addition were purchased by the City School Board for $1,200. The land became the present site of San Jacinto School. The building, designed by Edward Kneezell, would occupy a ground space of 148 x 75 feet.

At that time, the building was considered one of the best of the Southwest. It was, as it is today, a three-story, red brick building. It contained 21 classrooms, an auditorium and janitor's quarters. Originally, the windows were of

---

[79] http://www.episd.org/News/article.php?id=1133.
[80] Saucedo, Erca, *El Paso Ghost Stories*, El Conquistador, El Paso Community College, El Paso, Texas. October 24, 2002.
.

frosted glass, which was supposed to soften the rays of the sun. An innovation in construction was the deeply beveled window casings, which cast the least possible shadow.

San Jacinto School was named to commemorate the Battle of San Jacinto in which Texas won independence from Mexico. The school was opened on November 20, 1905. The pupils reported to their classes in Central School that morning, as usual, collected their belongs, and marched to the new San Jacinto. The school housed kindergarten through eighth grade.

In 1908, domestic science and manual training were added to the curriculum. These training programs were discontinued in 1933 due to the depression.

San Jacinto students took an active interest in athletics. The various teams won a number of trophies in soccer, football, basketball, volleyball, and baseball. The oldest trophy is a basketball shield that was won in 1910.

In 1974, the third through sixth grades were moved to Hart Elementary. In 1976, the remaining kindergarten-through third-grades were also moved to Hart. San Jacinto Elementary School was closed.

In 1978, the Adult Learning Center moved into San Jacinto and offered one class in English as a Second Language (ESL) and one class in General Educational Development (GED).

It was in 1979 that the Out-of-School Youth (OSY) program and the Adult Performance Level (APL) programs were located at San Jacinto. The adult training and retraining programs utilized classroom space and the Adult Learning Center experienced a slow growth until 1986.

That year, the Adult Learning Center accepted dislocated workers who were referred to San Jacinto by the Texas Employment Commission and the Private Industry Council. Since then, the Adult Learning Center has continued to grow.

Starting with longtime director Mr. Don Vickers, then followed by Mr. Gilberto Gutierrez, the San Jacinto Adult Learning Center continued to grow and expand; with our present director, Ms. Blanca Andrade, joining our staff in the Fall of 2000. At the present time, all existing classrooms are being used and more than 600 adults are enrolled in ESL and GED courses.

## THE GHOSTS

Many at San Jacinto Adult Learning Center say a pesky former teacher snoops around the principal's office. They'd call the police to get her out of there, but there's one problem — she's dead. The faint shadowy trace, who has been nicknamed "Mrs. Perez" by the employees, has been spotted sitting behind the principal's desk or flipping through paperwork. Some nights, lights have been seen on when nobody is in the building.

"Mrs. Perez" is a pleasant-looking slim silhouette with long, gray hair. She wears a dress with ruffles at the wrists and neck and glasses. Armando Flores has seen the mysterious lady twice — the first time she was inside the principal's office flipping through yellow notepads. And unless he had witnessed the viewing himself, he would have never believed it. He had heard the stories, but was always skeptical. When he did see her, he thought to himself, "No, I think I'm tired." But she wouldn't go away, and after Flores stepped away, he stopped and decided to look back and see if she was still there, he returned to find her calmly, flipping through papers. Flores said, "she looks like a ghost, but you can see every detail."

As far as San Jacinto Principal Blanca Andrade remembers, "Mrs. Perez" has been there as long as she has. Andrade recalls a time when a former student visited the school and his own chilling tale to tell. He described a teacher he once had. She was, he says, forced to retire and, somehow, perhaps of a heart attack, died at the school. His description of her eerily matched that of "Mrs. Perez."

## CHAPTER TWENTY-ONE
## CROSBY ELEMENTARY SCHOOL
**5411 Wren Avenue**
**El Paso, Texas 79924**

**Figure 39: Crosby Elementary School, showing the memorial under the tree on the left.**

This elementary is not nearly as old as El Paso or Austin High Schools, but still has its share of ghosts. The school is one of the older "modern" schools in town and sits on a side street off of Dyer on El Paso's northeast side.

I was asked to speak to some of the students and they all enjoyed it, even though after I left, some of the staff assured the students that they were no such thigns as ghosts and that even if there were such things, there were no ghosts at Crosby Elementary. Unfortuantely, the staff was incorrect on both counts.

An unbiased review of the of the evidence that has been amassed over decades by such writers as Hans Holzer leaves little doubt that something survives after death, call it a revenant, a spector or a ghost. It is certainly interesting to me how everyone becomes an expert when it comes to ghosts, makes me feel down right inadequate, since I try to find evidence upon which to base my beliefs.

As for there being ghosts at Crosby Elementary, let us start with the memorial that can be seen on the left side of the photo of the chool above. This memorial commenorates the death of a young lady that lived acorss the street. As I have asked questions about hauntings of this school a number of people have spoken of an unknown girl seen roaming around the school grounds. If approached she runs towad the memorial and then seems to vanish.

Inside the school, it is said that many times if you walk down the hall by yourself, you can feel what seems like someone walking aliongside so close that they brush up against you. A number have also said that they actually sense someone, a little girl they think, walking along beside them.

Then I have also been told that some of those who work past the end of the school day claim to hear footsteps when they are the only one in the building. One of two claim to have heard doors opening and closing and the soft giggling of a child.

# CHAPTER TWENTY-TWO
# THE EL PASO CLUB
## CHASE BANK BUILDING
### 210 E. Main
### El Paso, Texas

**Figure 40: The entrance to the El Paso Club, 18th Floor of the Chase Bank Building[81].**

In my first book, *Spirits of the Border: The History and Mystery of El Paso Del Norte*[82], I wrote about the Chase Bank Building at 210 E. Main Street. I didn't have much at the time, merely the story of a woman in a red dress being seen on the top floor and strange lights being seen late at night.

I now have more information on this haunting. I had occasion to speak to a group at the El Paso Club, an ating establishment which occupies the top floor of the Chase Bank Building Tower.

---

[81] This photo is from the author's collection.
[82] Hudnall, Ken and Connie Wang, The Spirits of the Border: The History and Mystery of El Paso Del Norte, Omega Press, El Paso, Texas. 2003.

**Figure 41: The Chase bank Tower, which dominates the El Paso skyline.**

I was discussing the ghosts of El Paso and then discussed the ghost of the woman in the red dress that haunts the El Paso Club and made a comment that they should be watching for that particular ghost. At that point, one of the members of the group who had been sitting quierly listening suddenly called the waiter over to his table and asked him if he had ever seen a ghost during the time that he had been working at the El Paso Club.

To everyone's surprise, the waiter confirmed that he had seen the ghost in the red dress. He said that some evenings he and others worknig there had seen a pretty lady in a red dress enter the dining room in which we were eating. She looked as real as anyone else and would generally go over to stare out the windows that looked toward the east. However, if anyone approached her or tried to speak to her, the woman would fade away.

He also went on to say that some nights when they were there late cleaning up from the evening's business, they would hear the glasses at the bar clinking as if someone was making a drink and sometimes they would hear what sounded like a large group of people talking elsewhere in the restaurant. The voices were normally pitched so low that while the sound of conversation could be heard, the actual words could not be understood.

He also confirmed that late some evenings if he happened to be in sight of the building, he could sometimes see what looked like lights burning in the Club at times he knew that the El Paso Club was empty.

# CHAPTER TWENTY-THREE
## YSLETA HIGH SCHOOL
**8600 Alameda**
**El Paso, Texas**

I wrote about Ysleta High School in volume one of this series, so this is in the way of an update. Without a doubt, there seems to be a lot of ghosts in that school. However, it is sometimes difficult to get people to talk about them. In the first volume, I discussed a seance that had been held in the gym, so I would recommend anyone interested in finding out more about this school to read volume 1.

I had a teacher who used to work at Ysleta finally tell me about some of her adventures. Sometimes she had to work late and one evening she went to the restroom by herself. While she was in the stall, she kept hearing someone move about the room and once or twice, someone knocked on the door to her stall. She responded that the would be out in a moment, but no one ever answered her. When she exited the stall, she was surprised to see that there was no one else in the room.

According to my information, a cheerleader committed suicide in the restroom after her boyfriend broke up with her. Many studnts claim to have seen her and it is said that every night she seems to appear in there.

This teacher also told me that she was one of those that had seen a little girl appear, looking lost. She went to the little girl to ask if she could help and suddenly the girl was gone. A number of students and teachers also mentioned to her in the course of the day that they had heard a girl screaming in the old gym, but no one ever found anyone there.

# CHAPTER TWENTY-FOUR
# THE RUIZ HOME
### 9108 Mount Shasta
### El Paso, Texas

**Figure 42: The Ruiz Home[83]**

I have written about many of the public buildings and schools that are haunted in this interesting city, but there are a number of private hoimes that seem to have invisible resident. This next story is about a small home off of Dyer that belngs to the Ruiz family. Built in the early 1950s on what had been empty desert, Tiffany Ruiz' grandmother, was the original occupant of this house.

The following is the story that was told to me by Tiffany Ruiz regarding the happenings at her home.

The house was purchased in 1952 by my grandparents, Wade and Violet Matthews. They are the original owners of the house, though they did rent it out for a few years while my grandparents were stationed in another city. Both of my grandparents were in the military, my grandfather being an Air Force Sgt., and my grandmother an Army Captain.

---

[83] This photo is from the author's collection.

Because of their rank, their relationship was highly unethical. We found out about a year ago that my grandfather had originally been in the Army, but transferred to the Air Force shortly after meeting my grandmother. They divorced when my mom and uncle were very young, and my grandmother raised the children on her own. I loved my grandfather dearly. He wrote the most

**Figure 43: The face of the grandmother can be seen behind the little girl.**

beautiful poetry, (my mom still has the poem he wrote for me when I was a baby). I remember being very young and visiting him at his house in Central El Paso, he always had Kit Kats for me and told me that, someday, I would be the next Dolly Parton. We lived in Germany at the time of his death, and though I was only 5, I still remember the day my mom got the call. My mother cried for three days and was unable to attend his funeral, due to the distance. I could not comprehend the concept of death, and had this vision of my grandpa leaning over a shiny stainless steel railing, looking down from the clouds.

Even though they were divorced, my grandmother took care of his final arrangements and had him buried at Fort Bliss National Cemetery. He was laid to rest under a tree, as he always wanted. On his marker his date of birth and death look almost like an error, if it were not for the year. He was born July 20th, and died July 20th. Perhaps the reason we were so close comes from the fact that my date of birth is also July 20th.

I have always had the feeling that he is still very close. My grandmother once told me that she woke one night to find him just standing at the foot of her bed, staring at her. I've told you how, shortly after we moved back from Germany, I saw him in the kitchen. What I neglected to tell you was, I believe that he looks out for us (my family). For example, the strangest thing happened a few days after bringing my oldest son home from the hospital. We were both finally asleep when I felt someone shake me, and say (clearly) "Get the baby". I responded to this by waving it off and mumbling "Grandpa, the baby's fine. I'm tired, go away". A few minutes later I was shaken again and I heard "Get the baby", more loudly this time. I ignored it, until finally I was nearly pushed out of bed and I heard "someone" yell "The baby is in DANGER!". I turned on the light, picked up my son out of his crib and checked him over. When I was laying him down, I noticed a large straight pin very near to where his head had been. Because I was not living at home when this incident took place, I believe that he watches over us every day.

My Grandmother did not have an easy life. She grew up on a farm where she "hoed and picked cotton" (her words). She left Arkansas at 18, went to nursing school and joined the Army. She served in the Korean War and was an inspiration to all military women. Here in El Paso, she was a nurse at William Beaumont where she mainly worked in Labor and Delivery and at one point she was the head nurse. That being said, she also divorced at a time when it was unheard of. (Imagine the talk from the neighbors!) She was very opinionated and that had a tendency to isolate her from other people. She frequently accused others of stealing her purse, money, her car, and toilet paper from her. At the end she was very lonely, her outbursts and fits of rage had also isolated her family.

I was living in New Orleans at the time of her death. I am more like my grandmother than I would care to admit, but needless to say I loved her more than anything. I finally understood why my mother cried for three days following my grandfather's death. I packed bags for my children (Adrian, Azsa, and Anthony), and headed for home to attend her funeral.

Even though I grew up in her house, it was the first time I had stepped foot in here in four years. It still had her presence, she frequently stood at the window watching the neighbors, and when she wasn't, she was sitting at the head of the kitchen table chain smoking. Even now, I still expect her to be sitting there when I walk through the back door. I always get the feeling that she is walking down the hallway, coming to check on me.

My mother was going to sell the house, she doesn't have pleasant memories of the place and it does hold a negative energy. I begged her to sell it to me, and in November of 2003, I purchased the house. I could not bear to have someone else living in the house that my grandmother worked so hard for. My mom is trying to get me to sell it and buy a new house, she doesn't like to visit me here.

This house has a presence of it's own. My son says that on days he walks home from school he hears someone knocking on the doors, in the hallway. There has been many times where I have locked my bedroom door (to keep the kids out) and a few minutes later it unlocks itself. There are so many strange things that occur in my house that it is really hard to keep track!

CHAPTER TWENTY-FIVE
## PEBBLE HILLS ELEMENTARY SCHOOL
**11145 Edgemere Boulevard**
**El Paso, Texas 79936**

A large urban K-6 elementary school in El Paso, Texas, Pebble Hills has a strong focus on improving student achievement. Pebble Hills has an extremely diverse student population, 78% Hispanic, 4% African American, .8% Asian and 18% White. Close to 25% of the students are limited English proficient and taught in bilingual classrooms.

Pebble Hills, a traditional school with average student achievement, embarked on a major reform initiative of instructional and professional development practices in 1995 with dramatic results. The school staff examined its instructional practices, student achievement data and current research on effective professional development. The staff established a professional development model that includes research-based practices, mentoring, model lessons, coaching, and problem solving around specific problems of the practice of teaching and learning.

Two instructional specialists support teachers at Pebble Hills in their effort. The instructional leaders facilitate conversations about "behind the glass" model lessons, in which teachers are observed by others. Teachers participate in weekly 45-minute instructional meetings. A "Professional Development Center" also is located on campus where weekly meetings are held and professional journals, books, and videos are available for staff.

The most apparent evidence of the success of the professional development model is the continual climb over the past four years of grades 3-6 student achievement as assessed by the Texas Assessment of Academic Skills. In addition, the campus developed a database of student assessments in literacy for its kindergarten through third grade students beginning with the 1998-99 school year. This charts the progress in literacy across time for K-3 students to assess program effectiveness and individual student progress in their primary grades[84].

According to what I have been told, a couple of years ago a teacher died in the bathroom. No one seems to know what the cause of death was but there was blood smeared all over the bathroom. I am told that there was a thorough investigation held but the results were never released. Now there's a picture in front of the school office commemorating her time as a teacher at the school and mourning her death. There are many students that maintain that no matter the

---

[84] Information from the U.S. Department of Education, Washington D.C.

picture was moved to, the eyes of the figure in the picture are staring directly at the bathroom where she died.

Former employees who had cause to work in the building after closing complained that the toilets would flush by themselves in the bathrom where the teacher died so mysteriously. Some also firmly state that a number of people had glimpsed the face of the dead teacher looking in the window of the classroom where she had spent so many years happily teaching.

## CHAPTER TWENTY-SIX
## CEMETERIES

It goes without saying that there may be many stories of hauntings and unexplained happenings connected with cemeteries. I do not suppose this should be surprising in view of the many tens of thousands of the dead that occupy these locations. To ask why the dead haunt cemeteries would call for an answer similar to that given by a famous Depression era gangster when asked why he robbed banks, His dry response was "Because that's where the money is!" Well, cemeteries are where the dead are. So what more likely place to haunt than the cemetery?

I do not think that anyone realizes just how many current and former Cemeteries exist in the El Paso area. It is documented hat areas around downtown El Paso such as the Popular Dry Goods Company, the El Paso Public Library and the Masonic Temple were very old burial grounds whose original occupants (in most cases) were relocated to Concordia Cemetery[85]. There are at least nine current major cemeteries and a large number of former cemeteries, some of which have been long forgotten.

Other locations include areas along West Missouri Street, Oregon Street, Mesa Street, the location of City Hall and Cleveland Square. Burials were also undertaken at the location of San Jose de Concordia el Alto, near the corner of Hammett and Rosa Street from about 1800 to 1923. There was another burial ground at the corner of Alps and Diana Streets.

---

[85] Hirsch, Dena, *The Last Roundup-Concordia Cemetery*, El Paso Today, January 1981.

The Herald Post of November 27, 1957 makes mention of another cemetery at Diana Drive just north of Pikes Peak Drive. The burial site that was known as El Paso's Boot Hill Cemetery is between Restlawn Cemetery and Diana Drive[86].

Although stanzas from Theodore O'Hara's elegiac poem, "Bivouac of the Dead," are inscribed on iron tablets found throughout some of the oldest units of this country's national cemeteries, there is little public recognition of this poet-soldier and his long-lived literary contribution to the memorialization of fallen troops. O'Hara's military service bridged the period from the Mexican War, whose action inspired the poem, to the Civil War, which led him to places where some of the first cemeteries were created. An elegy, or elegiac poem, expresses feelings of melancholy, sorrow or lamentation—especially for a person or persons who are dead. It may seem unusual that verse written about heroes of the relatively remote Mexican conflict was appropriated for the Civil War more than a decade later, but "Bivouac" had captivated the attention of a patriotic nation and would continue to do so for decades to come. Quartermaster General Montgomery C. Meigs (1816-92) recognized its solemn appeal and directed that lines from "Bivouac" grace the entrance to Arlington National Cemetery.

## THE POET

O'Hara was born in Danville, Kentucky, on February 11, 1820; thereafter his Irish Catholic family moved to Frankfort, Kentucky. Comfortable and able with academic study, his education was punctuated by accolades for his writing and oratory skills, which prompted O'Hara to study law. By 1845 he was employed at the U.S. Treasury in the nation's capital. As a captain promoted to brevet-major, he saw combat in the Mexican War (1846-48), including the Battle of Buena Vista; he served again in the conflict with Cuba (1850-51) until suffering an injury at the Battle of Cardenas. For the next decade O'Hara's career returned to one of words, and he served as editor of the Mobile Register, Louisville Times, and Frankfort Yeoman, sequentially. Volunteering for active duty again in the Civil War, O'Hara served in the Confederate Army as a colonel in command of the 12th Alabama regiment, and subsequently saw action at Shiloh and Stones River in Tennessee. After the war he briefly took up residence in the vicinity of Guerrytown (Barbour County), Alabama, but he soon fell ill and died on June 6, 1867. Described as a handsome bachelor, O'Hara spent his life traveling from place to place and never owned a home. This itinerant lifestyle of journalist and soldier may have masked frequent bouts with depression and an addiction to alcohol, according to some accounts. Upon his death at age 47, O'Hara's body was initially buried in Columbus, Georgia.

---

[86] From an undated document prepared by Ralph A. Guilliams, 3503 Volcanic Avenue, El Paso, Texas 79904.

Although O'Hara wrote "Bivouac" as a remembrance of the many casualties suffered by the Second Kentucky Regiment of Foot Volunteers who fought at the Battle of Buena Vista, the verse was produced as part of the dedication ceremony for a monument erected to these men long after the confrontation. The battle of February 22-23, 1847, saw 4,759 Americans under the command of General Zachary Taylor repulse an estimated force of 18,000 Mexicans led by President Antonio Lopez de Santa Anna. More Americans fell at Buena Vista—267 killed and 456 wounded—than any other battle in the war, which concluded with the United States compensating Mexico for the ceded Texas, and New Mexico and California becoming U.S. territories.

## "BIVOUAC OF THE DEAD"

The muffled drum's sad roll has beat
The soldier's last tattoo;
No more on life's parade shall meet
That brave and fallen few.
On Fame's eternal camping-ground
Their silent tents are spread,
And Glory guards, with solemn round,
The bivouac of the dead.

No rumor of the foe's advance
Now swells upon the wind;
Nor troubled thought at midnight haunts
Of loved ones left behind;
No vision of the morrow's strife
The warrior's dream alarms;
No braying horn nor screaming fife
At dawn shall call to arms.

Their shriveled swords are red with rust,
Their plumed heads are bowed,
Their haughty banner, trailed in dust,
Is now their martial shroud.
And plenteous funeral tears have washed
The red stains from each brow,
And the proud forms, by battle gashed
Are free from anguish now.

The neighing troop, the flashing blade,
The bugle's stirring blast,
The charge, the dreadful cannonade,
The din and shout, are past;

Nor war's wild note nor glory's peal
Shall thrill with fierce delight
Those breasts that nevermore may feel
The rapture of the fight.

Like the fierce northern hurricane
That sweeps the great plateau,
Flushed with the triumph yet to gain,
Came down the serried foe,
Who heard the thunder of the fray
Break o'er the field beneath,
Knew well the watchword of that day
Was "Victory or death!"

Long had the doubtful conflict raged
O'er all that stricken plain,
For never fiercer fight had waged
The vengeful blood of Spain;
And still the storm of battle blew,
Still swelled the gory tide;
Not long, our stout old chieftain knew,
Such odds his strength could bide.

Twas in that hour his stern command
Called to a martyr's grave
The flower of his beloved land,
The nation's flag to save.
By rivers of their father's gore
His first-born laurels grew,
And well he deemed the sons would pour
Their lives for glory too.

For many a mother's breath has swept
O'er Angostura's plain --
And long the pitying sky has wept
Above its moldered slain.
The raven's scream, or eagle's flight,
Or shepherd's pensive lay,
Alone awakes each sullen height
That frowned o'er that dread fray.

Sons of the Dark and Bloody Ground
Ye must not slumber there,

Where stranger steps and tongues resound
Along the heedless air.
Your own proud land's heroic soil
Shall be your fitter grave;
She claims from war his richest spoil --
The ashes of her brave.

Thus 'neath their parent turf they rest,
Far from the gory field,
Borne to a Spartan mother's breast
On many a bloody shield;
The sunshine of their native sky
Smiles sadly on them here,
And kindred eyes and hearts watch by
The heroes sepulcher.

Rest on embalmed and sainted dead!
Dear as the blood ye gave;
No impious footstep shall here tread
The herbage of your grave;
Nor shall your glory be forgot
While fame her records keeps,
Or Honor points the hallowed spot
Where Valor proudly sleeps.

Yon marble minstrel's voiceless stone
In deathless song shall tell,
When many a vanquished ago has flown,
The story how ye fell;
Nor wreck, nor change, nor winter's blight,
Nor Time's remorseless doom,
Shall dim one ray of glory's light
That gilds your deathless tomb.

## CONCORDIA CEMETERY
### Gateway West and Stevens
### El Paso, Texas

**Figure 44: The Graveyard Girls, found in Concordia Cemetery at Midnight. Kneeling from left - Samantha Carlos and Amanda Aleman. Top from left to right - Erika Salcido, Stephanie Castillo, Samantha Deucher and Heather Pomeroy.**

There are those who maintain that the only thing to be found in a cemetary is death, but I found six of the most lovely young ladies it has been my pleasure to meet. Since I met them in a cemetery, I have dubbed them the graveyard girls. These young ladies are actually students at Eastwood High School and on this particular night, there were hunting ghosts. Instead they found ghost stories. But more about these lovely young ladies in the section on Eastwood High School.

The cemetery where I found them is the infamous Concordia Cemetery. This well known repository for the dead had its beginnings as a large ranch settled by pioneer Hugh Stephenson and his wife, Juana Maria Ascarate. Sometime between the years 1830 and 1840, the settlement came to be known as Concordia, after the Missouri town in which Stephenson was raised. Born in Kentucky, Stephenson arrived in the area around 1824, one of the first Anglo-American settlers. A hunter and trapper, he later became a trader with mining interests in Mexico. There he met his wife, the daughter of wealthy landowners.

In 1854, a chapel and cemetery were built at the Stephensons' ranch. The chapel was named "San Jose de Concordia el Alto." On February 6, 1856, a pet deer gored Juana Ascarate Stephenson, and she became the first person to be buried in the Concordia Cemetery. Stephenson lost his land after the Civil War, but his son-in-law, Albert H. French, purchased the Concordia property at a federal marshal's sale in 1867. French sold each of the Stephenson's heirs an equal portion of the property for a dollar. By the 1880s, various groups interested in establishing cemeteries were contacting the heirs. The city of El Paso bought its first part of the cemetery in 1882 as a burial ground for paupers.

By the 1890s, sections had been purchased by different groups and were designated Jesuit, Catholic, Masonic, Jewish, Black, Chinese, military, city, county and other ethnic and social groups. Today, Concordia has about 65,000 individual graves. Historian Dena Hirsch refers to Concordia Cemetery as "a collection of privately owned, publicly owned, and non-owned burial lands" consisting of 54 acres. Thus, no one organization or person accepts responsibility for maintaining Concordia.

The history of El Paso can be found in the various sections of the cemetery. Various religious leaders are buried in Concordia. Reverend Joseph Tays, an Episcopal missionary who founded El Paso's first Protestant church, arrived in El Paso in 1870, a widower with two boys. C. L. Sonnichsen records the story that a month after he began his mission in El Paso, Tays sent word to Austin that he was "doing his best."

Tays was learning Spanish and at least one saloon keeper had closed his doors and found another vocation because of him. He not only preached and taught, he worked in real estate and served the county as surveyor. Tays laid the cornerstone of the first St. Clement's Episcopal Church on Christmas day in 1881.

Leon Metz writes that after having conducted the funeral of a smallpox victim, Tays contracted the dreaded disease himself and died after a week's suffering. Late in the evening of November 21, two men from the city wrapped Parson Tays' body in a sheet and delivered it quickly to Concordia. He was buried without ceremony in the middle of the night during a violent rain storm. The man who had helped so many in early El Paso was buried with only two grave diggers present.

The Chinese section includes the graves of early railroad workers who chose to stay in El Paso after helping the railroads reach the city. Older tombstones are rectangular and have only the person's name in Chinese engraved on them. More recent graves may contain more information about the deceased, but the name of the individual is engraved in Chinese.

The Jesuit section includes the grave of Carlos Pinto, S. J., founder of five Catholic churches, and other Jesuit leaders who established many of El Paso's Catholic schools, churches and social services in the 19th century.

Other prominent leaders buried at Concordia include James H. Biggs, World War I aviator for whom Biggs Field is named; Richard Caples, former mayor and builder of the Caples Building in downtown El Paso; former county judge and mayor Joseph Sweeney, who established the first paid fire department in El Paso in 1909; and Dr. M. P. Schuster, a founder of Providence Memorial Hospital.

Mexican Revolution leader and ally to Pancho Villa, Pascual Orozco, was originally buried at Concordia, but his remains later were moved to Mexico. Orozco's enemy, and former President of Mexico, Victoriano Huerta also was buried at Concordia, but his body was later moved to Evergreen Cemetery. Many other civic leaders, pioneers and war veterans lie buried in Concordia.

**Figure 45: Even in death John Wesley Hardin is behind bars!**

However, it is the grave of a notorious gunfighter that gets all the attention. John Wesley Hardin gained his reputation by supposedly killing more people than Billy the Kid and Jesse James. He was killed on August 19, 1895, at the Acme Saloon downtown by John Selman, a sometime lawman who had been on both sides of the law. Selman, in turn, was killed by another gunslinger. Ironically, Wyndam Kemp, who was Selman's lawyer, and Jeff Melton, Acme Saloon owner, are buried not too far from Hardin.

In 1995, descendants of Hardin came to El Paso to remove the gunfighter's remains and reinter them in Nixon, Texas. A court injunction stopped them and a judge has since ruled that Hardin's remains will stay in El Paso. Various groups have publicized the fact that several figures of El Paso's wild and wooly days are buried in Concordia. They are attempting to get the word out that Concordia is El Paso's "Boot Hill," and encourage tourists to visit the historical site. Once in El Paso, these visitors can learn of the various cultures reflected in the city and tour other points of interest in Texas, New Mexico and Mexico.

Since 1990, the Concordia Heritage Association has been working to preserve and restore the central El Paso historic cemetery. Establishing official boundaries for the cemetery will enable the Association to try for national historic cemetery status. This designation would allow the group to apply for federal grants to help pay for improvements.

El Paso has a 400 year history it needs to capitalize on. Part of this history is recorded in Concordia Cemetery. In the background is Mount Franklin and Scenic Drive, two other historical sites in El Paso. The success of the most recent Walk Through History seems to reflect a renewed interest in the cemetery, perhaps encouraging others to join the Concordia Heritage Association in cleaning and maintaining the historical site.


# EVERGREEN CEMETERIES AND MAUSOLEUM
## Two Locations:
## 4301 Alameda &
## 12100 Montana
## El Paso, Texas

Evergreen Cemetery on Alameda is a very old cemetery, rivaling Concordia not in age, but perhaps in the historical significance of those buried within its confines. Evergreen is the final resting places of personalities as diverse as gunslingers, such as Mannen Clements and Bass Outlaw, to a former President of Mexico, Victoriano Huerta, all of whom lie sleeping beneath the well tended grass of this old cemetery[87]. Even a personage as well known to El Paso as Joseph Magoffin, 4 time mayor of the city chose Evergreen as the site of his eternal slumber rather than the closer Concordia.

Also buried in this old cemetery are a number who chose to fight for the Southern Cause during the American Civil War. Periodically their sacrifices have been remembered on a little known Texas Holiday. Confederate Heroes Day was a formally approved Texas holiday celebrated on January 19th each year, also the date of Confederate General Robert E. Lee's Birthday. The remembrances, which have included raising the Confederate Battle Flag, known as the Stars and Bars, have been a cause of much dispute over the years as shown by various comments

---

[87] Martinez, Leonard, *Cemetery Tour Reveals El Paso's Long History*, El Paso Times, February 14, 2000.

included in an El Paso Times article of January 23, 1995, entitled *Service Raises Questions*[88].

Naturally, a cemetery that contains such diverse and dominate personalities as Evergreen Cemetery would be a natural place to also encounter ghosts and those creatures that walk the nights and haunt our dreams.

As you drive by the cemetery a number of people have sworn to me that sometimes you can see a boy standing on the sidewalk during the early hours of the morning. If you should stop to see if you can help the little boy, he will ask for a ride. But if you let him get in the car, he will slowly fade away.

There are railroad tracks that run behind the cemetery. In this area, if is sometimes possible to see a mist that hoevers around one specific spot. If you approach the mist, you will suddenly smell a strong order of rottig flesh, as if someone had died and was not decomposing.

## FORT BLISS NATIONAL CEMETERY
### Intersection of Fred Wilson and Jeb Stewart
### El Paso, Texas

Fort Bliss is located in El Paso County, Texas, within the Fort Bliss Military Reservation. The fort was first established in the late 1840s at the end of the Mexican-American war, when the United States gained possession of former Mexican territories in the Southwest. Due to its strategic location on the banks of the Rio Grande, Fort Bliss was originally used as an infantry post. During the Civil War, the fort was used as a Confederate garrison until the surrender of Gen. Robert E. Lee. Conditions at the desert fort could be arduous. One legend has it that Gen. Phil Sheridan, a resident of Fort Bliss at the end of the Civil War, declared, "If I owned both Hell and Texas, I would rent out Texas and live in Hell."

Although there are no definitive dates regarding the establishment of the first post cemetery, records indicate the first interment was made in 1883 and 16 burials had been made prior to 1890. In 1914, the status of Fort Bliss was changed from an infantry to a cavalry post. At that time, the area set aside as a post cemetery totaled 2.2 acres with a capacity of 800 graves, enclosed with a stone wall.

During World War I, Fort Bliss was used as a training center for cavalry detachments. It was first used as a gathering point for recruits at the beginning of the war and then as a demobilization camp after the Armistice. In the interwar years, 2.24 acres were added to the cemetery, increasing its capacity to 2,400 graves. Congress authorized the establishment of a national cemetery at Fort

---

[88] Hamann, Carlos, *Service Raises Questions*, El Paso Times, January 23, 1995.

Bliss in June 1936, but funds were not appropriated for construction until 1939. Had the funds been available, construction would have been delayed anyway, as the Fort Bliss commanding general and the Office of the Quartermaster General in Washington D.C., disagreed on the site. Finally, in March 1939, the quartermaster general approved a plan and the new Fort Bliss National Cemetery had its first interment a year later on March 7, 1940.

In addition to U.S. soldiers and civilians, there are a number of non-U.S. citizens interred at Fort Bliss. In fall 1944, Chinese authorities officially selected the post as the place of interment for Chinese air force cadets who died while training at the fort; 55 are buried at Fort Bliss. Others resting here include four German prisoners of war, three Japanese civilian internees who were disinterred from Lordsburg, N.M., and one German civilian scientist who had been conducting research at Fort Bliss during the war.

In 1955, the remains of Lt. Col. William Wallace Smith Bliss were moved from Girard Street Cemetery in New Orleans to Fort Bliss. Col. Bliss fought against the Cherokee, taught at West Point, served as chief of staff to Gen. Zachary Taylor in the Mexican-American War and married Taylor's daughter. The city of New Orleans notified the Army that all monuments in the Girard Street Cemetery must be removed because the land had been condemned to make way for a new building and a highway.

A number of visitors believe that they have seen barely glimpsed figures running among the tombstones around dusk. The sounds of laughter and conversation can sometimes be heard in the stillness of the approaching night, though it is impossible to tell the direction from which the odd sounds come. Do some of the ghosts still enjoy companionship with their peers?

## McGILL CEMETERY
### Intersection of Mount Baldy and Tetons
### Near Magoffin Park
### El Paso, Texas

The McGill Cemetery was also called the El Paso County Pauper Cemetery was located behind the Magoffin School. It was started by Judge Joseph McGill about 1890. A wood frame house owned by the Bull Family stood on the property until about 1950. A number of students that attended the Magoffin school talked about seeing figures standing in the grveyard staring toward the school building. Others swore that some nights there were dancing lights playing among the graves.

## SMELTER CEMETRY
### Corner of I-10 and Executive Boulevard

The little known Smelter Cemetery is one of the most poetic and eerie in El Paso. From 1882 until sometime in 1970, it saw is share of grief as the living brought the dead there to spend all eternity. Now, it sits forlorn and forgotten on a dusty windswept hill only a stones throw from two of the busiest thoroughfares in the city.

**Figure 46: The gate to the Smelter Cemetery.**

Just south of ASARCO Inc., high atop San Marcos Drive, off Executive Center, this reminder of times done by sits silent, unattended and unnoticed except by those who themselves live on the outskirts of civilization. In fact, the cemetery is completely surrounded by ASARCO property and the company has the actual deed to the land that became a cemetery back in 1882.

According to the records of the Catholic Diocese, which has responsibility for this cemetery, residents of Smeltertown are buried there along with some ASARCO workers and some residents of Sunland Park[89].

---

[89] Levin, Sondra, _Cemetery Evokes Emotion_, El Paso Herald-Post, July 21, 1979.

**Figure 47: One of the graves within the Smelter Cemetery.**

Smeltertown was once a thriving community located just south of ASARCO, boasting a school, a church and numerous houses. The primary residents were the workers of the various industrial plants in the area who found the commute from El Paso difficult and too time consuming. Naturally as travel conditions improved and the workforce expanded, many Smeltertown residents moved into El Paso housing. The town's Catholic Church, San Jose de Cristo Rey, operated the cemetery until the town was condemned in 1973 due to the discovery of high lead contamination in the land and high elevations of lead being found in the blood of some Smeltertown children.

The cemetery itself has also been a victim of time and the elements. The gates stand open, an invitation to enter and visit with those who have gone on before. Though there have been some efforts to preserve the graves, the area is generally as barren today as it was when the article was written in 1979. Though the hustle and bustle of the largest city on the border is just over the hill, the atmosphere within the cemetery is eerie and the silence broken only occasionally by and unusually loud truck accelerating onto Interstate 10 from Executive Center. Is it any wonder that there have been so many stories of odd happenings within and about the old cemetery?

Most of the graves are unmarked, those who sleep there completely forgotten and unmourned. Perhaps this is one of the reasons that those interned here do not seem to rest. There are a large number of stories associated with this cemetery and the nearby ASARCO plant.

## THE GHOSTS

The person that told me about the Smelter Cemetery also said that many nights shadowy figures are seen moving among the graves. Many h ave seen these figures, but they never leave any tracks or sign that they have been there. There are also mysterious lights that glimmer and dance about the hilltop in the thick darkness that cloaks this lonely place of the dead. Though whenever anyone tries to discover the source of the moving lights, nothing is ever found.

Even those living in Skull Canyon, a hidden enclave within the shadow of the high ground upon which sits the forgotten Smelter Cemetery rarely venture up to the graveyard after darkness covers the land.

Others tell of a lovely woman dressed in black who is seen to move silently and swiftly among the grave markers as if seeking one grave out of the many that dot the desolate hilltop. No one sees her come nor go, she is just suddenly there, alone among the many forgotten dead, searching, always searching..

There is also the story of the hound who sits at the gates of the cemetery. It is said that he is patiently waiting for his master who died. This big, loyal animal was his master's constant companion in life and does not seem to understand that his master is gone forever.

Just like the story of Blackfrairs Bobby of London fame, this large mastiff continues to seek the beloeved master that died so many years ago. Of course, I was sure that like so many others, this story was just a story. However, I was in for a bit of a surprise. When I was finally able to drive to the gates of this fogotten cemetery, I was amazed to actually see the hound I had heard so much about, sitting just outside the gates that stood open to the world as if he was actually waisting for someone.

I had been warned that no matter what I did I would not be able to take the picture of this elusive canine, but I was determined to try. Quickly getting out my camera, when I was far enough away that I did not think I would scare him, I tried to take his picture with a zoom lens, but it seemed as if the dog was equally determined not to allow me to suceed. Each time I would aim the camera toward this large dog, he would suddenly dart behind some obstruction, until finally he seemed to tire of this game and ran off toward the far end of the wind swept hilltop.

Not wanting to admit that I had been outwitted by this dog, I tried to follow him in my car, but to my surprise, he quickly outdistanced me and disappeared while crossing what seemed to be open ground. I never did find out where he went, but having only a little time to tour the cemetery. I returned to my mission. It was only as I was driving away from that silent repository of the dead that I saw this faithful companion of man in my rearview miirror returning to resume his eternal vigil for the beloved master who would never return. If only humans showed such loyalty.

## THE UNMARKED CONFEDERATE CEMETERY
Lot 33, El Paso Street
(corner of El Paso and Overland Streets)
EL PASO, TEXAS

**Figure 48: The first official flag of the Confederacy (1861-1863)**

As has been made mention of several times, in addition to the recognized cemeteries in El Paso, there have been many other areas that are now in the downtown area used to inter the dead at various times. One such undocumented area was used for the burial of a number of Confederate soldiers who died in El Paso during the Confederate occupation[90].

In the summer of 1861, the Confederate High Command sent the 2nd Mounted Rifles under the command of Lt. Colonel John Robert Baylor from San Antonio to El Paso. Lt. Col. Baylor's orders were to secure the frontier forts that had been evacuated by Union troops. Lt. Col. Baylor paused at Fort Bliss for a short period of time before pushing on to Mesilla and the capture of Ft. Fillmore and the occupation of Dona Ana and Robledo.

In December 1861, Brigadier General Henry Sibley arrived in El Paso with a Brigade of the Texas Mounted Volunteers. BG Sibley proposed to conquer the New Mexican Territory for the South. The Confederate's plan was sound, but the selection of the senior officer was an error. Brigadier General Sibley was not a suitable commander for such an audacious campaign.

The Confederate force enjoyed some early victories, but after the pitched battles at Valverde and Glorieta Pass, the Sibley Brigade was forced to retreat back into Texas. The destruction of the Confederate supply train at Apache

---

[90] Jenkins, Frank, <u>Confederate Burial Ground Search Proposal</u>, The Sibley Trail Association, El Paso, Texas.

Canyon by a Union force that flanked Sibley's main lines made it impossible for the Confederate force to continue the campaign.

Facing starvation as a result of the loss of their supply wagons, and weakened by the number of wounded and ill soldiers the Sibley Brigade was forced to withdraw to El Paso. Once safely back in Texas, the Brigade was reorganized and a hospital set up in the Overland Mail Station. The official records of this Confederate Field Hospital show that at least forty Confederate soldiers died there during and immediately after the Confederate evacuation of the New Mexico Territory. According to contemporary accounts, the dead Confederate soldiers were buried in the ground opposite the hospital. However, there has never been a monument or plaque showing the site of their burial on South El Paso Street.

The *Confederate Burial Ground Search Proposal*[91] includes three references that confirm the location of the Confederate Hospital in the Overland Mail Station at the intersection of Overland and El Paso Streets, the deaths of over forty soldiers at the hospital, and the ensuing burial across the street.

**The Location of the Hospital**: Confederate Private Alfred B. Peticolas kept a diary of the Confederate invasion of New Mexico. He also illustrated his diary with sketches of places that caught his interest. In his diary, he sketched what he labeled as "Hospital, C.S.A. Franklin, May 19th, '62". During this time period, El Paso was called Franklin and the sketch in his diary is very clearly a drawing of the Butterfield Overland Mail Station built in 1858 by Anson Mills.

**The Deaths**: Historian Martin Hall conducted a study of the actions of the Sibley's Brigade. Included within the records that he reviewed were a number of well kept entries for the period when the Overland Mail Station was being used as a hospital by the Confederate forces. From these records it is clear that in excess of forty deaths took place at the Hospital.

**The Burial**: According to the 1901 memoirs of William Wallace Mills, who acted as a spy and agent for the Union Army during this time period, of the three thousand five hundred Texans of the Sibley Brigade that invaded New Mexico, only about eleven hundred returned to Texas. The others were dead, wounded, sick, prisoners or deserters. Many were buried on the west side of El Paso Street, near where the Opera House now stands.

The property to the west of the Overland Mail Station was an empty block 33 where the Confederates would bury those that died in the hospital. It should be noted that Block 33 included lots 138 through 145. Though the Anson Mills plat from the time shows that El Paso Street had been opened as far south as the Magoffinsville acequia (the acequia ran through lots 141, 144 and the corner of 145), in all likelihood, the block was unimproved and covered with scrub brush making it easy to bury the bodies. Of course, there is also the question of whether the bodies were buried in separate graves or simply dumped

---

[91] Ibid.

into a common trench. Unfortunately, it is also not known just how far into the block that the burials were done, nor whether bodies were interned on just one side of the acequia or on both sides.

**Figure 49: Beneath this building and the others on this block lies the long forgotten Cnfederate Cemetery.**

In 1881, with the arrival of the railroad, improvements of block 33 began. The Conklin Fire Insurance map for this period shows a dance hall and saloon running through lots 139 & 140 to the alley and three small stores directly at the corner of Overland and El Paso Streets.

The dance hall and saloon referred to in the *Confederate Burial Ground Search Proposal*[92] was the notorious **Coliseum**, built in mid 1882 at the rear of the El Paso House Hotel, on El Paso Street[93]. This theater was 49 feet wide by 110 feet long, two stories high and contained 25 private boxes. There was a seating capacity of 500 people with room for six in each box (three men with girls on their laps). The Coliseum was known as the largest theater between San Francisco and New Orleans, but many called it a "honky tonk". The Coliseum was controlled by the infamous Manning Brothers. It was believed to be Jim Manning that shot and killed El Paso Sheriff Dallas Stoudenmire in front of the Saloon portion of the Coliseum[94].

---

[92] Ibid
[93] Jones, Harriot Howze, El Paso: A Centennial Portrait, El Paso County Historical Society, El Paso, Texas. 1973.
[94] Ibid.

After the incident regarding the shooting of Sheriff Stoudenmire, the Manning Brothers took off for healthier climes and the Coliseum fell into other hands. On May 19, 1883, the Coliseum was reopened under the name of the **National Theater** by Can Caddagan, former city Marshall of Albuquerque, New Mexico. However, by June 9, of that same year, Caddagan had lost the lease.

In January 1884, the National was reopened by Charles Body of Silver City, New Mexico and did a very good business. Even John L. Sullivan, the world champion boxer appeared in El Paso at the National in the spring of 1884 for an exhibition fight. However, in the summer of 1884, the National closed once again[95].

In September 1884, Mark Grayson reopened the National, but was forced to close it in November of that year. The National reopened in August of 1885 and operated profitably until June of 1886 when a benefit had to held in order to pay the salaries of the actors. By April of 1887, the once grand National Theater was reduced to holding cock fights. In July of 1886, however, Henry W. Myar bought the land for the princely sum of $17,250.00. He had big plans for this portion of Block 33.

By 1883, the branch acequia that ran through lots 141, 144 and 145 had been abandoned and the land used for the extension of First Street which came from the east. A few stores and a hotel were built below First Street and Second Street had been opened at the bottom of Block 33 along the edge of the Magoffinsville acequia. The west half of block 33, except for a couple of Chinese laundries and some small huts remained basically empty.

In 1887, National Theater and the attached saloon that occupied lots 139 and 140 were torn down and the Myar Opera House was built on this location. Henry Myar proudly opened his new establishment in December of 1887. The Opera House faced east on El Paso Street with a street frontage of 104 feet. There were four stores at street level and a central stair case that led to the opera hall located on the upper floors. There was also a full basement that ran to the alley in the center of the block.

On July 6, 1888, the dome of the Opera House and much of the interior collapsed into the basement due to the storage of 15 tons of beans in one of the stores located at street level. The Opera House was quickly rebuilt to become one of the best known Opera Houses in the country. From 1892 with the appearance of the Grand Spanish Opera Company from Madrid, Spain until May 19, 1905 with a performance of "Lucia di Lammermoor", the Myar Opera House presented the crème de la crème of talent to the citizens of El Paso. In 1905 the Myar Opera House was destroyed by fire[96].

---

[95] Ibid.
[96] Ibid.

By 1919, the land that had been occupied by the Myar Opera House was now filled with movie theaters and a newspaper printing plant[97]. Stores and lodging houses filled the rest of the frontage along El Paso Street from Overland to Second Street. The livery stable that had occupied the northwest corner of the block had been replaced by a hardware warehouse and an automobile garage. In the late 1930s, a saloon and a restaurant were built in the previously vacant First Street parcel facing Santa Fe Street.

Is it a coincidence that a number of the buildings in the vicinity of the old Confederate graveyard are haunted by figures that appear to be wearing civil war style uniforms?

So today, the citizens of El Paso live, work and conduct business over the remains of a number of Confederate soldiers who gave their lives in defense of an ideal. No one likes to be forgotten, so is it any wonder that some of these poor forgotten souls have been seen wondering through the structures that now exist over their graves?

# CHAPTER TWENTY-SEVEN
# FORT STOCKTON, TEXAS

**Figure 50: The original County Jail.**

If there is one thing that Texas has in an unbelievable amount it is history. In this volume, I have written about the hauntings at the Fort Davis historical site and now I am going to write about the other "local" military post, Fort Stockton.

According to the most compelte records that I can find, military scouts first camped near Comanche Springs as early as 1851. Continued military presence was placed in Camp Stockton by a detachment of twenty men consisting of personnel from the 1st and 8th Infantry Regiments, U.S. Army in December, 1858. Camp Stockton was formally established in March 1859. It was named in honor of Captain Robert Field Stockton, a prominent navy officer in the Mexican War. He was the grandson of Richard Stockton, a signer of the Declaration of Independence.

This military post protected travelers and settlers on the numerous roads and trails that crossed the rugged west and made use of the abundant water supply of Comanche Springs in West Texas. The first transcontinental trip

---

[97] Jenkins, Frank, <u>Confederate Burial Ground Search Proposal</u>, The Sibley Trail Association, El Paso, Texas.

initiated by the San Antonio-San Diego stage line passed by Comanche Springs on September 17, 1858. The next year the Butterfield-Overland Mail contracted to furnish through stages twice a week. The garrison formed detachments to protect the lines.

## THE CIVIL WAR YEARS

When the commander of the Department of Texas surrendered all of the propety of the Untied States Army to the Confederate States of America, the U.S. Army withdrew from Texas for the duration of the Civil War. As with Fort Davis, the Army also abandoned Fort Stockton in 1861. Confederate troops briefly occupied the site until the debacle of Sibley's invasion of New Mexico and then they too withdrew, in 1862.

**Figure 51: The original post guard house.**

In July 1867, Fort Stockton was re-established by four Companies of the 9th U.S. Cavalry Regiment on 960 acres leased from civilian landowners, one-half mile northeast of the original location of the first post. Companies A, B, E, and K of the 9th Cavalry begin construction of the new post under the command of Colonel Edward Hatch.

The 9th Cavalry was one of the new regiments organized after the Civil War staffed with Black enlisted men. When the 9th Cavalry was moved to New Mexico in 1875, Colonel Benjamin Grierson's 10th Cavalry took over the duties of protecting the westward migration and trade routes.

About 87 percent of all soldiers garrisoned at Fort Stockton from 1867 until 1886 were Black troops of the 9th and 10th Cavalry Regiments and the 41st, 24th and 25th Infantry Regiments. Surmounting obstacles of harsh living conditions, difficult pay and racial prejudice, they gained a reputation of tenacity and bravery. Stationed continuously on the frontier during the years of Indian hostility Black regiments played a major role in the settlement and development of America's western frontier.

On October 15, 1994, Barracks #2 (Quarters of Troop L 10th Cavalry) was dedicated at Fort Stockton.

## THE GHOSTS

There is so much history around the fort Stockton area that it would be unusual if there were not a few ghosts hovering about. The original guard house still stands as does one of the old jails where outlaws were held until they could be conveniently hung.

Just as with Fort Davis, there have been a number of figures seen moving among the ruins of the original post by local residents. However, there is one location that evenone agrees is haunted and that is The Fort Stockton Sutlery. The Sutler's store served the same pupose as the Post Exchange of today. It was a place where soldiers could buy items they desired that the army did not issue.

There is a strange, dark figure of an apparition has been spotted near this old building. When he is approach, he seems to disappear. Locals who have had the opportunity to see this mysterious figure call him "El Bulto" which means "the Figure".

I also found a listing of some of the other hauntings that fall generally within the area that I meant to cover in this book, but there are not close enough to warrant a detailed discussion. Therefore, I am taking this opportunity to lump all of these loctions under the Fort Stockton section. You can find a more detailed listing at the website http://www.lonestarspirits.org.

In San Angelo, something in Miss Hattie's Café on Concho Avenue tends to move things around and breaks glasses from time to time. The adjacent building that once housed a brothel named Miss Hattie's has a spook with a shoe fetish. The ghost moves a pair of men's slippers from room to room at night.

*Here's a sampling of other stories from West Texas, according to Lone Star Spirits:*

* Fletcher Hall at Sul Ross State University in Alpine: A dormitory room has showers and doors that operate on their own. A female apparition has been spotted there, named Beverly.

* Captain Shepard's Inn in Marathon: Doors open and close, and unexplained shadows are witnessed.
* Gage Hotel in Marathon: Guests in room 10 hear ghost music and are awakened at night by a ghost tapping on their shoulder. Some have reported ghostly poetry recitation and apparitions.
* Arcon Inn B & B in Marfa: "Emmeline" is seen gazing through the window of the north bedroom in her white dress. Doors open and shut, and cold spots are felt.
* Marfa Lights: More than 75 local legends are known to exist about the origin of these strange lights. As yet there is no definitive explanation for their occurrence.
* Monahans Sandhills State Park: Closed doors manage to slam themselves, shadows are seen in employees' peripheral vision, and disembodied shrieks can be heard.
* Reeves County Courthouse in Pecos: Footsteps on the third floor, footsteps descending stairs, and shadowy figures in peripheral vision have been experienced here late at night.
* Fort Leaton in Presidio: After having Edward Hall murdered in his own house, John Burgess moved into Hall's home (the fort). Burgess was killed in retribution by Hall's stepson. From time-to-time now one might find a female spirit rocking away in the rocking chair in the kitchen. No one knows if it is Mrs. Burgess or Mrs. Hall. Edward Hall can still be found, lingering in the room in which he was murdered.
* The School Building in Shafter: The older part of the building has experienced some whispers. The newer part has had ghostly footsteps of two children, and an occasional electrical disruption. The building is being converted into a private home.
* Landmark Hotel in Sterling City: Years after her death, a ghostly telephone operator would call the pay phone in the cafe downstairs. Ghostly footsteps have been reported, and mysterious business records would turn up in odd places.
* The Perry House in Terlingua: An unidentified female apparition has been seen in the house of the former cinnabar mining magnate.[98].

---

[98] http://www.oaoa.com/columns/gene103103.htm - Gene Powell Jr.'s column appears Fridays. E-mailed comments may be sent to oa@link.freedom.com.

# CHAPTER TWENTY-EIGHT
# FORT CONCHO

## SAN ANGELO, TEXAS

Since I mentioned this historic old post in the section on Fort Stockton, I thought it only far to explain a little bit about Fort Concho. Fort Concho, in San Angelo, was one of a number of United States military posts built to establish law and order in West Texas as settlers began to move in after the Civil War.[qv] A site at the juncture of the Main and North Concho rivers was selected in November 1867 for a new post to replace Fort Chadbourne, which lacked an adequate water supply. Company H of the Fourth United States Cavalry[qv] arrived there in December. The post's first commanding officer, Capt. George Gibson Huntt, named the post Camp Hatch after the commander of his regiment, Maj. John Porter Hatch.[qv] Later it was called Camp Kelly for the recently deceased Maj. Michael J. Kelly,[qv] and in March 1868 the post became Fort Concho, named after the Middle and North Concho rivers, which converge in San Angelo to form the Concho.

Built in 1867, Fort Concho was constructed to protect settlers and the transportation routes between a chain of forts in the heartland of Texas. Situated at the junction of the North and Middle Concho Rivers, the site selected for the fort was very strategic to the government's stabilization of the region because no less than five major trails passed nearby. Even though the fort was surrounded by miles of flat treeless prairie, it was considered to be "One of the most beautiful and best ordered posts in Texas." But order was anything but the norm in the post's early beginnings.

Confusion over the exact location of the post and the construction materials to be used to build the fort hampered early construction. The first site chosen for the fort was later rejected but not before 28,000 dollars had been spent to prepare the land for future construction. Once a site had been decided on, the next hurdle was what the fort would be built out of. Initially the fort's buildings were to be constructed out of pecan wood but it proved to be too hard and unmanageable. Adobe was the second type of building material put to the test. Soldiers with little or no experience in the making of adobe saw their work go down the drain when their stock pile of adobe bricks was melted away by heavy rains.

Finally it was decided that the fort would be constructed of sandstone from nearby quarries. As there were no competent stone masons on hand, private contractors were called in from Fredericksburg to do the work. Even this was plan was not fool proof. The stockpiling of materials was done in such a haphazard way that they generally arrived after the workers had been allowed to return to their homes in the east. Ongoing construction of the fort continued for the next 22 years but the never ending comedy of errors plagued the post. Even when the fort was later abandoned it was not completely finished.

Construction problems aside, several successful Indian campaigns against the Comanches were launched from Fort Concho. In addition, the post played a pivotal role in the suppression of illegal profiteering that was being conducted by Mexican and American traders known as "Comanchero's".

One of Fort Concho's most illustrious commanders was Colonel Ranald Mackenzie. Mackenzie was such a prominent character at the fort that it is said that he still attempts exert his command influence there from beyond the grave.

In September 1872, Mackenzie and his troopers successfully attacked a large Comanche camp. The attack caught the Indians completely by surprise. When the firing stopped, 23 Indians were dead and another 127 women and children had been taken captive. The captured women and children were then marched back to Fort Concho where they were imprisoned in the post's stone corral over the winter. The following spring the women and children were allowed to rejoin their families at the Indian reservation near Fort Sill, Oklahoma.

On the morning of September 27th 1874, Mackenzie and his troops were again thrust into battle with their Indian counterparts. As dawn was breaking, Mackenzie found himself looking down into Palo Duro Canyon. To his surprise hundreds of Indian tepees dotted the valley before him. Mackenzie immediately ordered his troopers to attack. The Indians would have again been caught by surprise if Mackenzie's "Raiders" had not been spotted by several of the Indians as they moved about the camp completing early morning chores. Despite the early warning, the Indians were routed and their village destroyed. In the army's wake, the carcasses of more than 1000 slaughtered horses and livestock lay scattered across the valley floor.

By the mid 1880's, it was clear that Fort Concho and its sister fort's, Fort Richardson and Fort Clark, had helped bring peace to the plains. Since Indian attacks no longer posed a threat, it was obvious that Fort Concho was no longer needed. On June 20, 1889, the post was abandoned.

In 1935, the city of San Angelo acquired Fort Concho and began restoring the fort to its former glory. The cities plans for reconstruction of the site were so successful that in 1961, the fort was designated as a National Historic Landmark.

## THE GHOSTS

One of the most haunted locations at Fort Concho is the officer's quarters also known as "Officers Row". Located across the parade ground from the enlisted barracks, this row of sturdy stone houses serve as the impetus for most if not all of the ghostly tales that are told about Fort Concho.

Fort Concho's most distinguished commander, Colonel Ranald Mackenzie, is said to haunt his old residence at the center of Officers Row. The ghost of Colonel Mackenzie has been seen by visitors and staff at the old house on more than one occasion. It is said that Colonel Mackenzie was fond of his house and its location because he could see almost everything that was going on in the fort at any given time. The house was also located in a position that afforded Colonel Mackenzie a full view of the old stone corral where his units 127 Indian captives were held over the winter of 1873.

While preparing for a winter event one December, a female staff member working in the Mackenzie house reported that she had heard the unmistakable sound of footsteps walking around the back of the room behind her. Just as the woman turned to see who was there, she was knocked up against a wall by an invisible blast of cold air. Frightened and disoriented, the women also noticed that the "unique sound of knuckles cracking" seemed to accompany the Another of the "row's" many distinguished families was that of Colonel Benjamin Grierson, regimental commander of the 10th cavalry. It is said that Colonel Grierson's, 12 year old daughter Edith died in the upstairs bedroom of one of the houses around her twelfth birthday. Over the years, many people have encountered Edith in the houses along officer row. In most instances, Edith is often seen quietly playing jacks.

Those people who have encountered her say that the first thing they notice is that the room where the girl is playing is substantially cooler than any of the other rooms in the house. Edith will acknowledge the presence of a person when they enter the room by turning her head and smiling at them before she turns her attention back to her game of jacks, but she will rarely say anything them.

One day, a florist delivered some flowers to one of the houses along Officers Row. The lady of the house told the driver to place two bouquets of flowers in the bedrooms at the top of the stairs, one to the right and one to the left. As the delivery man ascended the stairs with a large bouquet of flowers in each hand, he noticed that the temperature seemed cooler than in the foyer of the house. Reaching the top of the stairs, the man turned and entered the first bedroom on the right nearly tripping over a small girl playing jacks on the floor just inside the doorway. The man excused himself but the girl never appeared to even acknowledge his presence. The florist placed the flowers on the bedside table as instructed. Once finished, he left the room and placed the last bouquet of floors in the bedroom across the hallway.

Before going back down stairs, the florist looked in on the little girl across the hall and noticed that she was gone. He noted with some satisfaction that the flowers he had placed on the nightstand had been moved to a table in the corner of the room. He figured that the little girl had moved the flowers because he noticed that the girl's jacks were now laying on the table next to the bed.

Just as the florist was about to leave, he happened to see a picture hanging above the fire place. To the man's surprise, the little girl in the picture was a twin of the young girl he had just saw upstairs playing jacks. Believing that the small child was the daughter of the woman staying in the house, the florist mentioned that he had met the girl in the picture only moments before and commented on how she had moved the flowers from the nightstand. To the delivery man's surprise, the woman stated that she did not have a daughter and explained that Colonel Grierson's daughter Edith had died in upstairs bedroom where he had placed the flowers. Chuckling to herself at the delivery man's apparently look of distress, the woman informed the florist that countless others have seen the ghost of Edith in the house, and that he was not the first.

The Officers Quarters is not the only location at Fort Concho where ghostly activity has been report. The fort's headquarters building is also reputed to be a hot bed for paranormal encounters.

Once during one of the Christmas tours, Conrad McClure, a staff member working in the headquarters building saw a shadowy figure in a blue soldier's uniform brush past him while he was tending to the fireplace. Intrigued by his encounter with the unidentified ghost, McClure did a little detective work and learned that Second Sergeant Cunningham was the only soldier to ever die at Fort Concho. Cunningham was a chronic alcoholic who was hospitalized due to complications from liver disease. Knowing that he was going to die, Sergeant Cunningham requested that he be moved back to his barracks so that he could spend his last days with his friends and fellow soldiers. The end for old Irishman finally came one cold Christmas Day. Sergeant Cunningham suffered no more! After reading compiling all of this information, McClure was sure that the spirit he encountered in the headquarters building could be none other than that of Sergeant Cunningham.

Several of the other staff members believe that Sergeant Cunningham does not like females to be in the headquarters building but that he always seems to be looking out for the building and it occupants.

In addition to the ghosts of Colonel Mackenzie, Sergeant Cunningham, and Edit Grierson, several other lesser known but still active spirits have taken up residence at Fort Concho. The disembodied voices of Chaplain Dunbar and that of an unidentified officer's wife have been heard talking in the post's chapel and phosphorescent lights believed to be the ghosts of several drifters murdered in one of the officers quarters in the 1890's have been observed in what is now the museum's library.

No one knows why Fort Concho is so haunted. Clearly the post's ordered appearance does a good job of hiding the truth about the invisible figments that hide in its shadows. If you doubt whether ghosts exist, a visit to Fort Concho when the spirits are restless will make a believer out of you[99].

---

[99] http://www.militaryghosts.com/concho.html.

## A FEW OTHER EVENTS

In San Angelo, Texas the town across the river from the old fort, something in Miss Hattie's Café on Concho Avenue tends to move things around and breaks glasses from time to time. The adjacent building that once housed a brothel named Miss Hattie's has a spook with a shoe fetish. The ghost moves a pair of men's slippers from room to room at night.

The real ghosts, though, hang out over at Fort Concho. The San Angelo Standard-Times, has written several stories about ghosts at the old home of the Buffalo Soldiers. The most recent — by Editor Emeritus Perry Flippin — was rather intriguing. It seems the new assistant city manager moved to town and holed up in the fort's Officer's Quarters 1 for a few days with his family. Harold Dominguez and his wife, Andrea, had no prior knowledge of the Fort Concho ghosts. That, however, didn't keep Andrea from seeing a 12-year-old girl coming down the stairs unexpectedly at 4 o'clock in the afternoon on a clear day. "Coming out of the parlor and crossing the entrance, I looked up (the staircase) and there she was," Andrea is quoted as saying. "She was coming down, kind of in a pale peach dress. Very long dress. Her hair was long and light brown. Kind of pulled back. She looked about 12 years old. It was like she didn't know I was here. We just looked at each other and then she was gone."

There were other strange happenings while the Dominguezes were in OQ1. A loud, mournful wail outside their bedroom window that they grudgingly admit sounded like a woman. A chair being moved, and both Harold and Andrea denying they moved it. Doors slamming shut in the empty room directly above their bedroom.

To give you some background, let me tell you that a 12-year-old girl named Edith Grierson died of typhoid fever in OQ1 in 1878. She was the daughter of Col. and Mrs. Benjamin H. Grierson. He was the post commander. Flippin showed Andrea Dominguez a published portrait of Edith Grierson at age 12. In a hushed tone, skeptical Andrea said, "She looks like the girl I saw[100]." Spooky.

There waws a resident living in San Angelo near Fort Concho who had a few odd things happen. This individual lived only one block from Fort Concho and saw many strange occurences. On more than one occasion there were eyewitnesses to these events.The apparition of a soldier was seen by several witnesses on more than one ocassion. This was no foggy or distorted apparition, rather it seemed to be a real human being.

---

[100] **http://www.oaoa.com/columns/gene103103.htm** - Gene Powell Jr.'s column appears Fridays. E-mailed comments may be sent to oa@link.freedom.com.

This individual contributed the stories to http://www.lonestarspirits.org in the hopes that others who many ahave had encountered similar events would come forward.

According to this interesting story, one night the narrator and three friends were out on the porch talking. Suddenly the narrator heard the doorbell ring inside the house. All agreed that they had heard the doorbell ring through no one had touched the bell only a few feet from where they all sat talking. However, all of them could see that the doorbell light was blinking on and off as if it were being pushed. There was another person in the house who came to the door to see why they were ringing the bell.

The narrator's wristwatch always seemed to be missing. It would never be found where it had been put. However, it was always to be found inside one of the bathroom cabinets. There was an attempt made to ercord any electronic vouice phenomenon and a voice was heard to very clearly say "help me." The tape also picked up the sounds of doors slamming and the sounds of marching[101].

## CHAPTER TWENTY-NINE
## EASTWOOD HIGH SCHOOL
### 2430 McRae
### El Paso, Texas

Eastwood High School is not an old school, in fact, it was only built in 1961. However, in spite of its relatively young age, it seems to have acquired an assortment of ghosts that would amaze almost anyone who has spent any time there. In fact, when I began my research, I was assured by a number of people that Eastwood High School did not have any ghosts whatsoever. However, after my preliminary research, I am here to say that Eastwood High School does have its share of ghostly inhabitants.

Anyone sensitive to those from the other side get a hint of what is to come the moment that they step inside the front door of this bustling school. There sitting in the entry lobby is an antique canyon that has its own unique history and it may also be the reason for some of the spirits hovering around this school.

## THE HISTORY

Just inside the front door of this school sits a canyon. This is not a prop of some type or a nameless landmark. This canyon is famous in its own right and has a history so uniquethat it deserves to be told within these pages. This is the famous *Blue Whistler.*

---

[101] http://www.lonestarspirits.org/tales/ghostories7.html

The *Blue Whistler* was a Civil War era cannon that made a distinctive whistle when fired and thus its name. It saw duty, on the Union side, at the battle of Valverde in New Mexico (171 miles north of El Paso and 109 miles south of Albuquerque) during the Civil War and was captured along with a number of other artillery pieces by the Confederacy.

Figure 52: The famous Blue Whistler Canyon - Ames No. 39.

A short time later, when the Confederate Army was facing defeat, their 12-pounder howitzers were buried near Albuquerque, New Mexico, by the rebel commander, Captain Trevanion Teel. In 1889, Teel was reminiscing about his wartime experiences and recalled the buried cannon. He obtained permission from the city of Albuquerque to dig up the guns. The guns were given to several towns for various reasons but Teel kept No.39, the *Blue Whistler*.

A bronze 12-pounder M1841 howitzer has a tube length of 53 inches, a tube weight of 778 pounds, tube material of bronze, a tube bore diameter of 4.62 inches, a range at five degrees of elevation of 1100 yards, and used the following types of ammunition; Shell, Case Shot and Canister Shot.

An interesting sidebar note: Two bronze 6-pounder field guns (Ames Nos.250&255, both dated 1846) were buried by members of the Valverde Battery on the McCoslin Ranch outside of Fairfield, Texas and were dug up a few years ago. They are on display there by the ranch house. There are supposedly some more Valverde cannons buried on the ranch that have not yet been located.

Sometime after 1889, a 6-pounder cannon came into the possession of the McGinty Club of El Paso, Texas, a famed local musical organization. The club disbanded in the early 1900's, and the El Paso Pioneer Association acquired that cannon.

On St. Patrick's Day (March, 17) in 1911, the cannon was "kidnapped" by Madero sympathizers, Dr. Ira J. Bush, Ned Harper, Abraham Molina and Dr. Frank Thatcher, and was transported to Mexico on April 5, 1911, where it was used at the battle at Banderas (75 miles SE of El Paso near Van Horn, Texas), Ojinaga (April, 29) (200 miles SE of El Paso near Presido, Texas), and Santa Rosalía (SW of Chihuahua City?)

The "kidnapping" of the canyon took place very openly. One pre-dawn morning in 1911, while El Paso, Texas, was still asleep, an unobserved automobile backed up to the old Civil War cannon that had sat in the City Hall Plaza for almost a decade. The tail piece of the familiar landmark was hurriedly tied to the car's bumper. There was a muffled, "Let's go," and the famed Blue Whistler was whisked off to fight another war - a war across the border in Mexico.

Before it rattled away, The Blue Whistler, a 12-pounder howitzer, was already celebrated in fact and legend. It has served under two flags and avoided a sad fate several times. Perhaps this sojourn into Mexico to fight with Madero's army would be the denouncement of a long, strange career.

**The Birth of the Blue Whistler**

The chronicle of the Blue Whistler begins in 1846 at the N. P. Ames foundry in Springfield, Massachusetts. Under contract to fulfill an order according to specification in Army Ordnance Manual 1841, the firm cast in brass a series of barrels 53 inches long of certain configuration. Something about barrel No. 39, perhaps a slight imperfection within the four and one-half inch bore, caused at the moment of discharge a distinctive whistle as the projectile hurled through the air. This characteristic apparently was of no serious concern; otherwise, ordnance inspectors would not have accepted the piece.

That the whistling cannon would be amusing to the artillerymen who fired her was a foregone conclusion. So it was little wonder that she became known as the Blue Whistler while doing garrison duty at Fort Craig, New Mexico.

**Serving the Union in the American Civil War**

In time, war clouds on the horizon heralded a bitter conflict between non-slavery and slave states. With the out-break of the Civil War. Jefferson Davis, president of the Confederacy, gave his attention to the vast western territories and California. He had little doubt that if the few feeble Union forts strung along the Rio Grande were subdued the Confederacy could extend its domain to the Pacific Coast. As a transcontinental nation the Confederacy would have great prestige in Europe. Furthermore, gold from California mines would largely underwrite the cost of war. President Abraham Lincoln, however, was also aware of the fort's precarious situation. To meet the threat of the Confederacy he stationed General E. R. S. Canby with an army of 3,800 at Fort Craig - and just in time, for the Confederate force of 2,300 Texan volunteers under General H. H. Sibley was marching north from El Paso, Texas.

The battle began on the morning of February 21, at Valverde, near Fort Craig. Sibley's position was located on the east side of the Rio Grande where deep ravines and exposed lava beds, offered a favorable defense. To reach Valverde, it was necessary for the Union troops to cross the river.

A cannon duel preceded the crossing. As the rumble of cannons echoed over the water, the whistle of one cannon could be heard by anyone who listened intently. Captain Alexander McRae and his McRae's Light Battery of 12-pounders, including the Blue Whistler, succeeded in dislodging a Confederate battery, thus making possible a safe crossing. Thereafter, he attempted without success to dislodge a Texas regiment.

During mid-afternoon the Confederates began a flanking maneuver. General Canby hastily ordered McRae's battery, together with New Mexico Volunteers under Colonel Kit Carson, to a forward position. Too late, it was discovered they were sitting almost on top of an enemy battery hidden in an old river bed only 100 yards away. Discovery of the hidden Confederates came only when Texan artillery swept the Federal troops with a round of canister. A Texan infantry unit; giving a sustained rebel yell, charged over the river bank. The ill-trained New Mexico Volunteers, facing fire and bayonet for the first time, panicked and fled, leaving McRae and his men to their fate.

McRae's men, firing a double-shotted volley, repulsed the charge. The Texans regrouped in the river bed. Another volley of canister from the Confederate position followed. Again the Texans charged. Again McRae's double-shotted volleys repulsed them. On the third charge, the Texans had the presence of mind to drop to earth when McRae's artillerymen applied fire to the cannon's touch-holes, thus, they were spared the ordeal of direct fire. The courageous artillerymen met the Texans in brief hand-to-hand fighting. Captain McRae was slain on the barrel of Blue Whistler. While his blood was running out, Major Lockridge of the Texans likewise fell across the barrel. By now perhaps a hundred dead and wounded of both the Blue and Gray were piled around the battery. At that moment Union cavalry came to the rescue. McRae's survivors left the field of battle, leaving the 12-pounders to be taken by the enemy.

Because the New Mexico Volunteers failed to support McRae, the battle was lost. The Confederate victory, in turn, made it possible for Sibley to continue northward and capture Albuquerque and Santa Fe. Sibley's main objective, however, was to capture Fort Union Ordnance Depot to resupply his troops from the military stores there. The objective was thwarted by the timely arrival of Colorado Volunteers on a forced march from Denver. Strengthened, the Federals moved south and engaged the Confederates in two days of fierce fighting at Glorieta Pass and Apache Canyon. When Sibley's supply train was destroyed, his command became utterly disorganized. It was every man for himself, the sick and wounded were abandoned. Demoralized Texans straggled southward toward the sanctuary of El Paso. Those who did not die enroute arrived more dead than alive. This disastrous rout ended the Civil War in the west. The forts along the Rio Grande were never threatened again.

**Capture by the Confederacy**

When Blue Whistler and companion cannons involuntarily changed flags at Valverde, they came under the command of Captain Trevanion Teel. He promptly took them on the northward campaign. What was noticeable, and remained noticeable was that the blood of one or both fallen officers had fused into the hot barrel of one paricular canon, staining it a dusky rose color. From captured artillerymen at Valverde, Teel learned this particular cannon was affectionately called *Blue Whistler*. While other cannon may have remained nameless, *Blue Whistler* continued to live in fame among the Confederates.

In spite of added fire power from the captured cannon, the Confederates were turned back at Glorieta Pass and Apache Canyon. When the hard pressed, retreating Teel reached Albuquerque, he was faced with no other choice but to abandon the captured 12-pounders. He decided not to let them fall into Union hands. Instead, he buried the barrels. On a cold March night, he and a detachment of men dug a shallow trench in a corral. There, four of the 12-pounders were lowered into the deep trench and covered over. The dirt was soon tramped by hooves that would obliterate signs of the digging. The four other cannons were buried nearby at San Marshceell.

**Recovery of the Blue Whistler**

Time passed. The war that had so long divded this great nation ended. Those who survived began building a new nation. While the memory of conflict remained indelible for most veterans, few looked back to recall it except on occasions. It was not until August, 1889, that Teel had occasion to look back nearly 30 years to the night that he and his men buried the canon. When he did it set in motion the recovery of the buried cannon.

It was a long train ride from Kansas City to El Paso; Trevanion Teel, now a successful lawyer, was returning from a legal trip. On the same train was Charles Crawford, the "poet scout" of Union army fame. To pass the time, the two veterans began reminiscing about the war.

"By the way, Teel," said Crawford, "weren't you mixed up in burying some of our cannon?" When Teel told of how they were hidden away, Crawford asked, "Do you think you could still locate the spot where they were buried?" "I feel confident I can," replied the former Confederate Officer.

The upshot of the conversation resulted in the two men's meeting in Albuquerque. They were given permission by city officials to dig for and claim the cannon if they could be found. Teel discovered the corral no longer existed. Although the character of the land had changed considerably, still certain landmarks offered clues to the cannon's location. "Dig here," he told a helper.

The earth was quickly turned but no cannon were found. "All right, now try here," said Teel, indicating a place six feet away. Shovels struck metal. Moments later the cannon were lifted to the surface. Crawford wanted one cannon presented to Saint Joseph, Missouri, his hometown, and his request was complied with. Denver received a cannon as a memorial to the Colorado Volunteers whose timely presence saved the West for the Union. Albuquerque accepted a gift of another.

Regarding No. 39, Teel stated, "I am going to keep this cannon. The Federal soldiers called it *Blue Whistler*, because of a peculiar sound it made when discharged, and the Confederates adopted the name."

## Blue Whistler becomes a McGinty Cannon

Newspaper stories of Albuquerque's celebration of Teel's find prompted the McGinty Club of El Paso to wire Teel. Would he make the *Blue Whistler* available to the club, the telegram petitioned.

The McGinty Club, mainly a musical band replete with colorful uniforms, gave concerts at the Plaza in El Paso, played for funerals and weddings, and welcomed important visitors. It also had the distinction of welcoming President Benjamin Harrison and President William McKinley during their trips to El Paso. The *Blue Whistler* could be a companion piece to the 6-pounder mountain howitzer already owned by the McGinty Club. Two cannon, instead of one, would add emphasis to celebrations and especially the mock battles held on the Fourth of July.

Yes, replied Teel. In due time, the *Blue Whistler*, remounted on a carriage, was presented with appropriate ceremony.

## The McGinty Cannon goes to Mexico

Again time passed. Shortly after the turn of the century it was obvious "the good old days" of the McGinty Club were nearing an end. In 1901 the band made its last full-dress appearance. The *Blue Whistler* was given a new home at the City Hall Plaza where it remained an object of passing interest, until March 17, 1911. During that dark night it was spirited away.

"General belief is that insurrectos have El Paso's historic cannon," declared the El Paso Herald the following day.

The *Blue Whistler* was indeed appropriated to aid Francisco Madero's insurrectos in attempting to dislodge President Porfirio Diaz's government troops at Ciudad Juárez. Since the days of the Civil War, muzzle-loading guns had given way to breech-loading, and cannon balls were no longer used. But these drawbacks were of little consequence for Mexicans fighting for idealistic reforms.

To set the stage for the *Blue Whistler's* participation in the Madero revolution, the not-so-neutral United States unofficially permitted overt aid by American sympathizers in El Paso, Douglas, and other border towns. In El Paso, Dr. Ira J. Bush was the prime mover of American-Mexican intrigue. Sometime previously he had entertained Governor Abraham Gonzales of Chihuahua. The governor remarked, "We could use that gun if we had it in Mexico."

When Gonzales gave his blessing for the Madero revolution, Bush recalled the chance remark. With the help of Mrs. Monroe Harper, former wife of Major Teel, and her son Albert Hatcher, they "liberated" the old field piece. For a few days *Blue Whistler* was hidden in a barn. Black powder was needed for the howitzer and was obtained in a shipment from Denver. When it arrived, *Blue Whistler* was taken apart and loaded on the bed of a wagon. Added was a covering of hay and the household effects of a poor Mexican family. Completing the guise was the Molina family perched on top of the load. They were stopped several times by American militiamen patrolling the river road. The perfunctory searches failed to reveal the hidden cannon. After smuggling *Blue Whistler* across the Rio Grande, Molina wired Dr. Bush, "The baby has arrived."

Madero's ragtag army was made up mainly of Pancho Villa's insurrectos, and the soldaderas of General Pascual Orozco. While Madero's force numbered some 3,000, only two cannon supported the ranks. Aside from the *Blue Whistler*, Villa had an ancient Krupp field piece. The artillery was entrusted to a Frenchman. A reporter described him as, "a dainty little chap who wore a pair of kid gloves."

Before the revolutionary army closed in on Ciudad Juárez, it first had to reduce strongholds at Ojina and Camargo. This was accomplished with relatively little effort after *Blue Whistler* and the Krupp pulverized defensive adobe walls. Ciudad Juárez, however, was more formidable. The garrison commanded by

General Juan Navarro was strongly fortified, and armed with French machine guns.

At great risk, thousands of El Pasoans witnessed the battle raging in full view directly across the Rio Grande. American homes were peppered by stray bullets, and five Americans met their deaths in this manner.

One reporter described the scene. "The rebels moved in no formation

**Figure 53: The Blue Whistler on display in El Paso.**

whatsoever, just an irregular stream of them, silhouettes of men and rifles . . . . They would fight awhile and then come back to rest, sleep and eat, returning refreshed to the front."

Regarding the two-cannon bombardment, he wrote, "A shot struck the Federale's water tank in their barracks, a lucky hit which destroyed most of the defenders' water supply and which had much to do with the fall of the town."

Did the *Blue Whistler* fire the decisive round? Perhaps. At least it's a 50/50 assumption.

## After the Mexican Revolution

When the smoke of war cleared away and Diaz was dethroned, the peace of Mexico was assured for the time being. It was then the *Blue Whistler* came back to El Paso with all the honors of a conquering hero.

On the afternoon of August 18, 1911, the veteran field piece of two wars, adorned with Mexican and American flags, and pulled by two pair of mules, approached the international bridge. Accompanying the *Blue Whistler* were two companies of Mexican soldiers, together with bugles and drums, led by General Orozco and staff. Midway across the bridge the contingent halted before the mayor and dignitaries of El Paso. As townspeople of both nations looked on, General Orozco paid a glowing tribute to the part played by the *Blue Whistler*. The soldiers presented arms, and the formal presentation was made.

An automobile replaced the pulling power of the mules; the procession drove to the City Hall Plaza, and the *Blue Whistler* was home again, its mission completed. It remained there until 1936, when it was moved to the Texas College of Mines, now the University of Texas at El Paso.

Unfortunately while on display there, it was the object of a student prank. It was stolen, hitched to a car, and taken on a wild ride. It's carriage broken, the barrel was relegated to basement storage where it remained until 1961. Mr.Cole obviously was unaware of the September 24, 1942 presentation of the McGinty 6-pounder cannon to the Big Scrap Drive. Saved from destruction by this oversight, the historic old canon was then presented to the new Eastwood High School on McRae Boulevard, named for the Union Captain McRae who breathed his last breath lying acorss the barrel of this old dog of war.

Aware of McRae's dramatic death and the unusual history of *Blue Whistler*, the students at this new school adopted a Civil War motif for their band, and called themselves the "Eastwood Troopers." A fitting and meaningful school spirit has been built around *Blue Whistler*. Thus the venerable relic remains an object of esteem and affection.

## THE GRAVEYARD GIRLS

As I made reference to earlier, there are a number of spirits that haunt Eastwood High School. However, to my surprise, I discovered that very few of the students knew anything about them. I began my research in the usual manner, by going to the Ysleta School District Headquarters. I have found that tales of the unexplained quickly make there way to the powers that be, even though they are routinely denied when anyone asks about them.

To my surprise, no one knew anything about any ghosts at Eastwood High School, through I was informed about a ghost in the Library of the Ysleta Administration and Cultural Center that I will discuss in the next section. But then, I also discovered that no one at the school administraiton headquarters even seemed to know any of the history of the canon that sits in the lobby of Eastwood High School. I knew that I had my work cut out for me in regard to this school.

However, it seemed as if fate decided to step in and keep my attention focused on Eastwood High School. I was asked to spend the night in Concordia Cemetery on October 15th and tell stories about the hauntings of that old cemetery to memebrs of the Concordia Heritgage Society who were spending the night in the cemetery[102]. While sitting around the small fire that had been started for warmth, both the security guard and I spotted what looked like figures moving from tombstone to tombstone deeper in the cemetery[103]. The guard disappeared into the darkness and thenr eturned with six very pretty young ladies in tow as well as one very tired looking young man lugging a video carmer. These young ladies were ghost hunting. For sometime we talked about the various ghosts that are said to haunt Concordia and they invited me to come visit their class at Eastwood High School.

## THE GHOSTS

**Figure 54: Amanda Aleman on the winding staircase in the lower bookroom.**

During one visit to this school, I had the opportunity to talk to Bob Omspaugh and the head custodian. At first, neither admitted have seen anything out of the ordinary, but finally, the head custodian told me about have seen a

---

[102] October 16th was the date for the Concordia Walk Through History Event and many times vandals would try to disrupt the event by pulling stupid stunts the night before the event. So now to ensure that everything is under control, some members will spend the night in the cemetery the night before the event.
[103] See the section on Concordia Cemetery elsewhere in this volume.

Mexican Charro or vaquero walking down the hall. He is also not the only one to have seen this mysterious figure.

There was also a story that I was told about the piano being heard to play in the old choir room. Some said that the piano was being played the spirit of a teacher who had died, while others believed that a tape recorder of piano music had been left on.

As part of my research, I was referred to Ms. Rita Mae Brown, a very nice lady who is now the guadian of the entrance to Eastwood. She used to be in charge of the book room, but now the answers the phone and direts calls to the correct recipient. A number of people told me that she was a walking encyclopedia of events that had happened at this school.

I found Ms. Brown at her desk as well as the lovely Amanda Aleman, one of the graveyard girls. I was not sure that Ms. Brown would be willing to tell the many stories of which she was aware, as there seemed to be a common desire on the part of many of the school staff to play down such stories. However, Ms. Brown was very agreeable about talking with me.

**Figure 55: The door to the dumbwaiter.**

As I mentioned earlier, Ms. Brown had once been in charge of the bookroom for Eastwood. The design of the book room was somewhat unusual in that it was two floors. One floor was the office and the books were stored on the lower floor. It was in the lower bookroom area that a lot of manifestations seemed to take place.

She told me that there had been a number of people who had cause to go down the winding staircae to the lower book room and return to ask her who the man in the odd looking uniform was that was working on the pipes. She would go down to check for herself and there would be no man anywhere in the lower area working on anything.

Another incident involved a lady who was waiting for her husband, one of the custodians, to get off from work. While she waited, she sat in the reception office. She glanced up to see her husband talking to a girl in a long white dress. When she later asked him about the girl, he denied that he had been anywhere near the reception office until he came to get her. She also later learned that the description of the girl she saw matched that of a girl killed sometime before on prom night.

Finally, there was story I was told by another staff member of a girl working in the theater alone one afternoon when she glanced up to see a shadowy figure enter the door. The figure looked so odd that she immediately left and called security. After a search, it was found that there was no one else in the theater.

There is also a dumbwaiter connecting the lower bookroom to the upper for moving books between floors. It has not worked in sometime, so it was decided to repair it. While one workman had his uper body inside the shaft working on the cable, a wooden 2 x 4 came sailing down the shaft, barely missing his head. A later search revealed no place that a two by four could have come from.

I have also heard stories about night custodians seeing moving shadows when there is no one else around. There are also the sounds of lockers closing and footsteps as if someone is slowly walking down the h allway, though it is deserted. Why does the bookroom seem to be so haunted? Who is the ghost in the funny uniform?

# CHAPTER THIRTY
## J.C. MACHUCA APARTMENTS
### 1039 Sunland Park Drive
### El Paso, Texas 79922

I mentioned these apartments in the previous volume[104] as a place that

**Figure 56: J.C. Machuca Apartments.**

was alleged to be haunted, but at the time I had no address as I had been unable to even find that the apartment complex still existed. Well I am happy to report that I have found the apartments. Though I had searched for sometime when the first book hit the stands, I discovered that these apartments are so out in the open that they aer almost impossible to miss, even though I did. They are off of Sunland Park between Mesa and Doniphan, south of I-10.

## THE GHOSTS

Since writing about these apartments, I have had two or three people tell me stories about events that have occurred there. Everyone seems to be in

---

[104] Hudnall, Ken and Connie Wang, Spirits of the Border: The History and Mystery of El Paso Del Norte, Omega Press, El Paso, Texas. 2004.

agreement that these apartments where built on either an Indian burial ground or on land that was sacred to one of the local Indian tribes.

One person who had lived there for a short time confirmed that on many nights, when it was very late, he heard what sounded like heavy foot steps in his bedroom and one or twice, he was positive that he had seen ark shadowy figures moving about the living room in his apartment.

Others have told me that they had heard of things flying across the rooms and items being found moved from their original place, and put somewhere else.

# CHAPTER THIRTY-ONE
# KENNEDY BROTHERS MEMORIAL APARTMENTS
## 400 S. Zaragoza,
## El Paso, Texas 79907.

This very large low income housing area was built some years ago on lower Zaragoza. The number of units exceeded three hundred at one time and then was reduced to 240 in the 1980s. In the late 1990's, El Paso seemed to jump on the bandwagon of declustering these low income housing projects by demolishing 124 units of the 240 units that were then a part of the Kennedy Brothers Memorial Apartments.

According to some reports, the complex was riddled with crime, drugs and gangs. Unfortunately in early 2001, the original 124 units that were demolished were replaced with a new 174-unit development, which spans over 15 acres. The Kennedy Estates is a surreal complex made up of approximately 174 identical units, with some selling for $65,000, while the others are rentable units located near the remaining Kennedy Brothers.

## THE GHOSTS

There many of the old timers in the area who swear that the Kennedy Brothers Memorial Apartment Complex was built over another of the long forgotten cemeteries that dots the landscape in and around El Paso. In some units and common areas, loud footsteps can be heard as well as the crying of an infant.

Some residents have complained of seeing a little girl wondering around aimlessly as if lost, though if anyone tried to approach her, she will fade away. On the second floor, residents have been shadows moving where there are no people. Cabinets and doors open with no one nearby.

This apartment complex was designed to contain everything that residents might require. As a result, one area is a gym. Former residents have told me that late at night, the sounds of someone can playing basketball can be heard from this area, even though the court is empty and the basketballs are all locked up. There is also a stage area in the gym where a number of people have sworn that they can see what looks like someone standing in the middle of the stage as if waiting for an event to start.

The restrooms in the gym also seem to have a mind of their own. When someone enters, the faucets will begin to run and the toilets flush even though there is no one else in the room. The door from the restroom will slam as if someone has left.

Some who have come to the gym for periods of relaxation have reported that even though they are alone, they can feel rough hands push them and some have reported being continually tormented until they left the building. Security has been called to look into this a number of times, but they have never found anyone.

# CHAPTER THIRTY-TWO
## SKULL CANYON
### Off Executive on San Marcos
### El Paso, Texas

Skull Canyon is the perfect example of hiding something in plain sight. This small enclave is located just off of one of the busiest intersection in El Paso

**Figure 57: The Skull Canyon marker.**

but few seem to know where it is located. As one travels along executive toward Piasano, there is a small, partially hidden street to the named San Marcos. When you turn onto this street, it looks like it leads only to a metal fabrication company; but instead, this is the only entrance to both the Smelter Cemetery as well as the elusive Skull Canyon.

Just as mysterious creatures guard the entrance to a hidden fortress in the fantasy novels, so too does Skull Canyon seem to guard the entrance to the little known Smelter Cemetery. There are families living in this little visited are that can trace their ancestors having lived two or three generations in this sheltered alcove within El Paso.

There are a number of empty houses in this area andit is said that on some nights, you can see figures pasing by the windows. Prowlers are squatters are not options in this tightly knit little commuity. One of two told me that they had seen the spirits of people they know aer buried in the Smelter Cemetery, entering and leaving some of the empty houses. With a name like Skull Canyon, I guess anything is possible.


# CHAPTER THIRTY-THREE
## SACRED HEART CATHOLIC CHURCH
### 600 South Oregon
### El Paso, Texas

According to the records, Sacred Heart Catholic Church was built in 1892 at 600 South Oregon Street and claims to be the oldest continuing Catholic Parish in El Paso, though the congregation at the Immaculate Conception Church at 118 Campbell would dispute this claim since their church was also built in 1892[105]. Both of these churches were built on the site of the older St. Mary's Church, a small stone church, which had been built at the intersection of Wyoming and Oregon Streets by the Jesuit Order in order for Mass to be said in El Paso.

By the late 1880s, it had become clear the original St. Mary's was inadequate to accommodate all of the worshipers that desired to attend Mass and that there was a need to divide the American (English speaking) and Mexican (Spanish speaking) segments of the congregation[106]. Sacred Heart was built in order to allow those of the Catholic faith who preferred Spanish to be able to worship on the northern side of the river. Until the two new churches were opened, those who wished to worship in a Catholic Church where Mass was conducted entirely [107] in Spanish would have to cross the river by means of a

---

[105] Jones, Harriot Howze, El Paso, A Centennial Portrait, El Paso County Historical Society, Superior Printing, El Paso, Texas. 1972.
[106] Bond, Charles, The Catholic Churches in the Vicinity of El Paso, Western American, August 15, 1931.
[107] Ibid.

primitive ferry which was hauled, hand over hand, on a rope stretched from one bank of the river to the other.

The construction of the buildings of both churches followed basically the same plans, so they are very similar in design. In fact until sometime later, the priests of both churches lived in the former rectory of St. Mary's.

At the same time that Sacred Heart Church was opened, a one story school was built nearby. Later, this one story school has another floor added. This small school has become known as Sacred Heart School located at 610 South Oregon Street. The original school was built of adobe bricks, with earthen floors and windows covered with glazed muslin instead of glass, this early structure was the first parochial school in El Paso. The original enrollment was 500 students from El Paso, Juarez and Chihuahua, Mexico[108]

In 1923, it became clear to those in authority at Sacred Heart Church that the original building was unable to accommodate the congregation as it once had done. Therefore, a decision was made to raze the old building and build a new one on the same spot, more modern and better able to meet the needs of the parish. However, there was an uproar from the community over the destruction of the church that had played such an important role in the religious community. Therefore, a decision was made to use the bricks from the razed church to build the inside of the new structure, in this fashion, it could be said that the old Sacred Heart Church still lived.[109]

## THE GHOSTS

With such a long history, it is no wonder that there are many stories about hauntings associated with Sacred Heart Church. Strange sounds have been heard by some, such as a low chanting or a murmuring as if someone was talking to themselves, though no one is ever found.

There have also been many reports by parishioners of a woman wearing a turn-of-the-century bridal dress being seen and heard weeping in the side chapel of Our Lady of Guadalupe. It is believed by many that this young lady is the ghost of a young Mexican woman who was left at the altar by her intended husband. According to the story, she was so heart broken at being abandoned that she died not long after the day she was jilted.

She comes back, it is believed, in the hope that her deserting groom will come back to her.

---

[108] Normann, Debbie, *Sacred Heart Church Still Prominent*, El Paso Times, August 2, 1975.
[109] Bond, Charles, *The Catholic Churches in the Vicinity of El Paso*, Western American, August 15, 1931.

# CHAPTER THIRTY-FOUR
# FORT DAVIS
## Fort Davis Historical Site
## Fort Davis, Texas

In the 1850s the threat of Indian attack was the greatest fear of the settlers on the Texas frontier. The Wild and fierce Apache Indian struck like ghosts in the night, killing all who dared to oppose them. So in answer to the demands from the settlers for protection, the War Department began to build a series of military posts across the western territories of the United States from the Dakotas to the Texas border and from California to Kansas. One of the most important in this chain of fort was Fort Davis, built in 1854.

From 1854 until 1891[110], Fort Davis was strategically located to protect emigrants, mail coaches, and freight wagons on the Trans-Pecos portion of the San Antonio-El Paso Road and the Chihuahua Trail, and to control activities on the southern stem of the Great Comanche War Trail and Mescalero Apache war trails. Fort Davis is important in understanding the presence of African Americans in the West and in the frontier military because the 24th and 25th U.S. Infantry and the 9th and 10th U.S. Cavalry, all-black regiments established after the Civil War, were stationed at the post.

A key post in the defense system of western Texas, Fort Davis played a major role in the history of the Southwest. Today, Fort Davis is considered one of the best remaining examples of a frontier military post in the American Southwest. It is a vivid reminder of the significant role played by the military in the settlement and development of the western frontier.

As with many military decisions, the location of Fort Davis was selected to stop civilian harassment of the military brass over Indian attacks in the area. The settlers at Limpia Creek, Texas were continually being attacked by Apaches so to solve the problem General Persifor Smith selected the site for a new fort. The location for this post, named Fort Davis after the Secretary of War, Jefferson Davis was in a box canyon on the eastern side of the Davis Mountains near Limpia Creek and also near wood, water and grass. Unfortunately, in General Smith's haste to erect this new post, he chose a very vulnerable position for the new post. Due to its location inside the box canyon, it was possible for the marauding Indians to approach the post without being seen, which resulted in a number of attacks that were completely avoidable.

The fort was first garrisoned by Lieutenant Colonel Washington Seawell with six companies of the Eighth U.S. Infantry under his command. LTC Seawell had orders to build a permanent post, but due to the obvious liabilities caused by the post's location, he built only temporary quarters for the officers

---

[110] In spite of the best of intentions on the part of the Army, during the Civil War years, 1860 through 1865, the state of the garrison of Fort Davis was not a top priority to Washington.

and married soldiers, out of pine slabs set upright in the ground, with packed earthen floors and canvas or thatched grass roofs. For the enlisted men, however, he built six stone barracks buildings across the mouth of the canyon. The original post contained thirteen houses for officers and married soldiers, a hospital, a stable, a store and a billiard room.

## THE CIVIL WAR YEARS

From their arrival in 1854 until the outbreak of the Civil War in 1861, the troops of the Eighth Infantry that garrisoned Fort Davis spent much of their time in the field pursuing Comanches, Kiowas, and Apache raiding parties who terrorized travelers on wagon trains and stage coaches, murdered isolated settlers and attacked mail stations. However, just as the approaching storm clouds caused a disruption of relations between the north and the south, there were strained relations within the garrison of Fort Davis.

The officers from the North and the South found themselves taking sides and the ever rising tensions between the two factions had a serious detrimental effect on the effectiveness of the command. Records show that there were some officers that spoke to each other only when duty required it. When the south did finally break away form the Union, fully one third of the West Point trained officers stationed at Fort Davis left to offer their services to the Southern cause. As I will discuss later, it was this rising tension within the post that actually led to one of the best known hauntings of the post.

With the outbreak of the Civil War and Texas's secession from the Union, the federal government evacuated Fort Davis. As I have written earlier, Fort Bliss in El Paso and all Union fort located within Texas were surrendered to the Confederacy by the commander of the military department that included Texas. The fort was quickly occupied by Confederate troops from the spring of 1861 until the summer of 1862, when Union forces again took possession. Due to its location and the very real possibility of being cut off by Confederate forces still in the field within Texas, they quickly abandoned the post and Fort Davis lay deserted for the next five years.

## POST CIVIL WAR

The original post consisted of primitive structures which were located to the west of the present day Officers' Row. Not many of the fort's original structures remained usable in June 1867, when Lieutenant Colonel Wesley Merritt and four companies of the recently-organized Ninth U.S. Cavalry reoccupied Fort Davis. The building of a new post, just east of the original site, began immediately. By the end of 1869, a number of officers' quarters, two enlisted men's barracks, a guardhouse, temporary hospital, and storehouses had been erected. Construction continued through the 1880s. By then, Fort Davis had become a major installation with more than 100 structures, and quarters for more than 400 soldiers.

Fort Davis's primary role of safeguarding the west Texas frontier against the Comanches and Apaches continued until 1881. The danger from the deadly Comanches, the only tribe feared by the Apaches passed when they were soundly defeated in the mid-1870s, however, bands of renegade Apaches continued to make travel on the San Antonio-El Paso road dangerous. Soldiers from the post regularly patrolled the road and provided protection for wagon trains and mail coaches.

Though there were a long running series of minor engagements with the Apaches, the last major military campaign involving troops from Fort Davis occurred in 1880. In this series of engagements, units from Fort Davis and other posts, under the command of Colonel Benjamin Grierson, forced a large band of Apaches and their leader Victorio into Mexico. There, the Apache chief Victorio and most of his followers were killed by Mexican soldiers.

With the end of the Indian Wars in west Texas, garrison life at Fort Davis became more routine. Soldiers occasionally escorted railroad survey parties, repaired roads and telegraph lines, and pursued bandits. In June 1891, as a result of the army's efforts to consolidate its frontier garrisons, Fort Davis was ordered abandoned, having "outlived its usefulness. Seventy years later, in 1961, the fort was authorized as a national historic site, a unit of the National Park Service.

## THE GHOSTS OF FORT DAVIS

Today, twenty-four roofed buildings and over 100 ruins and foundations are part of Fort Davis National Historic Site. Five of the historic buildings have been refurnished to the 1880s, making it easy for visitors to envision themselves being at the fort at the height of its development.

There are a number of specters that call the Fort Davis Historical Site their home. There have been many reports that visitors have seen the ghosts of several soldiers still standing their posts in this historic old fort. For some reason, it would seem that old soldiers are loathe to finally stand down. The post hospital walls are said to change color, and some have claimed to have actually seen specters in several places. There have been a number of reports of a "presence" being felt in the hospital part of this fort, with a number of cold spots and a feeling of being watched.

I have also heard about the ghost of a young Army wife that is alleged to haunt the post. Though many have heard the story, and a number of tried to relate it to me, no one has been able to give me the entire history of the story of this unfortunate young woman who is supposed to have been killed by the wild Apaches who haunted the region around the fort. Then one day, I found the full story of what is supposed to have occurred that resulted in this tragic haunting.

According to the story, stationed at Fort Davis in the tense years leading up to the American Civil War was a Lieutenant Walpole, a young West Point educated officer from the State of Alabama. With Lieutenant Walpole at this posting was Alice Walpole, his beautiful young wife. It is said that Alice, a lovely gentle young woman, was the young privileged daughter of Southern wealth, more used to the wide green fields around her plantation home than the mountains and deserts of the American southwest. As was and is the case with many young Army wives, Alice was desperately homesick. The long dreary winters of west Texas were especially difficult for her to endure.

One April, just before the outbreak of the Civil War, her husband was out on patrol and the tenseness within the post was especially depressing to her. Rather than seek out some of the other southern wives for a chat, Alice took it into her head to walk outside the post, hunting the roses that she had heard grew in some spots within the mountains. Wrapping a long, bright blue shawl around her shoulders, Alice began her search for the roses that she somehow knew grew within the isolated recesses of the mountains around the post.

Using Limpia Creek as a guide, Alice moved further and further from the safety of the Fort. Though warned of the dangers that threatened even those assigned to the post, Alice thought she smelled the fragrance of her beloved roses and putting all thoughts of danger form her mind, she moved on into the wilderness.

She knew that the Apaches were an ever present danger, but she was certain that they stayed near the road leading to and from the post. She was nowhere near the road and felt relatively safe, besides, she knew that the smell of roses was getting stronger and their smell drew her on further and further from walls of the Fort. Step by step, she followed the winding course of Limpia Creek until she was well out of sight of the Fort, a veritable babe in the wilderness. Then she rounded a bend in the creek and came face to face with a band of Apaches who had come to this secluded spot to water their ponies. What followed could not have been pretty, but we shall never know as Alice Walpole was never seen again by those she loved and who loved her, alive or dead.

When her husband returned from patrol late that evening, he entered his quarters, calling for his lovely wife. He received no answer. Thinking that she was visiting friends within the post, he made the rounds. His concern growing as everyone he talked to said that they had not seen his wife that afternoon. Finally, he gave in to his fears and approached the commanding officer, Captain Edward D. Blake. Though Blake was a hated Yankee and Walpole was a southerner, the thought of Alice Walpole being taken by the Indians caused all political concerns to be put on hold. A search party left at first light the following day. Patrols scoured the entire region, but no sign of the missing Alice Walpole was ever found.

A few months after the disappearance of Alice Walpole, another Lieutenant was crossing the parade ground toward his quarters. He was somewhat surprised to meet a beautiful young woman in a long, bright blue shawl hurrying away from the officers' quarters. Not recognizing her, the Lieutenant none the less greeted her politely. Her response was so faint that it barely registered as she hurried past him. Suddenly he realized that he had met the missing Alice Walpole. He spun around, calling for her, but the beautiful young woman had vanished into thin air.

After that, the lovely young woman would periodically be seen near the quarters where the southern wives would gather to socialize. She never spoke to anyone, but those who caught a glimpse of her would smell the scent of roses or they would find a few wild white roses placed in prominent places within the quarters.

There is a report that when the South broke from the Union that seven southern officers called at the Post Commander's office to present their resignations. During this period of time, the Commander was startled to see a vase of white roses sitting on his desk that contained seven white roses. There was one rose for each of the southern officers that had handed in his resignation. No one ever admitted to seeing who placed the vase of roses on the Post Commander's desk.

The United States Army abandoned the post in 1861 and the Confederate forces immediately took possession. However after the Confederate defeat at Glorietta Pass in New Mexico, the Confederate forces abandoned Fort Davis and pulled back to the east. The Union forces did not occupy Fort Davis for any appreciable time until 1867.

There are those who say that when the United States Army returned to Fort Davis, so did the spirit of Alice. There were many who said that the ghost of this lonely young woman would return to comfort the lonely, homesick wives that accompanied their husbands to this out of the way Fort. She always did what she could to help those who felt the most alone. What a wonderful way to be remembered.

## CHAPTER THIRTY-FIVE
## SIX POLES.
### Located off I-10 West and Horizon Boulevard.
### Horizon City, Texas

There are many stories told of areas in the desert that are supposedly sacred to one spirit or another. Many of these tales relate to spirits that were sacred to one or more of the Indian tribes that once inhabited this area. However, there are a few areas that are said to be sacred to the spirit of evil, whatever he (or she) may be called, be it the devil or Satan or some other name. One of these areas is called by the unusual name of Six Poles and is said to be near El Paso.

According to one story that I heard, Six Poles is an area off the side of the freeway in the desert behind the Community College. When you are walking through the desert you will see a number of stray black dogs of all types. The Six Poles area is known to be a sacred Devil worshipping place. On many mornings evidence of sacrifice and rituals can be found at this location.

The name of this location alleged comes from the face that there are six poles made out of concrete nearby and a flat concrete slab that is said to have been used as a table that was supposedly used to lay victims upon. The table has some kind of Roman symbols and letters printed all the way around it and in the middle of the six poles is the Devil's star.

## CHAPTER THIRTY-SIX
## EL FENIX BAKERY AND GROCERY
### 8438 Alameda Avenue
### El Paso, Texas

According to the most accurate information that I can find, the El Fenix Bakery and Grocery was opened in the mid 70's. It is said that its owner died in the early 90's leaving his business to his children. This man worked 7 days a week and arrived at his bakery around 3:00 A.M every morning. Every morning, it is said that he would go outside and sweep the street and parking space for his customers. Up to now, people drive by and see this man's ghost sweeping and taking out trash. The bakery is closed at that time but you can see the man preparing his bakery for opening time at 6:00 A.M. Graveyard employees claim to hear noises coming from his office where it is said he spent hours doing paperwork everyday. They can hear the calculator and the cash register opening in the middle of the night. They hear footsteps, toilets flushing and often hear doors shutting. It is said that he has even spoken to customers who didn't know about his death. He welcomes them to the bakery and invites them to come in!"

# CHAPTER THIRTY SEVEN
# SAN ELIZARIO, TEXAS

**Figure 58: San Elizario Mission[111].**

San Elizario is at the intersection of State roads 258 and 1110, fifteen miles southeast of downtown El Paso in southern El Paso County. Don Juan de Oñate reached the Rio Grande at or near the site of present San Elizario on April 20, 1598, and ten days later took formal possession of New Mexico and all adjacent territory in the name of the Spanish king. A settlement known as the Hacienda de los Tiburcios was founded at the site where Don Juan de Onate claimed North America for his King. This small settlement was south of the Rio Grande and had a population of 157 in 1765. In 1789 the Spanish presidio, located in the Valle de San Elizario opposite Fort Hancock, was moved to the

---

[111] This photo was found in a box of photos of historic El Paso purchased at an Estate Sale.

Hacienda de los Tiburcios. The newly built presidio kept its old name, however, and the settlement that grew up around it became known as San Elizario.

The chapel was built near the fort to serve as a place of worship for both the garrison of the presidio as well as the Indian coverts living nearby. The original chapel was washed away in a flood and the current chapel was built in 1883. In 2853, a small mission was constructed at the site to serve the Piro, Manso, Tigus, Thaono and Gemes Indians who inhabit the area. This original mission was replaced in 1877 by a larger structure facing the plaza which was destroyed by fire in 1935. The current interior of the mission dates from 1944.

San Elizario was second only to El Paso del Norte among local towns for most of the nineteenth century. Merchant caravans passed through the town before the opening of the Santa Fe Trail, and Zebulon M. Pike and Peter Ellis Bean a survivor of the Nolan expedition, were held there in 1807. In 1821, after the Mexican War of Independence from Spain, San Elizario became part of the Mexican state of Chihuahua. Mexican troops still occupied the old presidio in 1835, and it served as a nucleus for a town which by 1841 had a population of 1,018. In 1830-31 the unpredictable Rio Grande changed course, placing San Elizario and its neighboring communities on La Isla, between the old and new channels of the river.

Members of the Doniphan expedition occupied the presidio in February 1847, and one year later, when the Treaty of Guadalupe Hidalgo established "the deepest channel" of the Rio Grande as the boundary between Texas and Mexico, San Elizario became part of Texas. The town lay on the Lower El Paso or Military Road from Corpus Christi to California, and hundreds of Forty-Niners passed through in the late 1840s. Many visitors admiringly described the local peaches, plums, and wheat, and the wine produced from San Elizario grapes was held in high regard. Companies of the Third Infantry under Jefferson Van Horne were stationed there from 1849 to 1852, and in 1850, when El Paso County was officially organized, San Elizario was selected the county seat.

Except for brief periods in 1854 and 1866, it remained the county seat until 1873. A post office was open in San Elizario from 1851 to 1869. During the Civil War troops of the California Column occupied the old presidio, but after the war it was finally abandoned for good.

The one story flat roofed adobe structure at the intersection of Main Street and Alarcon Road was the first County Courthouse and Jail in El Paso County. It is also the only jail that Billy the Kid ever broke into. According to the story, Billy the Kid's friend Melquaides Segura was in jail in San Elizario. At about 3:00 am, Billy the Kid knocked on the door of the jail. The guard called through the door to ask who it was knocking. Billy answered that it was the Texas Rangers. When the door was opened, the guard found himself looking down the barrel of Billy's pistol. Shortly, the guards were behind bars and Seure was free to cross into Mexico with his friend.

212\Spirits of the Border, Volume III

After 1873 as El Paso grow and prosper, San Elizario began to decline in importance. Perhaps the most notorious episode in the history of the town was the 1877 Salt War of San Elizario, in which several men died in a dispute over rights to the salt deposits just west of the Guadalupe Mountains, ninety miles to the east. After the Salt War many residents of San Elizario who had rebelled regarding the salt, fled across the Rio Grande to escape punishment further reducing the population. The final straw took place in 1881 when the town was bypassed by the railroad in favor of El Paso. In 1890 the estimated population was 1,500, and the town had two schools and a steam flour mill. In 1904 it still had an estimated population of 1,426, but ten years later that figure had declined to 834. In 1931 the estimated population fell to 300, but it climbed to 925 by the mid-1940s and to 1,064 by the early 1960s. In 1990 it was 4,385[112].

El Paso is not the only community where the spirits walk the night. It is said that San Elizario also has its specters. It is said that after midnight, on those nights when it feels like the earth itself is listening in anticipation, the ghost of a Spanish Viceroy gallops wildly around the plaza and then rides off into the night toward the east and home, Spain[113].

Then there is the story of *El Hombre-Perro*, or man-dog. According to those who claim to have seen him, if you are traveling on Socorro Road late at night toward San Elizario, this mysterious individual will be seen walking on the side of the road. Oddly he has a cat perched on one shoulder. If you are bold enough to stop and offer him a ride, he will turn to face you and his features are those of a dog. No one has reported picking him up.

San Elizario is a small community in El Paso County located some three miles beyond the city limits of El Paso, though it certainly predates El Paso itself. It also is home to some very interesting historic architecture as well as some very unusual ghosts.

This tiny village was the location of a Spanish Presidio that protected the El Paso area prior to the arrival of United States troops. San Elizario was the original county seat and the most important town on the North American side of the El Paso valley[114] until the railroad bypassed it in 1880. The original Spanish fort and the chapel were carried away by a flood in 1845.

Some ghosts seem to lose their personality after making the transition to the "other side" while others seem to remain in death very much as they were in life. This particular phantom haunts his former San Elizario home and is well known in the San Elizario area. It is said that he has retained that which made him well known as a ladies man[115] during his life.

---

[112] The *Handbook of Texas Online*, a joint project of The General Libraries at the University of Texas at Austin and the Texas State Historical Association.

[113] Flynn, Ken, *Men-dogs, Ghosts Lurk in San Eli*, El Paso, Times.

[114] Jones, Harriot Howze, El Paso: A Centennial Portrait, El Paso County Historical Society, El Paso, Texas. 1972.

[115] Kimble, Ed, El Paso Times, Kaleidoscope Section, October 31, 1978.

The house where he seems content to spend all eternity is a large, rambling adobe which dates back to the early part of the 19th century. The house, located near the Catholic Church was considered a mansion by the standards of the time in which it was built. The owner was Mauro Lujon[116], a very wealthy land owner, who was also very connected politically. He was also known as a man who loved the ladies.

Lujon was a dynamic individual who fancied himself as a leader of his people, and as such, he was continually having problems with the rulings powers of Texas. In fact, he seemed to have a penchant for looking for trouble. When the famous "Salt War" broke out in the El Paso area in 1877, it was at his beautiful home that the rebellious mob established their headquarters. This little escapade resulted in him becoming a prime suspect in the ensuing violence, thought little was proven against him.

After the death of this colorful figure in Texas history, his mansion was the home to a series of families. Unfortunately for them, even in death Mauro Lujon, or Don Mauro as he preferred to be called, had no desire to give up his beautiful home. He apparently had some reason to regret his somewhat infamous lifestyle as he returned to try and buy his way into Heaven.

Alejo and Maria de Ramirez were very happy when the opportunity arose for them to rent the beautiful home that had belonged to Don Mauro Lujon. They were happily settling into their new home when who should walk into the living room, but old Don Mauro himself. The couple was dumbfounded at the appearance of their visitor and not a little bit scared. However, their shock turned to joy when the wily old Don Mauro showed them the location of a cache of treasure hidden on the property. He told them that the money was theirs if they would use a substantial portion of it to have masses said for his soul. They naturally agreed and the ghost of Don Mauro left, happy to have met such generous people living in his old home.

For their part, in spite of their promise to Don Mauro, the Ramirez family knew exactly what they should do with their unexpected riches; they took the money and ran. As soon as they could get packed, they fled from their haunted home in San Elizario to the Mexican side of the Rio Grande where their ill gotten gains were used to start a grocery business. However, their business venture failed and Maria died soon after, showing that it is not nice to lie to a ghost.

According to the story, the next inhabitants of the former home of Don Mauro Lujon were an elderly couple named Maciel. It would appear that they knew nothing of the former owner, or if they did, the opportunity to live in such a nice home surely outweighed the possibility of living with a ghost. Naturally, they assumed that there is no such thing as a ghost. However, it was not long

[116] Sonnichson, Charles, *Mexican Spooks From El Paso*, Texas Folklore Society, 1937.

214\Spirits of the Border, Volume III

before Don Mauro made an unforgettable impression on Bonifacia Maciel, the wife.

According to the story that later came out, since her husband, Antonio, worked late, Bonificia always went to bed by herself each night. However, every night the ghost of a very old man with a long beard would crawl into the bed with her. The ghost refused to leave the bed even when the husband would come home, he would just move closer to Bonificia. In fact, the old man would so defend the bed that Antonio would have to ask the ghost's permission before he could even enter his own bed.

Bonificia later confided in a friend, Dona Tomasa Giron, and told her about the nocturnal visits by the ghost. It was Dona Tomasa that identified the ghost as that of Don Mauro Lujon. As she said, he certainly loved the ladies when he lived, so why should he change now? Bonificia agreed that he did seem to love the ladies as each night he would caress her almost to the point of distraction.

It is said that the lovely mansion of Don Mauro Lujon has long since fallen into ruin, but the amorous ghost is still said to look for lovely ladies to caress as they fall into their sleep. Perhaps he may choose another house in which to spend eternity enjoying the company of lovely ladies?

# CHAPTER THIRTY-EIGHT
# ALAMO ALTO

Alamo Alto is El Paso County's only ghost town. Alamo Alto is on State Highway 20 some 4½ miles southeast of Tornillo and thirty-five miles southeast of El Paso in southeastern El Paso County. The settlement was founded before 1931, when three businesses were reported there. Its estimated population grew from ten in the mid-1930s to twenty-five in the mid-1940s. The community consisted of a few scattered dwellings on maps in the early 1970s. In 1990 the population was twenty-five.

Today the town has vanished exept for the scattered ruins of the old school; except those that live in the area where it once existed claim that in the early hours of the morning, the shadows of what once was again graces the landscape. Several have sworn that they can see the lights of a small town where this ghost town once existed.

# CHAPTER THIRTY - NINE
# FABENS, TEXAS

Fabens is located on the Southern Pacific Railroad and State Highway 20 a mile southwest of Interstate Highway 10 and twenty-five miles southeast of downtown El Paso in southeastern El Paso County. The history of the town dates from the late nineteenth century, though in 1665 a mission branch known as San Francisco de los Sumas was established just southeast of the future site of Fabens, and a stagecoach station called San Felipe was in operation about three miles northeast of the site before 1870. In the 1870s Teodoro and Epitacia Álvarez owned a small farm on the actual site of Fabens, which was known as the Mezquital. In 1887 the townsite was sold to E. S. Newman by Sabas Grijalva and Diego Loya. The first permanent settler in what is now Fabens was Eugenio Pérez, who came from San Elizario around 1900. He owned a small farm and opened a small store shortly thereafter, when the Galveston, Harrisburg and San Antonio Railway built through the area and established a water-pumping station. In 1906 this store became the first Fabens post office. The town was named for George Fabens, an officer with the Southern Pacific.

Patrick O'Donnell, a native of Ireland working for the railroad, and his wife, Johanna, arrived in 1901 and lived in a section house. In 1910 Fabens had a few section houses and two stores, and in 1914 the estimated population was 100. The next few years brought to the area as many as 1,000 people fleeing the Mexican Revolution. The town site was laid out in 1911, but development of Fabens did not begin in earnest until the Fabens Town site and Improvement Company acquired it in 1915. The completion in 1916 of the Franklin Canal and the rise in cotton prices during World War I attracted a number of wealthy investors to the area. The estimated population rose from fifty in 1925 to 2,000 two years later, despite a major flood in 1925 or 1926. The price of cotton dropped during the Great Depression, and the estimated population of Fabens fell to 1,623 in the early 1930s, but it had risen to 1,800 by 1939 and continued to rise; it was 2,100 in the mid-1940s, 3,089 in the mid-1950s, 3,300 in the mid-1960s, 3,400 in the mid-1970s, and 5,599 in 1990.

In the summer of 1969 the University of Notre Dame sociology and anthropology department conducted a community study of Fabens. The study, published in 1970, called the town "basically unattractive," and noted that more than 40 percent of the families in Fabens were poor. Five-sixths of the local farms were owned by non-Hispanic whites, and virtually all the laborers on those farms were Hispanic[117].

---

[117] The *Handbook of Texas Online,* a joint project of The General Libraries at the University of Texas at Austin and the Texas State Historical Association.

However, what few know about this small community is that Fabens is the site of the first Mission built on the north side of the Rio Grande[118].

## VALLEY OF THE PYRAMIDS

Though Texas has been settled over 400 years, it might come as a surprise to many but the area around Fabens was not completely explored until after 1935. According to the El Paso Herald Post, it was in 1935 that the little known "Valley of the Pyramids" was found near the Indian Cliff Ranch[119]. The natural park with its beautiful, but highly unusual geographical fatures was found 13 miles noth of Fabens by County Commissioners L.J. Ivery, while for route for a new road. Acording to those who have entered this seculed valley, the natural wonder of this site makes McKelligon Canyon and Hueco Tanks look pitiful by comparison.

The finding of this unknown valley also solved the mystery of disastrous floods that had plagued the lower valley. The bowl shaped valley was a clay and sandstone formation. As a rsult, when it rained, the water did not seep into the, but ran off, evetually esulting in the deadly floods[120].

To make the mystery surrounding this discovery even more complex, one half mile north of the Valley of the Pyramids, an explorer found a piece of sandstone upon which was written an inscription[121]. The writing is in an unknown language and what is even moer unusual is that the location where this piece of sandstone was found is at leat 40 miles of any natural deposit of sandstone. There is no question that someone transported this piece of sandstone to this particular location. The answers to the riddle have yet to be found.

## THE GHOSTS

The Fabens area has many ghosts who seem to make regular appearances. There is a ghostly figure of a man that seems to run toward approaching cars on Alamenda Road between Clint and Fabens. Perhaps this unknown figure is runing away from something or someone, but we shall never known as no one has ever identified this unknown figure.

The next location, however, is very well known to everyone.

---

[118] Calleros, Cleofas, *Mission In Fabens First Built On North Side of Rio Grande*, El Paso Times, April 27, 1952.

[119] *Flood Riddle Solved With Finding Valley,* El Paso Herald Post, May 11, 1935.

[120] Ibid.

[121] Author unknown, *Ancient Writing May Tell Unknown Story of Valley*, World News, June 2, 1935.

## CHAPTER FORTY
## CATTLEMAN'S STEAKHOUSE
### Indian Cliffs Ranch
### P.O. Box 1056
### Fabens, Texas 79838

**Figure 59: The entrance to Cattleman's Steakhouse.**

There have been many stories brought to my attention regarding the Cattleman's Steakhouse in Fabens. However, no one knew anything more about the alleged hauntings other than the particular story that they wanted to relate to me. Therefore, in order to try and get to the bottom of the situation, I called the owner, Dieter Gerzymisch. Though I had never met the man and I was asked him questions that he had to think were somewhat crazy, I found him to be a very warm, open and friendly individual.

Dieter told me that he had owned the property for over 35 years and had never seen or heard anything out of the ordinary, but he invited me to come for lunch or diner and talk to the staff. Unlike many people with whom I have come in contact while writing this eries of books, Dieter literally gave me an open door to go anywhere on the property and talk to anyone I wanted.

According to the stories that I have heard there is an apparition of a man can be seen from the corner of your eye at night. This figure generally haunts the area around the bar, as well as the Bar, the Buffalo room and the Greenhouse room.

However, before I report on the information that I gathered about this well known easting establishment I want to first give the history of the place. The manager invited me to take any informatio from their website that I desired, so I am taking the liberty of relating the history in Dieter's own words.

According to what Dieter said on the website[122]:

*"Back in 1966, while still working in my father's shipping business in Germany, I was put in charge of moving the German Air Force School and it's soldiers to Fort Bliss. Business brought me to Fort Bliss and El Paso again in 1968. The unique flavor and the friendly people made such an impression on me, that I decided to make it my home.*

**Figure 60: The back dining room where so many things have happened.**

*That same year, trying to help out a friend who badly needed a job, I bought a string of livery horses at Hueco Tanks, which he rented to the public.*

---

[122] http://www.cattlemanssteakhouse.com

*Hueco Tanks was then still owned by the county of El Paso and I remember that I paid 10% in rent to the Tigua Indians every month.*

*In the fall of 1968, the county gave Hueco Tanks to the state of Texas and it became a state park. I needed a new home for the horses and that's how I wound up here at the Indian Cliffs, which gave the ranch it's name.*

*In the 1800's the entire area along the Rio Grande Valley was home to many Indians who made their living hunting and gathering. The "desert" looked different in those days. The old rancher who sold me a lot of the land once told me, "You know, I remember this well. You could ride on horseback all over this country and the grass would come up to your belt." To this day, Indian campsites, fire pits and piles of pottery chards are found all over the ranch. Indian campsites were especially frequent in the Dakota-style badland bluffs, which the locals call Indian Cliffs.*

*The San Antonio stagecoach route crosses the ranch just a mile and a half south of the Steakhouse and there was an adobe stagecoach stop at San Felipe Park. Butterfield stagecoaches also used the route for a short while as the Southern*

**Figure 61: The Greenhouse Room**

*Route. The cornerstone for our first building here, now the "Cantina" party facility, was laid in April of 1969. We had no water and no electricity in those days, just open land as far as you can see. The horse rental business grew and it became obvious that we needed a small place for our customers to be able to eat. So I started the restaurant building in 1972 and we opened in May of 1973.*

*Since I was still in the shipping business, I leased the restaurant for the first year and half. The Ranch Room was our dining area with some 50 seats, the Saddle Room was the bar and the present bar was the ranch office. Differences in regard to food quality and service forced me to take the restaurant operations over myself.*

*Over the years, the Cattleman's Steakhouse at Indian Cliffs Ranch grew and grew. Waiting lines were just too long and I decided to add on. In the summer of 1978, we built the Garden Room and Greenhouse with some 180 seats in exactly 4 weeks...and we are still growing, thanks to our customers.*
*My promise to you is:* **"Good Food! at a profit if we can, at a loss if we must. But always Good Food!"**

**Figure 62: The bar at Cattleman's Steakhouse.**

*I still buy every pound of beef every week myself and I personally see to it that our managers and employees never forget who makes the paycheck happen here: YOU, the customer.*

*When you get here, look around. Many of these young people work their way through college here. A chance they may never have had otherwise. We are here for you and we mean that sincerely.*

*Thank you for stopping by today and we invite you to be our guest at Indian Cliffs Ranch.*

*Dieter Gerzymisch, Owner*

There is no question that Dieter is absolutely correct about what he writes on the website. The Cattleman's Steakhouse serves some of the best food in the El Paso region and perhaps in the State of Texas. However, he is incorrect about something else, there are spirits that haunt the property as I shall relate in the following pages.

Dieter invited me to come up and talk to his staff and I took him up on the invitation. So, one afternoon, I drove to Fabens and sat down with members of the staff of Cattleman's Steakhouse[123].

One waitress told me that more than one couple has left happy, having had a good meal and then called back to say that they would not come back to Cattleman's anymore. In regard to one couple, they called and said that they had eaten a great meal, they lvoed the decour and the staff, but that they were never coming back again. When asked what hadhappened, they said that when the got to their car, they could see a little girl with what they called Shirley Temple blonde hair sitting in the back seat of their locked car. However, when they opened the car to ask the little girl how she had gotten inside, the girl was gone.

---

[123] I had taken a new tape recorder with me to record the stories of he staff. However, with many of the staff, there is a loud hum that can be heard on the tape. There was nothing humming at the restaurant.

One waitress was picked up by her mother one evening. When the girl was inside the car, she began to talk to her little sister who was sitting in the back

**Figure 63: The little girl is sometimes seen at the far end of this hallway.**

seat. Finally, the mother asked her who she was talking too. When she named her little sister, the mother looked at her in amazement and responded that she had not brought the little sister with her. The waitress looked over the seat and sure enough, it was empty. However, the waitress was adamant that when her mother had pulled into the parking lot, she had very clearly seen a small blonde head in the back seat.

One of the managers took me on a tour of the restaurant and told me that sometimes late at night, employees who have come from the restaurant's restrooms have seen a small blonde girl standing at the end of the long hallway that leads to the Buffalo Room from the restrooms. Thinking that some little girl has gotten lost, they will try to catch the girl, but she always disappears. Others have heard footsteps when they have been the only one in the area and still others have heard soft giggles like a little girl playing hide and seek with a friend.

One evening, several employees entered the rear dining room, making a

**Figure 64: The iron rod that holds the door open is solid.**

tour to ensure that everything was clean and ready for the next day and that all customers had gone for the day. The door through which they had entered was held open by an iron rod that it hooked over the handle. Someone must physically raise the iron rod for the door to be closed. One of the employees caught sight of a figure moving nbear the door and then the door slammed shut. The startled employees exited the room by way of the other door and began to thorough search of the bulding. No intruders were found.

Another story that had made the rounds of the staff involved an incident that took place at the main entrance to Indian Cliffs Ranch. According to the young lady who was telling me the story, a number of people leaving late have come upon a girl being beat up. The witness will, naturally, stop to help the girl and find themselves looking at an empty parking lot.

There is a ghostly figure that walked Cattleman's that is routinely mistaken for one of the managers. Generally, only management wore white shirts. The figure wears a whote dress shirt and is normally seen just leaving a room where some of the staff is working, or entering the doorway of another room. The staff will follow the figure into the room and find that there is no one there. To date, no one has been able to identify the mysterious figure.

One of the waitress staff walked into the new back dining room and saw a figure in the back of the room. The girl could see a black shadow of a man at the far end of the room. Suddenly the figure moved rapidly toward the far end of the room and exited the room.

Figures have been seen moving about in the Buffalo Room when there is no one there. This normally happens after closing when there are only a few people in the restaurant..

One night an employee flipped his car at the large tree in the curve heading toward Interstate 10. According to the story, one night a lady employee, driving home very late, was shocked to see the dead man standing on the side of the road near where his car had turned over. The sight scared her so bad that she had to return to the restaurant to calm down.

There was another female employee who was driving home alone, late one night. She glanced in the rearview mirror and saw two glowing eyes in looking at her from the back seat. The two eyes were looking up at her from between the seats. She pulled a u-turn and raced back to the restaurant where she had some male employees search her car. They found nothing.

No one knows the identity of these ghosts, but no one can deny that they exist. Too many people have experienced unearthly events to deny that anything happens. At the same time, Cattleman's makes up for some of this with some of the best steaks in the world. Perhaps, these spirits merely want a good meal.

# CHAPTER FORTY-ONE
## HEADSTART PROGRAM BUILDING
### Fabens, Texas

Then there are the ghosts that appear to haunt the old building used by the Head Start Program in Fabens. These apparitions appear to be guards, one stands at each corner of the building. In the dimly lit night, these figures look as if they are wearing old Mexican army uniforms and holding rifles. If you should catch them in the glare of your headlights, these figures fade into the night.

# CHAPTER FORTY-TWO
## OLD FABENS PORT OF ENTRY

At the Old Fabens Port of Entry there have been reports that ghostly horsemen ride charging across the border as if to run down the Border guards before fading away into nothing. These ghostly figures are said to cross the international border both ways. However, interestingly enough, on their way back to Mexico these spectral figures appear to fire revolvers both at bystanders and into the air.

## CHAPTER FORTY-THREE
## FABENS JUNIOR HIGH SCHOOL
### P.O. Box 697
### Fabens, Texas

There are said to be a number of ghosts haunting the Junior High School in Fabens. According to information that I have gathered, in the school auditorium there is supposed to be a ghostly figure that haunts the bathrooms. There have been one or two reports of a figure referred to as Bloody Mary appearing at the Junior High School.

## CHAPTER FOURTY-FOUR
## CLINT, TEXAS

On March 8, 1853, Texas governor P.H. Ball signed an act confirming the ownership of all of the land claimed by the inhabitants of Presidio de San Elizario. This land consisted of "4 leagues more or less" or approximately twelve square miles[124]. Clint, which was also known as Collinsburgh, is on the Southern Pacific Railroad at the intersection of State Highway 20 and Farm Road 1110, sixteen miles southeast of downtown El Paso in southern El Paso County.

The story of the town, which was named for early settler Mary Clinton Collins, began when the San Elizario Corporation sold the townsite to J. A. Cole, who sold it to Thomas M. Collins in 1883. For several years after the establishment of the Clint post office in 1886, the settlement was identified as the San Elizario station on the Galveston, Harrisburg and San Antonio Railway. In 1890 the estimated population of Clint was 100, and the town had a general store, a fruit grower, and a hotel. Clint soon developed into an agricultural center.

By 1896 the estimated population had increased to 150, including nine fruit growers and four alfalfa growers. The townsite was set up in 1909. By 1914 the estimated population of 400 supported three churches, two banks, a newspaper, and a tomato cannery. An estimated 600 residents lived at Clint in the late 1920s, but the number declined to 250 by the mid-1930s. By the late 1940s it had grown again to 550, then dropped to 417 in the early 1970s. In the late 1970s the estimated population was 1,120. It was 1,314 in the early 1980s and 1,883 in the late 1980s. In 1990 it was 1,035.

Unfortunately, as I related in the forward to this book, the attitudes of some of those living in Clint has not progressed much beyond that of the first settlers in 1853.

---

[124] Look at the Past, Pamphlet prepared for Clint Founders' Day, May 3, 1981.

# CHAPTER FORTY-FIVE
# CLINT HIGH SCHOOL
## 12625 Alameda Avenue
## Clint, Texas 79836

I had heard a number of stories about Clint High School. If a poll was taken among former students, I think that there would be no doubt in their minds that the building was, and is, haunted.

According to some of the stories, this school has also been the scene of some heinous crimes. As an example, according to a number of students, in the Old Gym above the Theatre, many have said that they have seen the naked body of a teenage girl hanging from the ceiling. According to the story, this unfortunte young lady was raped by a school janitor. After the rape, he hung her from a beam to keep her from informing on him.

Also in the Band Room in the room where all instruments are stored, several have said that it is possible to hear someone playing one of the musical instruments late at night. Everyone was unanimous that just being in the building at night, when it was empty of students give one the feeling that something does not want you to be there.

# CHAPTER FORTY-SIX
# FORT BLISS, TEXAS

This well known military post has become an integral part of El Paso, having been located here in one form or another since 1848. If has been an Infantry Post, the home of the United States Cavalry and now it is the home of the Air Defense Artillery.

As I related in *Spirits of the Border II: The History and Mystery of Fort Bliss, Texas*[125], in addition to all of its other claims to fame, this military installation is one of the most haunted in the Continental United States. In this second volume, I related a number of incidents that have taken place over the years, but some new ones have come to my attention.

I also want to report that the Army has decided to renovate the infamous Building 4 and move an agency into it. It will be interesting to see what the ghostly Captain thinks about his new visitors. However, there are even more stories of hauntings to occupy our attention while we wait for the Captain's reponse.

---

[125] Hudnall, Ken and Connie Wang, The History and Mystery of Fort Bliss, Texas, Omega Press, El Paso, Texas. 2003

# CHAPTER FORTY-SEVEN
# FORT BLISS REPLICA MUSEUM
## FORT BLISS, TEXAS

The Replica Musuem is an area created to look like Fort Bliss in the 1800s. Soldiers on duty claim to hear footsteps and crickett noises coming from the area where the office has been established.

At times water has been found on the floor of the restrooms, but when workers come back with mops to clean up the water, the water seen on the floor is gone. The water hose that are laid out to irrigate the grass have been found rolled up as if ready to be stored away. At other times, the hoses are found to have ben disconneted from the sprinklers.

# CHAPTER FORTY-EIGHT
# WILLIAM BEAUMONT COMPLEX
## BUILDING 7919

A number of military police have related stories to me about odd ocurrences that have taken place in some of the old buildings adjoining the William Beaumont Army Medical Center. According to several, events that have taken place in Building 7919 are some of the most unnerving.

A number opf Military Policemem (and Policewomen) have sworn to me that they have seen the lights of the building turning on and off during the night when the building is supposed to be unoccupied. Some have added that they have heard sreams coming from the building as if someone was being brutally murdered and on more than one occasion, the figure of a man has been seen hanging from the ceiling. More than one MP has stated very adamantly that they will not enter this building at night no matter what they see or hear.

# CHAPTER FORTY-NINE
# WILLIAM BEAUMONT ARMY MEDICAL CENTER
# 6TH FLOOR

During the Air Defense Artillery Veterans Day Gala, there is always a silent auction where some of the most unusual items can be found. One year I won a ghost tour of Fort Bliss and this led to the writing of *Spirits of the Border*

**Figure 65: The entrance to the Alternative Medical Clinic on the 6th Floor.**

*II: The History and Mystery of Fort Bliss, Texas*[126]. Last year I won a tour of William Beaumont Army Medical Center to be conducted by Colonel Mitchell, the Hospital Commander.

---

[126] Ibid.

Due to my status as a 100% disabled veteran, I have had a great deal of interaction with various clinics within Beaumont, but I have never been able to

**Figure 66: This room is still haunted by a stubborn spirit that refuses to leave.**

confirm whether or not the Hospital had any ghosts wondering about. Oh, it is true that when I do book signings at the Veteans Administration Medical Clinc that is attached to Beaumont, I have heard a number of stories about strange occurrences taking place at Beaumont, I have never been able to get any concrete information. During this tour, I was able to get all of the information I had ever wanted to obtain about the ghosts of Beaumont. Not only is the building haunted, but the hauntings were of such an intensity that the extremely conservative United States Army had to conduct a psychic cleansing of this historic old hospital before part of the 6th floor could be used.

Now previously, I had been told by one surgeon, who hid his nametage so that I could not see his name, that in one of the Operating Rooms of Beaumont Hospitasl that a nurse who had died some years ago perodically returns to assist with surgery. This unexpected help sometimes results in the living staff abandoning the Operating Room until the spectral nurse leaves. In spite of this unusual set of circumstances, I am told that they have never lost a patient.

However, when the Hospital renovated the 6th floor, which had been a surgical ward, problems arose that the Army was not equiped to handle. It seems that a number of spirits of those who had died after surgery had remained on the floor. These unhappy spirits felt that they had died needlessly and they were definitely not happy with the creation of a clinc dedicated to alternative medical treatments and these angry ghosts apparently went out of their way to interfer with the living.

Finally, having run out of ideas, the Military authorites arranged for a psychic cleansing in a last ditch effort to reclaim this portion of the hospital. I was told that religious leaders from several different religions, to include a Native American Shaman were brought in to try and remove the unhappy spirits.

The ceremony, I am told, was a partial success as all of the spirits but one agreed to leave to begin the long journey to the next world. That one spirit still haunts the Alternative Medical Clinic on the 6$^{th}$ floor of William Beaumont Army Medical Center.

# CHAPTER FIFTY
# REPLICA POOL
# FORT BLISS

The stories of strange occurences at the Fort Bliss Replica Pool were given to me by a very attractive young lady who desires to remain anonymous. So I am repeating the tales just as she told them to me, omitting only her name.

I heard that a woman died in Replica Pool, that she drowned and her body was discovered floating on the bottom at closing time. I'm not sure it it's true, but if it is, maybe it would explain some of the things that I have seen. Here are my stories. Please let me remain anonymous.

Replica Pool, April 2002

One night after the pool had closed another lifeguard and I were cleaning. Since there was only two of us, we decided each one would clean a locker room. I took the girls locker room and he took the boys. I went around the locker room, picked up all of the trash and closed all the lockers. Then I began to wipe down the sinks. All of a sudden it got really cold and I couldn't move. Then I felt a hand grab my left arm. It was cold and all I could do was stand there. After what felt like eternity, the coldness faded away. I turned around and all the lockers were hanging open. I ran into the guys locker room to grab the other lifeguard. When I took him back to the girls locker room, some of the lockers were open and some were closed. Nothing else happened that night.

Next story:

One night after a birthday party, three other lifeguards and I decided to stay and swim for a while. I went to the far end of the pool and turned off the slide and then came back to the shallow end. Three of us got in and one guy sat at the edge of the pool with his feet in the water. We were all just standing there talking when all of a sudden the slide at the deep end of the pool turned back on. We were all shocked. We decided that someone had to go see if someone was in the pool, and I was elected to go. I took the guy who wasn't swimming and walked to the deep end of the pool. We couldn't see anyone so I turned the slide off again. After the water had stopped running, we still heard splashing coming from the bottom of the slide. It sounded like someone was drowning, but we couldn't see anyone or anything. Then the splashing stopped. For some reason we both looked towards the girls locker room and watched as wet footprints ran inside. Curiosity got the best of us and we followed them in. We looked everywhere but we never saw anyone. At that point we decided to le

## CHAPTER FIFTY-ONE
## HOSPITALS OF EL PASO

It is not only military hospitals that have their share of spirits who are too angry at having died to let go of the earth. There are a number of specters that haunt the civilian hospitals of El Paso as shall be seen in this section.

**Figure 67: The Pest House**

The first record of an actual hospital existing in El Paso was from an article appearing in the Lone Star Newspapers on February 11, 1882[127]. The facility being discussed was what was referred to as The Pest House, a facility used to treat such infectious diseases as smallpox and tuberculosis. The Pest House was more formally known as the City Eruptive Hospital. The news article resulted in a public demand for a newer more modern facility, so in late 1882, a 48' x 20' building was erected and a director hired. However, it was not long before it

---

[127] Jones, Harriot Howze, El Paso: A Centennial Portrait, El Paso County Historical Society. 1973.

232\Spirits of the Border, Volume III

became apparent that this new building was not really suitable for the purpose for which it was being used.

In 1884, a new facility was built, but in March of 1893, it burned to the ground as a result of a spark from a chimney. The only survivors of the disastrous fire were the "keeper" and one patient.

For the next few years, El Paso had no formal hospital facilities, but in 1898, over the objections of the smelter, a new Pest House was established in one of the barracks remaining at the former Fort Bliss that had existed near Hart's Mill. In spite of assurances by the medical staff that there was no danger of spreading infection, the owners of the smelter operation continued to object to the presence of this potential biological time bomb being so close to their employees so the city fathers began to look for other locations in which to locate this very necessary facility. Finally, in 1891, it was announced that since there had not been a new case of smallpox diagnosed in over 45 days that the Contagious Disease Hospital at Old Fort Bliss would be closed. Once abandoned, the old barracks in which it had operated for so long was burned to the ground to ensure there would be no risk of any becoming infected.

When it became clear that there was a continuing need for such a facility, the Hospital was later located near the reservoir in Sunset Heights and later on Conception Avenue, one block north of the Galveston, Harrisburg and San Antonio Railroad line. However, once the City-County Hospital was built near Washington Park, the City Eruptive Hospital was moved to that location.

The Pest House was, of course, designed specifically for the treating of infectious diseases. Naturally, there was a need for a facility to treat those with less drastic ailments, so in 1882, the women of the churches of El Paso got together to create the Ladies Aid Society of El Paso and founded a hospital in a long wooden building located on Oregon Street near the Santa Fe Depot at South Santa Fe and West Fifth Streets.

This hospital was designed and intended to be a group effort of all of the churches in El Paso. So it was that each denomination treated their ill in varying levels of comfort. For example, the Jewish ladies furnished a room with a number of comforts that were unusual for the time to include upholstered furniture. This room was used only for "their sick[128]."

As time progressed and El Paso grew, this medical facility supported by the Ladies Aid Society became the Indigent Hospital of El Paso. Such were the conditions of the times that the number of sick always threatened to overwhelm the ability of this private effort to meet the demand for medical care. So it was that in 1893, plans were made to build a new, modern facility, however, with the advent of Hotel Dieu in 1894, such plans were tabled and responsibility for the treatment of the indigent of El Paso was passed to the new hospital.

The somewhat shabby treatment of those who contracted the many contagious diseases that found a home in El Paso caused much bitterness in those

---

[128] Ibid.

who found themselves ill. Such was the fear of smallpox that those with the disease were literally shunned by their friends and relatives, most were just left on their own devices to die. Once shut up in the Pest House, their chances of survival were slim. In fact this was the topic of the article in the Lone Star. According to the text of the article,

"*Four of the five smallpox patients who were sent to the miserable hovel at Old Fort Bliss have died. The one who did not die, after he had been taken there, got up and walked back to town. It is nothing less than murder to send patients to such a place. The house has neither window nor floor.*"

As a result of the terrible treatment received by the patients, the various locations in which the Pest House was situated retain some of the dark anger and sadness that was experienced by those poor unfortunates during life.

This is especially true of those who occupied the Pest House when it was located at Old Fort Bliss. Where the barracks was located that became the medical facility, there have been a number of figures seen wondering in the night, their bodies wasted by the diseases that afflicted them during life. Several small figures, representing some of the children who contracted these terrible diseases and died, have been regularly seen wondering along the river.

Since this time there have been other hospitals in El Paso and each has left their own indelible mark on both the community as well as the spirit world as almost without exception, each had more permanent residents who were loath to quit this world. Over the next few pages we shall review a few of them.

## CHAPTER FIFTY-TWO
## HORIZON HEALTHCARE CENTER OF EL PASO
### 2301 North Oregon
### El Paso, Texas

I wrote about the ghosts that are said to haunt the Mesa Hills Specialty Hospital in book one of this series, but a great deal of new information has come to my attention. One of the nurses, Veronica Vega, agreed to talk to me about some of the happenings she has witnessed and been told about for this new book. The story is even more fascinating that I originally thought that it was, as you shall see as you read on.

Veronica Vega told me that for four years, she used to work on the 3rd

**Figure 68: Horizon Healthcare Center of El Paso.**

floor of the building, which is actually part of the Nursing Home, now known as the Horizon Healthcare Center of El Paso. She and the other nnurses on duty would sometimes see the faint impressions of three tall, dark, men standing at the very the end of the 3rd floor hallway. These three figures always wore tophats, and never left their positions at the end of the hall.

Sometimes the nurses would here the three men call their names and on more than one occasion, one of the three mysterious figuers has called for help, in Spanish. Each time the nurses would hear the soft whispery voices calling for help, they would check all of the patients, but they would find nothing out of place and none of the patients needing help.

In room 308 or 310 the ghost of a lady in a white dress would appear to patients staying in the room. Staff would always know when she was about as they would always small a strong scent of frsh roses in the room. The female patient staying in the room told staff that one one occasion she had gotten up in the night to go to the restroom and the lady in white was in the room just staring at herself in the mirror. On another night, when the patient opened the door to the restroom and turned on the light, the lady in white had dashed from the restroom, going right through the patient. The patient said that she felt a moment of intense cold as the spirit of the lady in white passed through her body.

One patient asked them to cover her feet one evening. When the nurses came back the patient's feet were uncovered. The patient complained that the tall lady in white would not leave her alone.

One night a CNA was leaning over to to something at the foot of the bed in this room and a hand grabbed her shoulder. The CNA did not turn to see who was there, but just said leave me a lone. The hand was removed. When she did turn, there was no one there.

Once, Veronica and another nurse were sitting at nurses station and there was also a CNA sitting near the wall. Suddenly, they all heard the sound of someone walking down the hall and the jingling of keys as if the person coming down the hallways had a ring of keys hanging on their belt. The sounds of jingling keys and footsteps continued down the hall and passed the nurses' station, though none of those present could see anyone in the hallway. At other times, the elevator doors will open and stay open for long periods of time as if someone was holding down the button to keep the elevator on the floor.

Another ghost is a little girl about four or five years old with blonde curly hair. She sits on the siderails of the hall and watches the activity in the hallways. Then sometimes she will go into the rooms of patients wanting to play. The really bizarre part of this haunting is that when the little girl appears, the next day a patient would die. There are a lot of strange things that happen on the third floor of this old building.

On the fourth floor nurses would see the doors to rooms opening and closing with no one near them. However, no one has ever seen any figures.

One evening on the third floor, a patient had died. Two CNAs, not knowiong that the patient in that room had died, went into the room and changed the sheets. The patient was in the bed as always and even requested that they make the bed a certain way as the sheets kept coming up. Later on when one of the CNAs was on rounds with one of the nurses, they entered the room and the patient was not there.

Connie Wang was on duty that night and when she was asked where the patient had gone, she told the CNA that the patient had died the previous evening. This was before the CNA had helped change the sheets for a dead man.

Then, later, a nurse saw a CNA that had been known as a perfectionist changing the linens in some of the rooms on the floor. She thought nothing of it until she realized that the CNA she had seen had recently died in a car wreck. When she went back and checked the rooms she had seen the dead CNA come from the linens in both had ben changed and the CNA on duty had not yet gotten to those rooms. Even I death, he wanted to make sure that his job was done well.

Then the day shift on the third floor saw someone enter one of the rooms and so one of the nurses went to see who had entered the room. The patient assured the nurse that no one had entered the room even though several people saw a figure go in the door. This was the room where the Lady in White spent her time.

Finally, one evening Veronica was in a room checking on a patient when someone tugged on her jacket. The patient was trying to look around her as if someone had entered the room. Veronica turned and thare was no one behind her/ Later she bent down to check something on the chart and someone placed a hand on her shoulder. She immediaetly spun around and there was no one behind her.

Veronica and Conie Wang both maintained that they had worked with patients for so long that they could smell death. Unfortuantely, their record is very good. A most unusual talent.

# CHAPTER FIFTY-THREE
# PROVIDENCE MEMORIAL HOSPITAL
## Upson and North Santa Fe Street
## El Paso, Texas

**Figure 69: Providence Hospital in 1915[129].**

In 1902, Drs. M.P. Schuster, M.O. Wright, Alward White, A.L. Justice, H.M. Shught, H.T. Thompson and J. Shelton Horsley purchased the Rio Grande Congregational Training School property located at Upson and North Santa Fe streets. At this location they founded The Providence Hospital, maintaining that it would be very beneficial to get their patients away form the noises of the city and let them enjoy clean, fresh air[130]. The first two nurses, Lucy Houghton and Marion Farmer joined the staff in October 1904.

The original two story building had two open wards, one for male patients and one for female patients, with a large number of single beds. The

---

[129] This photograph came from a box of old El Paso photos purchased at an estate sale.
[130] Ibid

original building later had a third story added due to the growth in both patient demand as well as services being offered by the medical staff.

By the late 1940s, it had become clear to the management of the hospital that the original buildings were no longer satisfactory. As a result on March 7, 1949, work was started on a new Providence Hospital at the intersection of Blacker and Oregon Streets. The new building opened on January 14, 1952 and began to immediately receive patients while the old building was razed to make way for the construction if Interstate Highway 10.

In only a relatively short time, the demands of the patients began to strain the ability of the new hospital to meet the needs of the city. Deciding that it was time to expand, so a new portion called the Sam Young Tower, comprised of four stories and two basements was completed in September of 1972.

Providence Hsopital has become one of the best known of the hospitals

**Figure 70: Providence Hospital today.**

in the El Paso area. It is not as large as some of the others, but it offers excellent care to its many patients.

## THE GHOSTS

There is no question that the nurses that staff this hospital are some of the most dedicated in the city. Some are so dedicated that not even death can stop them from carrying ot their duties. I met a lady at an event who had been a nurse at Providence until she retired a number of years ago. She told me about an incident that literally scared her to death.

One morning she reported for duty, coming in the rear entrance from the employee parking area as was normally her custom. When she entered the elevator, there was one other person already in the car. Though she did not now this nurse, she greeted her warmly as the staff of Providence has always been close. The oddly dressed nurse failed to respond, she the lady telling the story turned to face the front of the car and pushed the buton for her floor.

According to my informant the other nurse was dressed in a startched white uniform of a type that had not been worn in a number of years. She had the little white hat on her head, her nursing pin on her collar and she was wearing white nursing shoes with the raised heel. The lady telling the story said that she felt a little uncormtable when she glanced back and noticed that the other occupant of the car just stared straight ahead, her face expressionless.

When my friend reached her floor, she said that she turned to try once more to be polite to the other occupant of the car and saw to her shock that the car was empty. There had been no stops and no way that the other nurse could have disappeaerd. Not really knowing what to say, she made her way to the her assigned nurses' station. One of her friends noticed her shocked expression and asked her what had happened. When she related the story, her friend nodded and patted her shoulder. You've just met Bertha, she was told. According to her friend, Bertha was a nurse at Providence a long tmie ago who died one night. She still comes back to check on the patients!

# CHAPTER FIFTY-FOUR
# DEL SOL MEDICAL CENTER
## 10301 Gateway West
## El Paso, Texas 79925

 

    This ultra modern, state of the art medical center has a very checkered past. Before becoming Del Sol, this facility was known as Columbia East and before that it was Vista Hills Hospital and then finally, it was known as Eastwood Hospital. Oddly, very few seem to remember that this hospital was also once referred to as the Death Hospital. The current facility has 342 beds, 500 physicians and a staff of 1,325. Del Sol Medical Center also has seven ancillary facilities that provide specialized care. However, by whatever name it is known, this hospital has a long history of hauntings.
    Veronica Vega, the nurse currently working at Mesa Hills Specialty

**Figure 71: Del Sol Medical Center**

Hospital who told me about some of the hauntings there also told me about somethings tht had happened to her friend who was working at Del Sol, back when it was Columbia – East.
    According to Veronica, her friend was asked to stay in the room with a lady who had the habit o getting out of the bed at night. The problem was that the lady would fall and hurt herself. So a number of sitters had been hired to sit with the lady to ensure that she stayed in the bed. To everyone's surprise, each sitter would quit, complaining about very scary things happening in the room at night. So finally, Veronica's friend was hired to be a sitter for this lady, but was told to

sit right outside the lady's hospital room door and only go inside the room if she heard a noise that indicated that the lady had gotten out of bed.

Her friend heard sounds inside the room two or three times as if the lady had goten out of bed, but whenever she would check, the lady would be in the bed. She waited at the door until she heard the noise again and she immediately opened the door. What she saw shocked her down to her shoes.

She saw that the bed, and the patient in it, were now elevated some feet off of the floor. She screamed and a nurse and a security guard came running. She left the room as the guard and the nurse ran inside. She does not know what the two of them saw inside that room, but whatever it was scared the two of them so badly that they both quit.

There is another ghost that seems to haunt the medical/surgical floor. This ghost is a little boy with very white skin who is seen running in and out of the rooms of the various patients. One of the nurse techs even said that the staff would see people who had no business being on the floor wandering around. If approached, they would fade away.

Another of the CNAs could see ghosts and usualy was the first one to be aware if the little boy was on the floor. One night, the CNA reported that the little boy went into a particular patient's room. Two of the nurses decided to see if there was anything to the story. They went into the room that the CNA had indicated that the little boy had entered. Before either of them could say anyting, the patient asked them if it was their little boy who had come into the room. One of the nurses asked what little boy and the patient said the little boy standing beside you.

Oddly enough, the patient saw the little boy, but the nurses did not. The patient described the little boy as wearing clothing from the early 1900s. A number of patients complained that the little boy likes to play around by removing the blankets from the bed. He seems to like to torment certain patients. He especially seems to like room 552. The unfortuante thing is that ever time the little boy is seen, some patient dies.

The interesting thing is that this little boy can be seen on the security cameras running from one room to another. The security staff searched the floor, but found no one. In another situation, a nurse took a picture of a pressure sore on a patient's foot. When the picture was developed, rather than a pressure sore, the photograph should the face of a little boy.

In another incident, which took place in room 552, the call light for this room kept ringing. The patient in the room was comatose and certainly could not have pushed the button for the call light. Thinking it may be a CNA needing help with the patient, the nurse at the nurses' station went down to the room several times to answer the call light. Each time, there was no one in the room except for the patient who certainly could not push the call light.

The next time the call light turned on, the nurse used the intercom to ask what the situation might be. The voice of the comatose answered saying the he had been calling for help, but no one had come to help him. The nurse ran to the room, but the patient was still comatose and the call button was well out of his reach, even had he been conscious.

Who is the little boy? Why does he haunt Del Sol? Is he a harbinger of death?

# CHAPTER FIFTY-FIVE
# HOTEL DIEU

It is my belief that the building being discussed in the following article was formerly Hotel Dieu, one of the older hospitals in El Paso. After Hotel Dieu closed this old building sat empty for a good many years before the city tore it down. The building was U-shaped with two wings, one of which bordered Yandell and one was on the west side of the buildnig.

## Whispering and Tapping Mirror

This building that I am about to reveal is very little known of. It was built near Downtown El Paso (Texas) and has already been demolished by the City. It was allegedly that it was haunted possibly by two unknown nature. It was revealed that the property where it stood was a family cemetery, don't ask me why. Read on.

To give you an idea, this was an "U" shaped building and we called three wings: West, Yandell and East, the East being longer than the West wing. The location of the front office is right on the very corner of East and Yandell Wings. During my junior high and high school years, I attended many social events at this building when it looked new. All occassions, you name it, took place here. I'll refer this as the Center.

During my term as Treasurer of the Board of Directors in 1996, I volunteered my time to provide guidance and transitition for the newly hired Executive Director. We were in the process of moving into a brand new building a few miles north near the University of Texas at El Paso (UTEP, my alma mater).

A little after 6 am on a cold dark December morning, I was the second person to arrive at the Center. The Chief Financial Officer (CFO) was already diligently at work while others groaned their way out of their warm beds, y'all know what I mean.

The condition of the building was in disrepair and was too expensive to renovate; it was wiser to invest in a newer building facility. The heating unit does not work at all so the CFO had a pair of electric space heaters warming up this huge office with glasses enclosing three sides and a solid wall on one side of the office. From this office, you could barely see the Yandell wing but clearly visible of the East wing.

While I was sipping on my 7-11 bought coffee and reviewing some financial transactions, the CFO asked me if I've ever heard of any unusual sounds before or after hours. I simply shook my head and asked why. She mentioned that she had heard a faint whispering prior to my arrival at the Center. She kept thinking she was imaging things and tried to ignore it. During this period, we were in the office, she asked me if I had whispered something to her a few seconds ago. I denied that I have. She gave me a very perplexing look on her face and became distracted. She swore she had heard a whisper. She stated that while she was hearing it, she glanced over at me and noticed that I was indeed tightlipped. She begged that she would feel comfortable if I'd take a look-see around the Center which I happily obliged, but a little worried.

I thought that someone has silently broke into the building because it had happened twice. I haven't heard anything. I was dreading at the fact that I had to check each and every room in the Center, especially West and Yandell. Here are where it was claimed to be the most spooky and haunted part of the building. Regardlessly, following my natural instinct, I progressed to investigate. I instructed that she should stay behind and to be ready to dial 911.

I locked the front office door and I tiptoped my way up East wing towards the Dance Hall/Conference Room. I didn't want the plops of my cowboy boots to be heard. Upon entering this room, I had chills running down my spine and could feel hair standing all over. I instantly turned on the light because it was awfully pitch black. Imagine a haunting ugly face only inches from yours? AAAAAY! Anyways, I checked the door which was secured and took a peek outside. Didn't see anything. I hurriedly walked out of the room. I returned to the front office and gave an "OK" sign through the glasses and I progressed to investigate the Yandell/West wings. I feel my fear began to grow to the point where I could almost hear my heartbeat pounding and at my throat. I tiptoed all the way through both wings wishing I had my .45 Colt (revolver). I simply turned on all lights and glanced into each rooms hoping to not see anything spooky.

When I was done, I hurriedly walked back to the front office and told her that all is clear. I paused at the lobby and mouthed that I was going to wash my dusty hands.

I entered a private dim lighted restroom. While I was midst of washing my hands, I suddenly heard an audible whispering and tapping from behind the mirror right where I was washing them. I gasped and was reeled backward toward the closed door. I couldn't see anything on the mirror but myself and I was hearing it from behind the mirror!!! I was so desperate to get out that I kicked the door then I got the door open and I bolted out running.

I ran to the front office. She dialed 911. She could see clearly that I was terrified! She stated later on that I was pale with fear!!

Believe it or not, within 1.5 minute or less, the El Paso County Sheriff's Department cruiser wailed through the streets and arrived with flashing lights. We were somewhat relieved because of a quick response. The bulky Sheriff's deputy exited his patrol car with a shotgun in his hands. I wanted to just grab it and start to wildly blast where ever the sounds were coming from!! The deputy couldn't enter the front entrance as it was locked. My adrenaline rush made it all possible for me to run out and opened the door. The deputy ordered us to get out of the building. I merely pointed and told him what I heard. The deputy was waiting for the back up unit to arrive. Feeling adrenaline overwhelming me, I told him that I'd go in with him which he refused. His back up arrived and both went in. A minute later, the El Paso Police Department arrived silently. Two young rookie police officers and not as bulky as the deputies, they entered with pistols drawn. Somehow, being overwhelmed with adrenaline rush, I followed after them inside to take a good look-see. They didn't see me follow in, but the deputy whirled and cracked, "Sir, get out of here!" I reeled backward outside on the street.

After three additional patrol units and 45 minutes of searching. They found no culprits.

A police sergeant stated that he had responded to same incident at the same building a few months prior with an exception it was late in the evening. He had stated that at least 7 folks have heard unexplained noises and one sighting of a shadow moving around quietly and quickly. They didn't find anyone. I was skeptical, but still got the chills down my spine.

Two months later, we moved to our new facility. This one is much nicer and so modern. It was much larger and the Dancing Hall is huge enough to hold a capacity of nearly 440 heads.

At the new facility, the hall looks spooky and has a huge basement, I wonder if I'd hear it again? You be the judge.

## CHAPETR FIFTY-SIX
## EYE, EAR, NOSE AND THROAT HOSPITAL
## A/K/A/ ROLSTON PRIVATE HOSPITAL
## A/K/A/ EL PASO MASONIC HOSPITAL
### 200 Block of Wyoming AND
### Corner of North Piedras and Montana
### El Paso, Texas

Figure 72: Masonic Hospital[131]

What became known as the Masonic Hospital at the corner of North Piedras and Montana has had a long and eventful history. The property has also had several names.

Initially, Dr. Eugene R. Carpenter built the first house on the south side of the 200 block of Wyoming in 1908 and founded an Eye, Ear, Nose and Throat Hospital[132]. In 1911, Dr. Carpenter sold the property to Miss Margaret H. Rolston, R.N. who served as superintendent of the newly named Rolston Private Hospital. Then in 1912, Miss Rolston sold the property to Mrs. W. M. MacDonald, R.N. who acted as supervisor of the Rolston Private Hospital while Miss Rolston continued to live at the hospital and act as a staff nurse.

---

[131] Photo taken from a postcard purchased at an estate sale in El Paso.
[132] Jones, Harriot Howze, El Paso: A Centennial Portrait, El Paso County Historical Society. 1973.

Eventually this hospital was sold and a new $50,000.00 red brick colonial style building containing four stories and a basement was opened at the corner of North Piedras and Montana in 1916. The new Rolston Hospital continued to operate under the ownership of William M. MacDonald until 1922 when the facility was purchased by the Masons. At this point the name was changed to the El Paso Masonic Hospital, a hospital which became an integral part of the life of so many in this city. Efforts were made to expand the Masonic Hospital to meet the ever growing demand for medical care, but in 1946 as a result of the Emergency Federal Work Agency forbidding expansion, the 65 bed hospital was forced to close[133]. So ended an era of the city's growth.

**Figure 73: The "new" Rolston Hotel located at Five Points (Piedras and Montana)[134].**

The next reincarnation of this site began when it was sold to a "Chicago woman" for $125,000.00. This lady clearly had a head for business as she very quickly made a deal with Sears, Roebuck and Company to place a new store on the site of the Masonic Hospital.

---

[133] Ibid.

[134] Photo obtained from the El Paso County Historical Society.

Today, this site houses the Headquarters of the El Paso Police Department. Though the mission of the structure has changed a number of times, some things remain consistent such as the ghosts that haunt the facility.

## CHAPTER FIFTY-SEVEN
## MASONIC HALL
### El Paso Lodge 130
### 1505 Magruder
### El Paso, Texas

**Figure 74: El Paso Lodge 130, 1505 Magruder[135].**

On January 21, 1854, Lodge 130 was founded in San Elizario, the county seat at that time. This was one of the first lodges to appear on the Western frontier, 600 miles from the closest one in San Antonio.
El Paso Lodge meetings were suspended between 1859 and 1866 during the Civil War. Lodge 130 resumed work in July 1866, and a formal meeting was held at the Grand Central Hotel. During the following years, El Paso Lodge 130 rented different places in which to hold its meetings until they could erect a one-story adobe building at San Antonio and Mesa Streets.
The history of the El Paso Lodge is intertwined with the history of the city. In 1870, judges and Masons Gaylord Judd Clarke and A.J. Fountain founded St. Clement's Episcopal Mission, the first Protestant church in the county.

---

[135] This photo came from the award winning website of Lodge 130.

El Paso Masons first met at Judge Simeon Hart's residence, or Hart's Mill. Journalist Ken Flynn says Hart's flour mill was probably "the first real industry on the America side of the river." Parts of Hart's mill and residence are preserved as historical landmarks and are now home to La Hacienda Restaurant. Hart was also one of the founders of the El Paso Times.

For several years, Masons owned the Ralston Hospital at Five Points until they decided to support the new Providence Memorial Hospital. Later they built the Masonic Hospital, in service until the mid 1940s.

Members of the Lodge also contributed to the economy of El Paso. Benjamin Dowell set up a combination grocery store, saloon and billiards hall, and his business also became the city's first official post office. Joseph Magoffin, who, like Dowell, was mayor of El Paso, served as Collector of Customs. His home is now a state park. Masons Maury C. Edwards and O.T. Bassett were associated with the lumber business for years.

Masons helped establish the public education system in El Paso. In 1870, M.A. Jones, a Mason and lawyer, set up a day school in his law office where he taught American and Mexican children to read and write. In 1882, the school board was formally organized, with Edward C. Pew, Joseph Magoffin and Samuel Freudenthal, all Masons, serving as members. In the 1800s, Masons as a group lobbied for the establishment of state supported education and federal land grant colleges.

While most Masons are members of the three aforementioned levels, others advance through about 100 other rites composed of 1,000 higher degrees worldwide. The two most popular rites in the United States are the Scottish that awards 33 degrees and the York that awards 10, including the Order of Knights Templar, similar to the highest degree Scottish Rite Mason. Many African-Americans belong to the Prince Hall Grand Lodge.

Other orders include the Veiled Prophets of the Enchanted Realm (the fraternal fun order for Blue Lodge Masons) and the Ancient Arabic Order of the Nobles of the Mystic Shrine. The latter are thirty-second degree Masons called Shriners, noted for burn institutes and hospitals for crippled children. Two such charities are the Texas Scottish Rite Hospital for Crippled Children in Dallas and the Shriners Burns Institute in Galveston.

Shriners also are identifiable by antics in their tiny cars during community parades and their sponsorship of the Shrine Circus. The circus raises money for the hospitals, and free seats are given to local needy children.

Charity is at the heart of Masonic teachings of growth and development of individuals. Compassion, honor and integrity unite Masons in a brotherhood also known for its emphasis on fellowship. Masonic organizations for women include the Order of Eastern Star and Amaranth. Girls may join Rainbow, Job's Daughters, Triangle or Constellation and boys enter DeMolay.

Like other fraternal societies, the Masons use symbols and rituals. The most widely known symbol is the Square and Compasses, with the former representing things of the earth as well as honor, integrity and truthfulness, and the latter symbolizing things of the spirit, including the importance of self-control. The G in the middle of the symbol stands for geometry, the science which the ancients believed most revealed the glory of God and His works.

Over the centuries, the Masons have encountered much opposition. Masons have never been permitted in some Catholic countries such as Spain, and the Church still discourages its members from joining the order. The Masons do not bar Catholics, however, and many lodges are active in Latin America. In the United States, short-lived opposition came in the form of the political anti-Masonic party established in 1828 that nominated William Wirt to run for president against Andrew Jackson. Jackson won handily over Wirt, ironically himself a Mason. The party lasted only until 1834.

Masons have done much to influence the nation, the state of Texas and El Paso. Although most fraternal organizations have lost membership in the past few decades, Grand Lodges across the country are working to make the organization more appealing to prospective members.

## THE GHOSTS

Almost every Mason that I have spent anytime with has shown an unbelievable loyalty to their Lodge. So it does not surprise me that a ghost might return to haunt his lodge. I have had several people tell me that the ghost of a Mason who was known for always ensuring that the Lodge was straightened up after a meeting has been seen cleaning up this particular Lodge.

## CHAPTER FIFTY-EIGHT
## EL PASO ZOO
## 4001 E. Paisano
## El Paso, Texas

The El Paso Zoo is an eighteen-acre home to more than 600 animals of over 250 species in a variety of natural habitat exhibits including a Reptile House, South American Pavilion, Americas Aviary, Paraje, Birds of Prey, American Biome, Forest Atrium, Asian Grasslands, Asian Endangered Walk, and an Elephant Complex.

The ticket booth for the Zoo closes at 4:00 PM each day so by 5:00 PM,

**Figure 75: The El Paso Zoo Entrance.**
**(The raised structure on top houses the security office.)**

the guests have gone for the day and the animals are settling down for night. Security guards patrol the locked Zoo, more to protect the animals than to protect anyone who might try to break into this facility. However, it now appears that the security guards are not the only entities who wander through the gathering dusk.

## THE GHOSTS

Of all of the places I had thought about being haunted, the El Paso Zoo was certainly not one of them. However, Joe O. Cabrera, the security guard hired to patrol Concordia Cemetery the night prior to the Walk through History had worked security at the Zoo and had a lot of stories about events that had taken place there after the guests leave for the day.

According to Mr. Cabrera, there wre normally two security officers on duty each night. They sat in a booth, watching the grounds visually as well as monitoring a bank of alarms. Most nights, the duty is boring and it is a chore to stay awake, but then on other nights all hell breaks lose.

The security office is in a taised structure on top of the entrance as shown in the picture above. The security office is reached by a wodden staircase that winds around the outside of the building. There are normally two security officers on duty. When patrols are done, one will stay in the office and the other will patrol the internior of the Zoo. Quite often, the officer remaining in the booth will hear someone mounting the wooden stairs and see the doorknob turn, through no one enters the booth. If the guard in the booth opens the door to see who is at the door, no one is ever seen. Then later the actual security guard who conducted the patrol will enter, denying having been on the stairs earlier.

One evening, a female security guard needed to go to the restroom. The

**Figure 76: The Zoo restrooms where the female security guard had her scare.**

male officer on duty offered to go with her, but she retorted that she was old enough to go to the bathroom by herself. Boldly, the security guard descended the steps and vanished into the Zoo compound. A few minutes later, the guard in the booth heard the female guard screaming and, looking out the window of the security booth, saw her running toward the booth, her pants still down around her lower legs.

When the female guard had calmed down enough to talk, she told her companion that she had been in the stall attending to business when someone knocked on the stall door. She thought it was the other guard, but couldn't figure out why her had felt it necessary to come into the ladies' restroom. She told him to go away that she was fine. For a moment there was silence and then the knocking on the stall door was heard again.

This time, the female guard pulled her pants up and jerked the stall door open, but to her surprise, she saw no on else in the restroom. There was no way that anyone could have gotten fmo the stall door to the outside without her seeing him. Not really knowing what was taking place, she erturned to her stall, settling back to finish her business. For a few moments, all was peaceful and quiet.

Then, without warning, an ice cold hand came under the stall and grabbed her ankle, literally scaring her to death. What made it even worse was that though she could feel the grip of the hand, she could not see anything.

**Figure 77: The Mexican Wolf habitat.**

Letting out a horrendous scream, she pulled up her pants just far enough to run and bolted for the outside.

Though there was no doubt in the young lady's mind that a hand had grabbed her ankle, a thorough search by both guards revealed that there was no one in the Zoo compound but the animals, who were unusually restless, and the two guards. What had grabbed her ankle?

I have been told by several people that years before the El Paso Zoo had ever been though of that thre was a cemetery on this spot. Perhaps, just like at the Library downtown, when the property was put to use by the City of El Paso that all of the bodies were never moved. Perhaps as you tour the zoo and look at the animals in their native habitats, you are walking over the bodies of those who were once buried here.

There have also been many stories of figures seen moving near the section of the Zoo that holds the mexican Wolves. Whenever the mysterious figures are seen, the animals literally go wild, just like the police dogs at El Paso High School whenever the phantom pep rally starts. Though the guards have tried, they have always been unable to catch any of these mysterious figures.

Who are these figures seen roaming the Zoo compound after dark? To date, no one has been able to shed any light on the situation.

## CHAPTER FIFTY-NINE
## EL PASO/JUAREZ

This story was told about the Bishop of Durango and an event that occurred to him when he was a young priest living on the border between Juarez and El Paso[136]. Not until the very end did he realize that he was dealing with the supernatural. Everyone that he met looked and acted as if they were among the living and not the dead.

One night as he was getting ready to retire for the evening, three men knocked at his door. When he answered, they begged him to come quickly as a young woman was dying and in need of the services of a priest. He asked if it could not wait until the morning, but the three men hastned to assure him that the young woman in need of his services might not last the night. When he agreed to minister to the young woman, the three men gave him very detailed instructions on how to get to the house where she lived and then the three good Samaritans disappeared into the night[137] leaving the young priest to make his own way to the stricken female.

As quickly as he could, the young priest dressed and gathered what he would need to minister to a dying person. His concern for the dying woman he wanted to help overcame any trepidations he may have had about going out at night on what might be a wild goose chase. Outting all other thoughts out of his mind, the young priest followedthe directions he had been given until he arrived at a modest little house siauted near the border. Slowly, he crossed the clutered yard to step onto the porch.

---

[136] West, John O. Dr, American Folklore Series. 1938.
[137] Many supernatural events seem to involve three mysterious individuals. I would direct the curious to the numerous stories of the three men in black who appear to many witnesses to U.F.O. phenomena.

Gathering his courage, for it appeard to him that either the house was abandoned or that no one was home, he softly knocked on the door. No one answered, but he kept knocking. Finally, he reached down and tried the door knob which turned in his hand. Slowly he pushed the door which opened with a loud creak.

The young priest called out, asking if anyone was home. All he heard in response was a half yell, half moan from the rear of the small house. Slowly, he walked through the rooms. He noted that the house was clean, but showed signs of great age. The furniture was old, but serviceable. Finally he came to a bedroom door through which he could see a young woman in the bed who appeared to be quite ill. However, the moment she saw the young priest, her pale face was covered with a smile. Weakly she raised one hand toward him.

Though he could tell she was so ill and weak that she probably would not last the night, the young preist set about ministering to the young woman as best he could. Finally, after doing his best to make her comfortable and administering the Last Rites just in case his belief that she was dying was correct, the young priest stopped to rest. He was so tired that he knew that he should return home before he fell asleep in the chair in which he sat.

Making sure that the young woman was sleeping peaceably, the priest finally left for home and h is own bed. The next day, he returned with a doctor of his acquaintance. Though the young woman was not one of his parishners, the young priest wanted to do his best to help her. However, he was in for a bit of shock.

Arriving back at the house the next day, the young priest was completely baffled at the changes he saw. The modest house in which he had adminstered the Last Rites the night before was now a complete wreck. The windows were gone and the roof was caved in. The yard was overgrown to the point that it was difficult to even see the porch on which he had stood the previous evening.

Concerned and not a little frightened, the Priest, followed by his friend the doctor, fought his way across the overgrown yard to reach the porch. The previous night, the porch had been sagging but still firm. Now, most of the porch had fallen in, making it difficult to reach the door, which also sagged inward, held up by only one hinge.

Finally gaining access, the two men made for the bedroom where the priest had seen the young girl the night before. The bed was there, but the mattress was gone. Only the springs, rusty and fragile to the touch reminaed. The aged but neatly maintained room from the preiovus evening was now a cluttered disaster. The young priest was totally confused, he knew that this was the house he had been in the previous night, but nothing was the same. It looked as if no one had lived here in many years.

Finally, leaving in total confusion, the priest and the doctor went to the house of the closest neighbor, hoping to get some answered. The elderly woman that answered their knock was able to give them some answered but not ever answer that they needed. The old woman said that a young woman had indeed lived there many years ago, but she had died of a very high fever. Sadly, the young woman, who had been very beautiful, had been struck down so fast that there was not even time to get a priest there to give her the Last Rites. No one had lived in the little house in many years.

So that is the story. Who had the priest administered to in that little house? Was it the young woman, unable to rest until she had the Last Rites? We shall never know for sure.

# CHAPTER SIXTY
# BURGESS HOUSE
### 603 Yandell
### Sunset Heights
### El Paso, Texas

**Figure 78: The Burgess House**

This stately home on Yandell Street in El Paso is now known as the Jane Burgess Perrenot Research Center. This is the mecca for anyone wanting to specialize in El Paso and Southwestern History. Built in 1912 for Richard F.

Burges by J.E. Morgan, this historic home was remodeled by architect O.H. Thorman in 1927[138].

Richard Burgess was a prominent attorney in El Paso. Four generations of the Burgess family have lived in this two story home. The last of the Burgess family to livein this house was Jane Burgess Perrenot. At her death, she willed the home to the El Paso County Historical Society to be used as their headquarters.

I have been told a number of stories about things seen in and about this home by a lot of people over the last year or so. According to one of Mrs. Perrenot's granddaughters, one evening a security guard saw a Nun come from the detached house located in the backyard and cross the yard to vanish at the gate to the drive that runs up the side of the property.

On another occasion, a body was seen hanging from one of the huge trees located in the backyard. There are legends that Pancho Villa spent a great deal of time in the Sunset Heights area and that he buried money in the area. He is alleged to have hung the figure seen haning fom the tree.

## CHAPTER SIXTY-ONE
## OTHER COMMUNITIES IN EL PASO COUNTY

## VINTON, TEXAS

Vinton, Tx River fifteen miles northwest of downtown El Paso in northwestern El Paso County. The town, which was named for J. C. Vinton, a surveyor for the Southern Pacific, was most likely established when the railroad built through the area in the early 1880s. A post office opened there in 1892 {From: Texas Handbook of Texas Online]

## SAN LORENZO, TEXAS

San Lorenzo was located in what is now southeastern El Paso, in southwestern El Paso County. Its origins date to September 1680, when Spanish and Indian refugees fleeing the New Mexico Pueblo Revolt settled in the El Paso area. By October 9, 1680, they had established a camp at San Lorenzo, where Governor Antonio de Otermín established his residence. In the early eighteenth century San Lorenzo developed into a prosperous agricultural community, and by 1750 the population consisted of 150 Suma Indians and a like number of Spanish.

[138] Jones, Harriot Howze, El Paso, A Centennial Portrait, El Paso County Historical Society, Superior Printing, El Paso, Texas. 1972.

In February 1751 the mission lands that had been in the hands of the Franciscans were assigned to the Indians, but by 1754 the Sumas had revolted against Spanish authority. In 1760 the population of San Lorenzo consisted of 192 Spanish and only fifty-eight Indians. The community still existed in the 1860s but was no longer shown on maps of the 1940s, having been superseded by the community of Ascarate, which was later absorbed by the city of El Paso.

## SMELTERTOWN, TEXAS

SMELTERTOWN, TEXAS is an industrial area on Interstate Highway 10, U. S. Highway 80, the Southern Pacific and the Atchison, Topeka and Santa Fe railroads, and the east bank of the Rio Grande, just west of downtown El Paso in western El Paso County. The community came into being with the construction in 1887 of the Kansas City Consolidated Smelting and Refining Company (called ASARCO) copper and lead smelter, after which it was named. In the 1880s the Mexican employees of the smelter began building houses west of the smelter, beside the Rio Grande. San Rosalía Church, named after the Chihuahua town from which most of the first parishioners came, was built in 1891, and E. B. Jones School was established later. The church burned in 1946 and was replaced by the San José de Cristo Rey Church. In 1938 the population of Smeltertown was estimated at 2,500; a post office was established the following year and closed four years later. Smeltertown included a cluster of small adobe dwellings with dirt floors and windows without glass. In 1970, when the population of the community was approximately 500, the city of El Paso filed a $1 million suit against ASARCO, later joined by the state of Texas, charging the company with violations of the Texas Clean Air Act. In December 1971 the El Paso City and County Health Department found in early 1972 tests found that seventy-two Smeltertown residents, including thirty-five children who had to be hospitalized, were suffering from lead poisoning. The city sought to evacuate Smeltertown but many residents resisted. A number of the residents also did not want to give up their homes, many of which had been in the same family for several generations. A 1975 study found levels of "undue lead absorption" in 43 percent of those living within one mile of the smelter. In May 1975 an injunction ordered ASARCO to modernize and make improve-ments. Against their wishes the residents were forced to move; their former homes were razed, leaving only the abandoned school and church buildings and cemetery to mark the site of El Paso's first major industrial community.

## MAGOFFINSVILLE

MAGOFFINSVILLE, TEXAS was established by James Wiley Magoffin in 1849 about a half mile north of the Rio Grande on a site within what is now El Paso, Texas, in El Paso County. Magoffinsville was known as the American El Paso in contrast to the Mexican city across the Rio Grande, El Paso del Norte, now Ciudad Juárez, Mexico. Magoffinsville consisted of a group of adobe buildings around an open square and was watered by an acequia that ran from the river to the square. Magoffin resided in a large, elegant house, in which he lavishly entertained army officers and government officials. John R. Bartlett was among Magoffin's guests, and predicted that Magoffinsville would remain the center of Anglo-American settlement in the El Paso area.<P> A post office operated at Magoffinsville in 1852 and 1853. In January 1854 an army post was established there, with four companies of the Eighth Infantry under Maj. Edmund B. Alexander quartered in buildings rented from Magoffin. In March 1854 the post was officially designated Fort Bliss. Most of the buildings at Magoffinsville, including the fort, were destroyed or severely damaged by a Rio Grande flood in 1868, the year Magoffin died and by 1870 it was described as "only an old dilapidated ranch." The site was incorporated into El Paso in 1873. In 1875 Joseph Magoffin James's son, built a home a short distance west of the site of Magoffinsville, on property that had belonged to his father.

## Isla

LA ISLA. When Mexico became independent in 1821 a chain of six towns in the El Paso area situated from three to five miles apart stretched along the southern bank of the Rio Grande. In the early 1830s the capricious river formed a new channel south of the old one, thus placing three of them-Ysleta, Socorro, and San Elizario-on an island some twenty miles in length and two to four miles in width. For the remainder of the Mexican period this area was called La Isla, "the Island." The Rio Grande continued to flow primarily through its new channel, and by 1848, when the river became the boundary between the United States and Mexico, water had ceased to flow in the Río Viejo, or old riverbed. A flourishing agriculture existed on the Island that featured a fertile soil mixed with a sandy loam and irrigated by a network of acequias, or irrigation canals. The principal products were corn, wheat, fruits, and vegetables. The quality and flavor of the grapes, wine, and brandy produced by the vineyards ranked with the best to be found in the viceroyalty of Spain, according to almost every official who visited the area. Most of the land, haciendas, ranches, and farms-with the exception of the ejidos, the communal holdings of the mission Indians, was owned by the wealthy Paseños of El Paso del Norte (Ciudad Juárez) across the river, the largest town and political capital of the area. Supplementing the Island's agricultural base was the Chihuahua trade along the historic Old San Antonio Road,qv a natural extension of the Santa Fe trade with Missouri that began a decade earlier. sleta and Socorro were established as missions by refugees of the Pueblo Revolt in New Mexico in 1680-Ysleta for the Tiguas and Socorro for the Piros. Both missions were swept away by the flooding river in the early 1830s, but they were at length replaced by the present structures-Socorro in 1843 and

Ysleta in 1851. San Elizario, a presidio that was moved upriver to the El Paso area in 1879, became the nucleus of a town. According to a census of 1841 the total population of the three Island settlements was 2,850. Socorro was the largest with 1,101, San Elizario was second with 1,018, and Ysleta had 731 residents. Each town was governed by an alcaldeqv appointed by the ayuntamientoqv of El Paso del Norte, which was controlled by the landowning and mercantile aristocracy. Most heads of families on La Isla were farm workers or servants. Indians were dependents, and poverty was widespread. The two-room adobeqv structure was the general pattern for all. During the Mexican Warqv Col. Alexander Doniphan's force brought the El Paso area under United States control. The Treaty of Guadalupe Hidalgoqv of February 2, 1848, which officially ended the war, provided that the new international boundary was to be "the Rio Grande . . . following the deepest channel . . . to the point where it strikes the southern boundary of New Mexico." American officials declared theIsland to be United States territory, and in November 1848 Col. John M. Washington, military governor of New Mexico, appointed T. Frank White president and directed him to extend his jurisdiction over all of the territory east of the river that had formerly been a part of Chihuahua. In February 1849 Mexican officials reported that an armed force of the United States had occupied Ysleta, Socorro, and San Elizario and had taken possession of all the lands, including ejidos. Mexican protests proved futile. Meanwhile, by mid-1849 the discovery of gold in California had brought into the El Paso area hordes of immigrants, many of whom decided to remain. By late 1849 five settlements had been established by Anglo-Americans-Frontera, Hart's Mill, Coon's Ranch, Magoffinsville, and Stephenson's Ranch. These five, together with the three Mexican settlements on the Island, indicated that a bilingual, bicultural complex was taking shape at the Pass of the North. That the Mexican town of San Elizario should become El Paso County's first county seat is significant.

## Anthony

ANTHONY, TEXAS (El Paso County). Anthony is in El Paso County on the border of Texas and New Mexico and is located on the Atchison, Topeka and Santa Fe Railway and State Highway 20 sixteen miles northwest of downtown El Paso. It was reportedly named by a Mexican-American woman who built a chapel to St. Anthony of Padua sometime before 1884. A post office was established on the El Paso County side in March of that year but was never in operation. The Texas community later became known as La Tuna, after the Federal Correctional Institution located there, at which a post office was open from 1932 to 1965. In the early 1940s the population was estimated at only twenty, but ten years later, after the community incorporated as Anthony, the population estimate had grown to 1,200. It declined to 1,082 in the early 1960s, then grew to 2,154 in the early 1970s, 2,640 in the early 1980s, and 3,328 in

1990. A post office was established in Anthony in 1981. In 1988 the Anthony Chamber of Commerce named the town the Leap Year Capital of the World, and the Worldwide Leap Year Birthday Club, open to anyone born on February 29. Leap Year Birthday Club had more than 100 members by 1992.

## YSLETA

Ysleta, now part of the city of El Paso, is perhaps the oldest town in

Ysleta Mission
1910

**Figure 79: Mission at Ysleta.**

Texas. It was one of several agricultural communities started on the Rio Grande by Spaniards and Indians after the Pueblo Revolt in New Mexico in 1680. The Tigua Indians, who were brought from their pueblo at Isleta, New Mexico, in 1680-82, have occupied the area continuously since. The new Ysleta del Sur ("little island of the south") was located a league and a half east of Guadalupe Mission at the site of present Ciudad Juárez. The first Mass was celebrated near Ysleta on October 12, 1680. By 1691 a temporary church was replaced by an adobe building that was later washed away by a flood in 1740, rebuilt four years later on higher ground.

The roof and bell tower were damaged by fire in 1907. The mission's name has been changed several times, recently to Our Lady of Mount Carmel. Between 1829 and 1831 the Rio Grande cut a new channel, which placed Ysleta on an island formed by the old and new channels. When the deepest channel became the international boundary in 1848, Ysleta became part of the United States. The population of Ysleta showed steady growth numbered 560 (429 Indians and 131 others) in 1760, and 8,550 in 1960. Henry L. Dexter became the town's first mayor in 1859. This city government did not survive nor did one that operated in the early 1870s. An election in 1880 approved incorporation, and in 1889 the town council declared Ysleta a city. After a stormy period of squabbles over water supply, land grants, limited resources, the town government dissolved in 1895. In 1873 Ysleta replaced San Elizario as the El Paso county seat. The coming of the railroads in 1881 changed the population center of the county, and made El Paso the county seat. A bridge was built across the Rio Grande in 1929 linking Ysleta with Zaragosa, Mexico. In 1955 El Paso annexed Ysleta, although residents of the smaller town had voted against the move. The annexation was upheld by the United States Supreme Court. Ysleta Independent School District was allowed to retain its identity. The Tiguas, who helped the United States military as scouts during the Indian wars, were recognized as a tribe by the state of Texas in 1967 and by the United States Congress in 1968. They have established a housing area and various business enterprises on their reservation in the oldest part of Ysleta.

## CANUTILLO

Canutillo is an incorporated community on the east bank of the Rio Grande and on U.S. Highways 80 and 85 about twelve miles northwest of downtown El Paso in northwestern El Paso County. The community also was on the Atchison, Topeka and Santa e Railway. The story of the town begins in June 1823, when the Canutillo land grant was assigned to Juan Maria Ponce De Leonqv and twenty-nine other citizens of El Paso del Norte (what is now Juarez, Chihuahua, Mexico. A small agricultural settlement was established in 1824, but Apache raiders forced residents to abandon it in 1833. The site remained vacant until after the arrival of Anglo-American settlers in the mid-1800s. The Canutillo ranch became a principal source of income for James Wiley Magoffin but in 1855 Jose Sanchez and others established their ownership as descendants of the original grantees. The state of Texas recognized their claim in 1858, and the land grant was surveyed by Anson Mills two years later. In 1874 a court order divided ownership of the grant among Joseph Magoffin, Josiah F. Crosby, William W.

Mills Anson Mills, John S. Watts, and Sanchez. The Canutillo Townsite and Land Company was chartered in 1909, and a post office was established there two years later. In 1914 Canutillo was identified as a rural post office and had four general stores to serve the surrounding population. The community's estimated population was 300 in 1925. By the mid-1950s its estimated population was 1,326, and by the early 1990s it was 4,442.

# CHAPTER SIXTY-TWO
# UPDATE ON THE
# GREAT FORT BLISS/WHITE SANDS TREASURE

I wrote about the White Sands Treasure in the first volume of this series and have had numerous questions directed at me about what happened to this supposedly vast treasure. My best answer is found within this story that ran in Freedom Magazine in 1986.

### The Mystery of the $30 Billion Treasure
#### Part I
#### From Freedom Magazine, June 1986

You are about to read a story that strains the imagination. It is about the disappearance of a fortune of up to $30 billion in gold bullion. When it was first presented as a "tip" to a Freedom Magazine reporter in El Paso, Texas, in 1981, it was discounted as beyond belief. However, when dozens of unrelated, independent sources began to corroborate the story, it could no longer be disregarded, no matter how bizarre. The following story, constructed from personal interviews, documents and confidential reports, is the result of a five-year investigation.
By Thomas G. Whittle

In one of the most closely guarded crimes of recent history, hundreds, perhaps thousands, of tons of gold bullion were secretly and illegally removed from caverns on White Sands Missile Range in New Mexico, the beneficiaries allegedly including former President Lyndon Johnson and individuals connected with the U.S. Army, the Central Intelligence Agency and organized crime.

The caverns are located in and around Victorio Peak, in a remote, rugged section of south-central New Mexico. The peak, named after a 19th century Apache war chief, apparently served as a repository for immense quantities of gold mined centuries ago by Spaniards and Indians and smelted into tens of thousands of crudely formed bars.

Between 1937 and 1939, Milton Ernest "Doc" Noss (left) and his wife, Ova (right), working with family members and trusted associates, reportedly removed up to 350 gold bars from the depths of Victorio Peak.

An investigation by Freedom has probed the history of that region, particularly the nearly 49 years since gold bars were first found in that area in November 1937 by a man named Milton Ernest "Doc" Noss, as fascinating a character as ever held a six-gun.

Background research into the enormous wealth contained in the caverns of Victorio Peak revealed many eyewitness reports of the gold.

In 1937, the peak was miles from nowhere. Its occasional visitors included hunting parties, and Doc Noss and his wife, Ova, were on one such expedition in search of deer. They had trekked in from Hot Springs, New Mexico, a town since renamed Truth or Consequences.

According to accounts from members of the Noss family, Doc bagged no deer, but he found something that whetted his appetite for the area — a shaft near the top of Victorio Peak

**Figure 80: Doc and Ova Noss**

which led into the bowels of the mountain. Doc mentioned nothing of his find to the group, choosing instead to return to the site a couple of days later with Ova.

Using ropes for support and guided by his flashlight's wavering beam, Doc Noss descended a series of interconnecting chambers which led downward for 186 feet.

Years later, in 1946, Doc discussed his exploration with Gordon E. Herkenhoff, field representative of the New Mexico State Land Office. In a four-page confidential report entitled "Field Examination of Noss Mining Claims, Hembrillo District," Herkenhoff recorded a description:

"Dr. Noss claims that beyond the 186-foot depth, there is an incline downward at 45 degrees for 72 feet.... Beyond that there is supposed to be another incline upward at about 30 degrees for some distance (40 feet as I remember it) where entrance is gained to a cave some 2700 feet long which contains many evidences that the cave was occupied as living quarters by a large group of humans for many years."

The group evidently had some grisly practices, for the first thing Doc Noss encountered was a row of skeletons, 27 in all. Each skeleton had its hands bound behind it to a large wooden stake driven into the ground. Doc later brought one of the eerie things out.[2]

Doc's object at the time of discovery, of course, was more than old bones. Passing through the large cavern, he came to a series of smaller caves — "rooms," he called them. In one "room" he discovered a large stash of old swords

264\Spirits of the Border, Volume III

and guns, papers and letters from the 19<sup>th</sup> century, and a king's ransom in jewels and coins.

Returning through the main cavern, he noticed an immense stack of metal bars off to one side. There were thousands of them, covered with old, dusty buffalo hides.

After he got back to the surface, Doc told Ova what he had seen, and almost as an afterthought mentioned the long row of metal bars. He also told his wife that there were "enough gold and silver coins to load 60 to 80 mules."

Ova convinced Doc to return to the big cave and bring one of the heavy bars back up. Begrudgingly, he did so.

After scraping a small section of the bar clean, she exclaimed, "Doc, this is gold!"

Letha Guthrie, Ova's eldest daughter from a previous marriage, described the next few years as a very happy time for the Noss family, one of simple, hard work with a bright, limitless future. Deferring to Doc's belief that the gold would all be taken by the government should his find become too broadly known, the work force was confined to the immediate family and a couple of handfuls of trusted associates.

Ova Noss, her two sons, Harold and Marvin, and her two daughters, Letha and Dorothy, helped Doc in the strenuous task of removing the bars, one at a time, from the depths of the peak. Letha told Freedom that she herself handled 12 to 15 of the bars, "and I even put one up and hid it for four days."

Six men who worked with Doc in removing the gold — C.D. Patterson, Don Breech, Edgar F. Foreman, Leo D. O'Connell, Eppie Montoya and B.D. Lampros — later signed sworn affidavits regarding their experiences.

Lampros, for example, described having his photograph taken with Colonel Willard E. Holt of Lordsburg, New Mexico; each held an end of a bar while it was being sawed in half.

Joe Andregg, an electrician from Santa Fe, New Mexico, reflected on the days when he worked with Doc Noss in the late 1930s. "I was just a kid, about 13 or 14 years old," he told this writer. Asked about the bars, he said, "I sawed one in two with a hacksaw."

One person who worked with Doc Noss inside the cave was Jose Serafin Sedillo of Cuchillo, New Mexico. He told this writer that the gold bars in the cave were "stacked like cordwood."

The bars that Noss and his crew removed from Victorio Peak were, in general, crudely formed, indicating the use of primitive smelting processes.

Estimates vary on the number of bars removed, ranging up to 350 or so.

According to members of the family, there would have been more, but Doc's work was abruptly and unexpectedly brought to a halt in August 1939 when a dynamite blast, set to enlarge a narrow passage, instead caved the passage in, sealing off the main cavern.

Doc Noss spent the next 10 years in intermittent efforts to regain access to the hoard, in vain. He worked with a succession of partners, the last of whom,

Charlie Ryan of Alice, Texas, shot and killed Noss in an altercation in Hatch, New Mexico, on March 5, 1949.

The night before his death, perhaps sensing that a business deal was going sour, Doc enlisted the aid of a cowboy named Tony Jolley to shuffle the locations of various stashes of the bars. There were 110 gold bars moved that night, according to an affidavit obtained by this writer and sworn to by Jolley.

The affidavit states, in part: "In March of 1949 I handled 110 rough [sic] poured bars of gold in the area which is now White Sands Missile Range which is now the area of Victorio Peak. On the night of March 4, 1949, I went with Doc Noss and dug up 20 bars of gold at a windmill in the desert east of Hatch, New Mexico, and reburied them in the basin where Victorio Peak is. We took 90 bars ... stacked by a mine shaft at Victorio Peak and reburied them 10 in a pile scattered throughout the basin with the exception of 30 bars that we buried in a grassy flat near the road we came out on."

After the death of Doc Noss, Ova and her family continued efforts to regain access to the big treasure room. The U.S. Army, which gained control of the area when it was converted to a bombing range during the Second World War, refused her request to bring in an excavation firm and ultimately ordered the Nosses to stay out of the area.

Word of the Doc Noss treasure spread, and keeping people out of the area was no easy chore. In November 1958, a team of four weekend gold seekers rediscovered the hoard.

Led by U.S. Air Force Captain Leonard V. Fiege, the four had done extensive research on Victorio Peak, poring over old documents and records, and even traveling south into Mexico to check stories there regarding a man who has often been linked with the origin of the gold, Padre Philip La Rue.

All four men — Fiege, Thomas Berlett, Ken Prather and Milleadge Wessel — were, at the time of their find, employees at Holloman Air Force Base in New Mexico. This writer conducted extensive interviews with Thomas Berlett. According to Berlett, the four men proceeded down a fault into the peak for about 150 feet, at which point their progress was stopped by a large boulder. They dug under it, and Berlett and Fiege moved past it for another 100 to 125 feet, coming eventually to what Berlett described as a small cavern, approximately eight feet wide by 10 or 12 feet long.

In the room were two large stacks of gold bars, each roughly six feet high, three feet wide and eight feet long. A third, smaller stack, pyramidal in shape, stood about three feet high.

Berlett and Fiege had found a different passage into Victorio Peak, leading into a different chamber.

The room had been undisturbed for so long that the dust, according to Berlett, lay several inches thick. The slightest movement stirred up a cloud. Nearly choking, the two men hastily marked their claim and made their exit.

Before leaving, both men had observed an old wooden cross on one of the walls. Berlett viewed this as substantiation for the theory that Spaniards had been responsible for stashing the gold.

In September 1961, Berlett and Fiege swore to the specifics of their discovery in detailed affidavits provided to federal officials. They also were given — and passed — lie detector tests.

Among those who attested to the accessibility of the peak's treasure was Lynn Porter, a businessman now residing in San Diego, California.

On the night of September 1, 1968, Porter drove to the peak with a friend and a civilian security guard from White Sands Missile Range named Clarence McDonald. The three men had been on a hunting party when McDonald, who reportedly had imbibed several cans of beer, began talking freely about a huge stash of gold. Porter and his friends were amused at his story and McDonald, to prove that what he was saying was true, took the two other hunters on a moonlit drive to Victorio Peak.

A narrow passage through rocks kept the bulky Porter from following the other two men into the depths of the peak. He stood guard while McDonald and the other man descended into a large cavern, returning with a crudely formed gold bar roughly 2 ½ inches wide by 7 inches long.

The gold, Porter's friend stated breathlessly, ran in a tremendous stack along one side of the cavern — stretching for approximately 200 yards. The two men told Porter they had taken one of the smaller bars from the stack because they felt it would be easier to handle than one of the large bars in moving through the long and sometimes difficult passage.

After some discussion, the men decided that Porter should take the bar to a close friend of his who worked in the provost marshal's office in nearby Fort Bliss, Texas. Possession of gold was against the law at the time, and the men reasoned that the bar would provide evidence to bring about an authorized, legal expedition to remove the vast quantity of gold. The men believed that Porter's friend was in a good position to help arrange an official government expedition to claim the gold.

Porter subsequently brought the gold bar to the close friend, who was an Army major.

The major took the bar and told Porter to check back with him in a few days. He did, only to find that in the short, three-day interim the major had been whisked away, transferred to the Pentagon. His wife and his two school-age children had also abruptly left.

The gold bar had disappeared without a trace. No one in the provost marshal's office to whom Porter talked would admit to knowing anything about the gold, and he was warned by the provost marshal that any future "trespassing" would be dealt with severely.

There is evidence to indicate that many gold bars were removed from Victorio Peak a short time after Lynn Porter brought the bar to the Fort Bliss provost marshal's office.

Going public with information about the gold stored in Victorio Peak or removed from it, however, is something that people familiar with the subject are generally reluctant to do. And for good reason.

Chester Stout, for example, a retired Army sergeant, traced the removal of two large truckloads of gold from Victorio Peak, but later had to move out of New Mexico; his life was threatened because, as he was told, he "knew too much."

In all, eight persons told this writer they had received direct threats against their lives or against the lives of their families. Sam Scott, for example, a retired airline pilot, was warned in 1977 to keep clear of anything regarding Victorio Peak for at least five years under pain of having his home firebombed and his wife and daughter killed.

The sources of this threat, according to the man who relayed the threat to Scott, were two agents of the U.S. Central Intelligence Agency.

The daughter of another man, Harvey Snow, died from a gunshot wound in the head after Snow had disregarded repeated warnings in regard to the peak.

Thayer Snipes of El Paso, Texas, swore to an affidavit regarding another death. The affidavit states:

"I, Thayer Snipes, first being duly sworn, on my oath state:

"That in the latter part of 1972, I had stopped by the Airport Chevron Station at the corner of Airway Blvd. And Montana Ave. in El Paso, Texas, to visit with a friend, Frank Foss, owner of the station.

"That while visiting Foss, a man we both knew, E.M. Guthrie, drove in to the station in a late model Ford Thunderbird.

"That I had known E.M. Guthrie for about three years prior to this meeting and knew him to be the husband of Letha Guthrie, stepdaughter of Milton Ernest 'Doc' Noss.

"That I knew E.M. Guthrie had taken an active personal interest in the fate of gold located in Victorio Peak by Doc Noss.

"That I walked over to E.M. Guthrie on this occasion in 1972, greeted him, and invited him out to dinner with myself and Frank Foss.

"That he seemed very disturbed, nervous and agitated, and refused my invitation to dinner, saying, 'I'm running for my life.'

"That he also said, 'The Mob is after me.'

"That three or four weeks later Frank Foss told me that E.M. had called him and said he was in Central America.

"That about a month after that, I heard E.M. had been beaten to death in California.

"That after he had been beaten to death, according to the information I received, his body was put back into his car, the car was doused with kerosene or gasoline, and then set aflame."

Another source confirmed the manner and the circumstances of E.M. Guthrie's death, noting that "it was listed as just a natural death, but he'd been worked over with a baseball bat." This source said that he had hired a team of experienced investigators to dig into Guthrie's death and more than 30 other deaths in connection with a massive, continuing cover-up of the removal of gold from Victorio Peak.

Bill Shriver, an international dealer in precious metals who proved very helpful in the initial stages of this investigation until his death, brought the total still higher. According to a close relative interviewed by Freedom, Shriver was "murdered." The relative said that Shriver "was beaten up in California, beaten about the kidneys and the head" and subsequently died from his injuries.

The cloud of death shrouding Victorio Peak has reached far.

Edward Atkins of Decatur, Illinois, had been a claimant to the peak's gold and was vigorously pursuing that claim via attorney Darrell Holmes of Athens, Georgia, when Holmes died under mysterious circumstances.

According to Atkins' son, John, Holmes possessed key materials which were being used to press the Army into allowing Atkins and Holmes access to Victorio Peak. These materials, including tape-recorded sessions wherein Lyndon Johnson discussed the disposition of some of the gold bars on his ranch, disappeared from Holmes' office at the time of his death in February 1977.

Edward Atkins himself died, reportedly of a heart attack, in April 1979 while returning to Illinois from El Paso on a matter pertaining to his claim. At least one close relative was convinced that Atkins' death was not accidental and that it was directly related to his getting too close to the true story of Victorio Peak.

Lyndon Johnson's name loomed large in the information that Freedom uncovered, with various sources claiming that the president was instrumental in the planning and execution of the removal of the gold. The charges concerning LBJ's involvement included the following:

• A retired White Sands Missile Range security guard, residing in El Paso, Texas, indicated that he observed Johnson and former Texas Governor John Connally spending about 10 days in the desolate area around Victorio Peak in the late 1960s. According to the security guard, Johnson and Connally headed a team which brought in sophisticated excavation equipment to remove gold from the peak, "the most modern I've ever seen," he said. "They even brought in their own security guards," he added.

• A retired U.S. Army officer said that while on duty at the provost marshal's office on White Sands Missile Range during the period of LBJ's presidency, he was visited by four men in a late model Cadillac Fleetwood Brougham who sought permission to drive to Victorio Peak. One man, a Mr. Moon, said that he was from the White House Secret Service detail and he showed the officer a green, laminated card which stated "Secret Service, Division of the White House." Another man, an engineer named Dick Richardson, told the officer that he was a boyhood friend of Lyndon Johnson's and that he had personally counted 18,888 gold bars in one stack in a cavern at Victorio Peak, each bar weighing about 60 pounds.3

• Bill Shriver, before his death, told this writer that he had a copy of a transcribed order from Lyndon Johnson describing in detail how the president wanted a military escort to handle the supply of gold taken out of Victorio Peak and taken to his ranch. Shriver also said that he had copies of other "presidential messages, several initialed by LBJ," dealing with the clandestine, illegal removal of the gold.

• A source interviewed in Mexico stated that it was common knowledge in the towns of Jimenez and Camargo that Johnson's 110,000-acre ranch in Chihuahua served as a storage area for a very large amount of gold flown in by a four-engine, propeller-driven aircraft in the late 1960s.

• Still another source reported knowledge of aircraft movements of the gold from Chihuahua to Vancouver, British Columbia, during the period of Johnson's presidency. According to this source, a B-24 was used to transport at least seven loads of the peak's gold, with up to 20 tons of gold moving in each load.

• Another source, who asked to remain unidentified, stated that he had personally interviewed several men who had brought a large load of the peak's gold to Johnson's ranch.

According to this same source, Victorio Peak "was just like a private vault to certain high-ranking people." They would "go in periodically and get what they wanted. They would have the proper persons on guard duty."

Possession of gold by private American citizens was illegal under federal law throughout the period of the Johnson presidency. In addition, Victorio Peak lay on land owned by the state of New Mexico, and removal of gold without permission of the state violated New Mexico law.4

A number of sources also independently named Major General John G. Shinkle, the commander of White Sands Missile Range from June 1960 to July 1962, as knowing about the movement of tons of gold from Victorio Peak. Reached for comment in Cocoa Beach, Florida, General Shinkle adamantly denied any knowledge of the gold and refused to comment at all on the story.

Large movements of bullion from the peak went on for nearly a decade, with the largest single removal of gold occurring in 1976, according to Bill Shriver. This was shortly before a much-publicized expedition, entitled Operation Goldfinder, took place at the site in March 1977.

Shriver estimated the total amount of gold removed from Victorio Peak at 25 million troy ounces, of which 10 million came out in 1976. The gold, he said, was removed and "smelted into old Mexican bars, 50-pound bars." The gold in its new form, he noted, had no marks to identify its origin.

The gold was then shipped to Switzerland and sold in a new form in Zurich. "The buying entity was a Middle Eastern principal," Shriver said.

The actual movement of the gold in this last, largest shipment, Shriver said, was "done by [U.S.] military aircraft." Independent of Shriver, another source traced a number of large removals from Victorio Peak. He estimated the total amount of gold coming from the peak at a staggering 96 million troy ounces, worth, at $320 an ounce, nearly $31 billion.

Army spokesmen have consistently dismissed all reports of Victorio Peak gold as "rumors." An apparent propaganda campaign, in fact, has been conducted for many years by the Army in order to dispel these reports and to keep treasure seekers away from the missile range.

Part II: The bizarre history of Victorio Peak continues to unravel as the Army, the Treasury Department and the Secret Service authorize a top secret operation aimed at locating and bringing out the gold.

Ova Noss, Leonard Fiege and others don't listen when they are told to "shut up" — and they pay the price.

References:
1 Freedom Magazine obtained copies of the 1946 New Mexico land office correspondence regarding Doc Noss' claim.

2 Chester R. Johnson Jr., "Explorations at Victorio Peak," Division of Research, Museum of New Mexico, 1963. The official version of this report, released after U.S. Army censorship, deleted numerous key references to gold bars and to secret government activities contained in Chester R. Johnson's original report. The author obtained copies of both the official version and the original, uncensored report.

3 While the purity of the gold cannot be accurately assessed at this time, the mid-1960s value of this stack, which was about one-third of the total amount in that cavern, would be more than $400 million at $32 per troy ounce. At a 1986 value of $320 per troy ounce, that stack alone would be worth more than $4 billion.

4 Those who took the gold were also taking it over what had been claims filed by Doc Noss, members of his family and others who had staked claims to the gold with the state of New Mexico as early as the 1930s. U.S. Army rights to use the land did not include mineral rights, which were retained by the state.

## The Mystery of the $30 Billion Treasure
## Part II
## From *Freedom* Magazine, July 1986

**Figure 81:** *According to Freedom's sources, hundreds — perhaps thousands — of tons of gold were secretly and illegally removed from Victorio Peak on White Sands Missile Range in New Mexico between 1964 and 1977.*

*In the first part of this series, **Freedom** reported the bizarre story of a fabulous hoard of up to $30 billion in gold bullion sequestered in a remote location on White Sands Missile Range in New Mexico.*

*A large number of sources had reported to **Freedom** that the gold was secretly and illegally removed from its underground chambers by a combination of interests that allegedly included the U.S. Army, the Central Intelligence Agency, organized crime and former President Lyndon B. Johnson.*

*The peak's modern history began in November 1937 with the discovery by Milton Ernest "Doc" Noss of an immense quantity of gold bars. Over a period of about 21 months, Noss removed a large number of gold bars from one of the caverns, a fact attested to by more than a dozen people who worked directly with him. Estimates on the number of bars removed by Doc Noss and his co-workers range up to approximately 350.*

*During an attempt to enlarge a passage to the gold in August 1939, the shaft caved in, leading to frenzied and unsuccessful efforts by Doc, his family and a few close associates to regain access to the hoard through hundreds of feet of rocks and rubble.*

*Nineteen years after the cave-in, in November 1958, U.S. Air Force Captain Leonard V. Fiege led a team of treasure hunters who discovered a second, smaller treasure in another Victorio Peak cavern.*

*As described in Part I, Fiege and Airman Thomas L. Berlett found three stacks of gold bars that had lain undisturbed for so many years that they were covered by several inches of thick dust.*

*Freedom* also unveiled some of the further history of Victorio Peak, including numerous reports by eyewitnesses and others that a tremendous quantity of gold bars were secretly and illegally removed from the mountain over a period of years, principally from 1964 to 1977.

In this article, *Freedom* continues the story.

By Thomas G. Whittle

The clandestine removal of tons of gold from Victorio Peak left legitimate claimants to the treasure with no money and little recourse. Principal among these unlucky individuals were Ova Noss and Leonard Fiege.

Ova had been with Doc Noss when he made his 1937 discovery of the tremendous stash of gold bullion inside Victorio Peak.

Fiege, Thomas Berlett and their companions — Ken Prather and Milleadge Wessel — were, at the time of their find, employees of Holloman Air Force Base, located just east of White Sands Missile Range.

As leader of the four treasure hunters, Fiege worked within the Air Force chain of command to get permission to legally return to Hembrillo Basin — the large, bowl-shaped area surrounding Victorio Peak — in order to recover the treasure.

In seeking to return to the site of his find, Fiege solicited the assistance of Holloman's staff judge advocate, Lieutenant Colonel Sigmund I. Gasiewicz.

The aboveboard attempts by Fiege, Berlett and their companions were stymied, however. The White Sands commander, Major General John G. Shinkle, refused all requests for permission to enter the area, including one made by Air Force Major General Monte Canterbury on behalf of Fiege and his companions.

In August 1961, after forming a partnership with three Air Force attorneys, the men were allowed to meet in Washington, D.C., with senior representatives of the Department of the Army, the Department of the Treasury, the Secret Service and the Bureau of the Mint. Chairing the meeting was the director of the Bureau of the Mint. At the meeting, the four treasure hunters and the three lawyers stated their case. And, nearly three years after the discovery, the men were finally allowed to return.

The operation itself, a five-day affair in August 1961, was "carried out as a top secret project," according to a heavily censored Secret Service report.

Those accompanying the four treasure hunters included General Shinkle and agent Liliburn "Pat" Boggs from the Secret Service's Albuquerque office.

The passage used by Fiege and Berlett in reaching the gold was found. Unfortunately, as noted in the Secret Service report, the final 40 feet to the gold "was blocked by large boulders that could not be removed by hand or shoveled away." Although the expedition had General Shinkle as a supervisor and 14 armed military policemen as guards, no equipment heavier than shovels and picks had been brought. It ended fruitlessly.

A heavily deleted August 31, 1961, Secret Service memorandum obtained by *Freedom* shows that on that date the missile range's provost marshal met with Pat Boggs in the Albuquerque Secret Service office. The provost marshal stated that he was seeing Boggs at the order of the missile range commander.

According to the memorandum, the commander, General Shinkle, "was anxious to determine the degree of interest" of the Secret Service in the gold.

In the memorandum, Boggs records that the interview with the provost marshal was interrupted by a telephone call from the Holloman commander, who wanted to know whether the Treasury Department would "permit exploration of the tunnel on weekends."

Boggs resumed his interview with the provost marshal. The provost marshal "stated that should any gold be recovered from the tunnel, he would immediately notify the writer [Boggs] so that possession of the gold could be taken by this Service for delivery to the Federal Reserve Bank Branch at El Paso, Texas."

After a flurry of additional memos, reports and top secret conferences, work at the site continued, this time with heavier equipment.

In the interim, Fiege and Berlett had authenticated affidavits they had previously written regarding the gold they had found by taking, and passing, lie detector tests. After those tests, the order to dig came — not from General Shinkle, but from Secretary of the Army Elvis J. Stahr Jr.

New Mexico law is quite clear on the point that there can be no mining or treasure troving on any land in the state without approval of the State Land Office. In carrying forward with this top secret project, neither the Army nor the Secret Service had consulted with that office.

On October 28, 1961, word of the digging leaked out after four civilians — friends of Ova Noss — "wandered" into Hembrillo Basin.

News of the Army's activities quickly reached Ova, who wasted no time in telling Oscar Jordan, general counsel of the State Land Office in Santa Fe, that her claim was being jumped.

Jordan sent S.A. Floersheim, supervisor of the State Land Office's Lands and Minerals Division, to investigate. Floersheim, in a memorandum dated November 6, 1961, wrote that he contacted Colonel Jaffe, the White Sands staff judge advocate.

Floersheim told Jaffe that he wanted "to make an investigation of the land down there in question to determine if any activity on the part of unauthorized persons had taken place."

The colonel, in Floersheim's words, "was not too cooperative."

When Floersheim indicated that if necessary he would secure a court order from a U.S. district judge, Colonel Jaffe "attempted to assure me that there was no operation, that it was all a myth."

The "myth," however, was quickly shown to be fact. The four men who had visited the peak — Ray Bradley, Bob Bradley, Hugh Moreland and R.B. Gray — had drawn up notarized affidavits of what they saw and heard. The affidavits were specific, down to the serial number on one of the jeeps.

Before Jaffe was confronted with the affidavits, he told essentially the same story to Ova Noss and her attorney, and on a separate occasion to Ova's son, Harold Beckwith.

According to a later account, "When informed of the affidavits, he [Colonel Jaffe] became quite upset."

Eventually, Oscar Jordan and S.A. Floersheim got the digging to stop. The Army's less-than-straightforward practices, however, were not corrected.

A report, for example, entitled "Explorations at Victorio Peak," was prepared by the Museum of New Mexico in 1963, summarizing the highlights of the peak's history. This report was heavily censored by the Army. All references to Captain Fiege's 1958 discovery of gold bars and to the subsequent illegal excavation efforts by the Army — two full pages of material — were removed from the final report.[1]

Furthermore, the Army misrepresented some important excavation work in 1963 done by the museum and Gaddis Mining Company of Denver, Colorado. The museum had obtained permission to conduct an expedition to Victorio Peak in 1963. As a key part of the expedition, extensive digging was done by Gaddis Mining Company in an attempt to contact a passage that would lead to one of the caverns.

The Gaddis team ran out of its allotted time and money before it could reach the shaft that would have led to a cavern. The team, therefore, was forced to leave the site before completing its work.

The man who supervised the work for Gaddis on the 1963 expedition, geologist Loren Smith of Denver, was not happy with the results and wanted to return to finish the job. As recently as 1981, Smith wrote a letter to the secretary of the Army requesting permission to conduct a 90-day search.

"We didn't give up," Smith told this writer in reference to the 1963 expedition. "We just ran out of money. We had spent $100,000, and when we ran out we were getting close to where Fiege found the bars."

The Museum of New Mexico also wanted to get back in. In a 1965 application to return to the peak, the museum stated, "The results of the exploration program conducted in 1963 proved the existence of a number of open cavities within Victorio Peak similar to those described by the individual who claimed to have been in the caves and seen the artifacts and treasure."

And yet, through the 1960s and 1970s, the Army would repeatedly and falsely state that the 1963 expedition had "proved" there were no caves or caverns.

According to Sam Scott, a retired airline pilot who with his brother, Norman, led another expedition into the area in 1977, the Gaddis effort got very close to the fault which led down to the main cavern — the passage which Doc Noss had apparently used to haul up hundreds of bars of gold.

The Army consistently misrepresented what occurred on the Gaddis expedition, citing the "negative results" of the 1963 expedition as a reason all future treasure searches would forever be banned as a matter of official policy.

The reason was never sufficient, however. In the late 1960s and into the 1970s, pressure for a bona fide search for the treasure continued to mount.

Among the leaders in the push for a new expedition was nationally known attorney F. Lee Bailey, who represented a group of some 52 claimants to the gold. A search of at least a cursory nature seemed inevitable.

Another expedition to the peak was finally mounted. With a twist of irony, this very limited search was dubbed by the Army "Operation Goldfinder." Although brief and tightly constrained, it became the ultimate excuse to ban people from Victorio Peak.

The ostensible purpose of Goldfinder, as expressed at the time by expedition leader Norman Scott, was to "validate or not validate" stories about the gold and other treasure.

When contacted, Scott said that he and his company, Expeditions Unlimited Inc. of Pompano Beach, Florida, had been "used" by the Army.

Asked to elaborate, Scott expressed the theory that he had served as a "patsy" to give the appearance of a search in order to release the tremendous pressure that had been brought to bear on the Army by F. Lee Bailey and others.

One of the claimants to the gold who was there during Operation Goldfinder was Joe Newman of El Paso, Texas. Newman told this writer that he had found three piles of gold bars in a small cave within the peak in November 1973. He counted the bars in one pile — there were 600. The other piles were identical. Each bar, he said, weighed up to 60 pounds. They were roughly formed, as though from a primitive smelting process.

Newman provided photographs to *Freedom* showing extensive activity around Victorio Peak shortly before Operation Goldfinder. According to Newman, the photographs demonstrate that Victorio Peak gold was removed just weeks before the expedition.

By the time of Operation Goldfinder, the entrance Newman used to gain access to the small cavern was covered up by the Army. All possible entrances to the peak, according to Newman, had been sealed with concrete, steel bars, steel plates, mounds of earth, or two or more of those in combination.

"There was no way in hell we could get in there without heavy equipment," Newman said. " And then we showed up there without bulldozers, without backhoes, without anything but picks and shovels."

When heavy equipment finally did arrive at the site, both Newman and Sam Scott charge, its use was restricted to locations where "we knew there wasn't any gold."

Attorney F. Lee Bailey had similar words. Bailey acknowledged that his group — one of a half-dozen claimant groups on the expedition — had been stopped in its efforts to dig at Bloody Hands, a site in an arroyo by Victorio Peak so named because of five red hand prints on the arroyo wall.

B        ecause those he represented couldn't look where they wanted to, Bailey told this writer that the expedition "didn't really prove anything one way or another."

There was universal agreement among all of the participants interviewed — except for Army spokesmen — that the 1977 expedition had been poorly executed and had not satisfactorily explored for gold.

Sam Scott charged that the expedition was "conceived to fail." He continued, "I originally made arrangements for a 60-day expedition. The Army cut that down to 30 and then to 10."

Nearly 19 years after he had made the dramatic three-stack find, Leonard Fiege crawled down the long passage which led to the same room. In the intervening years, much had changed.

As Fiege told newsmen during Operation Goldfinder, "It's entirely different. There are timbers in there now. It's all shored up." And the gold was gone.


Ova Noss continued to press the family's claim to the treasure after Doc Noss was shot and killed in 1949. Here she makes a point during Operation Goldfinder in 1977.

Ova Noss climbed to the top of the peak. In the same place she had scraped the crusty covering from the first bar Doc had brought out of the mountain in 1937, 40 years before, the 81-year-old Ova shouted to the wind, "Goddamn Army took the gold!"

While the gold had apparently been removed right from under the claimaints' noses, Operation Goldfinder was important in that it provided high-tech proof that Victorio Peak harbored a very sizable cave. Using sophisticated ground-penetrating radar, a team from Stanford Research Institute headed by Lambert Dolphin determined that there indeed was a very large cavern situated right at the base of Victorio Peak. "It's about where Doc Noss said it is," Dolphin told this writer.

The geological structure of the peak is odd, according to Dolphin. Regarding the cavern, he said that "It's an unusual geological formation, more or less a freak of nature, but it's there."

Dolphin is one of the many Goldfinder participants who sought to return to the site. His scientific interest was not shared by the Army, which summarily turned down his 1977 request for re-entry.

Dolphin would like to reach the big cavern, and he had the idea of lowering a remotely operated television camera through a shaft in order to see what remains in the cave described by Doc Noss as being "big enough for a freight train."

Expressing a thought echoed by virtually everyone interviewed for this article, outside of military spokesmen, Dolphin said that the Army had been very active in and around the mountain. "Everybody who was there would like to know why the Army dug up the mountain so thoroughly," said Dolphin. "You could see they went in through the existing openings, explored them, and then covered them over."

One source familiar with Victorio Peak's history who asked to remain unidentified described the mountain as being "like a hotel." There were "five layers of caverns in that mountain," he said.

The top caverns or rooms held "as little as 10 or 15 tons" of gold, according to this source. The bigger caverns were not all cleared out until the 1970s.

Operation Goldfinder "was all basically a show," said Sam Scott. "Something the Army could turn around and say — 'See? This proves there's no gold!'"

But, at the time, the Victorio Peak show was one of the hottest things around. Scores of reporters from various news media were on hand, including CBS-TV's Dan Rather.

According to several sources, Lady Byrd Johnson, the widow of former President Lyndon Johnson, reportedly called White Sands every day during the expedition in order to be kept posted.

This writer endeavored to reach Mrs. Johnson but was told that any questions had to be submitted via a staff assistant in Austin, Texas.

The answer that came back was that "Mrs. Johnson has no knowledge about that [the phone calls] at all." The assistant said that Lady Byrd "was entertaining friends here" at the time of the expedition, and, she asserted, "Mrs. Johnson just doesn't do things like that. It would be out of character for her."2

By the last day of Operation Goldfinder, a carefully orchestrated public relations scenario had apparently done its work. Those most closely connected with the treasure had seen their dreams trampled and their claims ridiculed. For them, the 1977 expedition must have represented the end of any hope of confirmation of what they knew to be true.

One of these people was Leonard Fiege.

Sam Scott and Fiege were close friends. According to Scott, "Fiege was threatened. He didn't like to talk about it. But that's why he left the 1977 expedition early."

In an affidavit in the possession of Freedom, Thayer Snipes of El Paso, Texas, confirms the threat and sheds some additional light on the overall situation.

The affidavit states that Snipes first met Dr. Robert Welch of Denver, Colorado, around 1975 or 1976. Welch, according to the affidavit, went to Snipes' home on several occasions to buy turquoise for jewelry .

On one of these occasions, the affidavit states, Welch gave Snipes his business card. The card identified Welch as a medical doctor and a psychiatrist, although he jokingly referred to himself as a "head shrinker."

The subject of treasure at Victorio Peak came up on one occasion. On this occasion, according to Snipes' affidavit, "Dr. Welch stated that a U.S. Air Force captain had been sent to his office by the military."

Snipes continues, "Dr. Welch stated that 'the military wanted this man to be put away,' which he further explained as meaning locked away in an insane asylum.

" ... Dr. Welch stated that on numerous occasions he hypnotized the captain.

" ... while under hypnosis, the captain told him he had found gold bars in a cave in Victorio Peak.

" ... also while under hypnosis, the captain stated he had held gold bars in his hands and had covered up stacks of gold bars with rocks and dirt, intending to return later and retrieve the treasure legally.

" ... Dr. Welch stated that he felt he could not put this man away because he was telling him the truth about the gold, and that he could not lie while under hypnosis."

Snipes' affidavit states that "I later met U.S. Air Force Captain Leonard V. Fiege while on the March 1977 expedition to Victorio Peak.

" ... while on the expedition, I told Captain Fiege the story in front of several witnesses.

" ... Captain Fiege's reaction to the story was one of extreme surprise and shock.

" ... Captain Fiege said he remembered being sent to a psychiatrist named Robert Welch by the military, but that he did not realize that he had been hypnotized."

According to the affidavit, "Captain Fiege said he had been shipped overseas after finding gold in Victorio Peak, and that he had been 'harassed ever since' by the military."

The affidavit states that Fiege "said he was going to investigate the matter of his visits to the psychiatrist and see what had happened during those visits."

The affidavit closes with the statement that "Captain Fiege left the expedition a couple of days later, saying that he and his family had been threatened with death if he continued his efforts to prove gold had been in Victorio Peak."

Fiege did leave the expedition, but, as described by Sam Scott and others, threats did not shut him up.

Scott signed a sworn affidavit regarding the harassment and intimidation leveled at Fiege which only ended with his death in 1979.

According to this affidavit, "I can recall many occasions (probably 10) that Leonard told me about his harassments and the threats to his and his children's lives. For example, the time that Leonard spoke to a Lion's Club luncheon in Milwaukee, only to be threatened that night on the telephone. Then there was the time that he was told at supper time what his kids had for lunch in the school cafeteria, their route to and from school, times, etc. Again, a nasty voice on the telephone — a threat on their lives."

In a personal interview, Fiege's daughter, Jan, confirmed for this writer the fact of the threats which plagued the family. In 1971 or 1972, for example, shortly after moving to Denton, Texas, she received a phone call from her father telling her that he had just received a call threatening all three of his children if he did not keep his mouth shut about Victorio Peak. Fiege had called her to see if she was all right. The caller knew where all three of his children were, Fiege told his daughter. He even knew that Jan had just taken a job at a diner in Denton. The bewildered Fiege told his daughter that with the operator's help he had been able to trace the call to Kansas City, Missouri — hundreds of miles from himself in Wisconsin and from his daughter in Texas.

According to Jan, she returned to the family home in Eau Claire, Wisconsin, not too long after that and heard a threatening voice on the phone there herself. The male caller told her that unless her father shut up about Victorio Peak, someone was "going to die."

Similar threats were made to others. Harvey Snow, for example, was told over the phone where each of his five children were by geographic coordinates — including a son who was on a U.S. Navy ship in the Pacific at the time. Snow was told to stay away from White Sands Missile Range or his children would be killed. Snow disregarded the warning, and his youngest daughter was found shot to death shortly thereafter.

A grandson of Ova Noss described an apparent attempt on Ova's life to Freedom. Shortly after the expedition, someone entered her house at night by forcing a window. The intruder turned on the gas on the stove. "If we hadn't gotten there," the grandson said, "in 10 or 15 minutes, she would have had it."

As it was, Ova had to be hospitalized. The grandson mentioned that after the expedition, Ova's home was broken into two or three more times. Various items connected to Doc Noss' treasure were stolen.

By the end of 1979, both Leonard Fiege and Ova Noss — the two major living claimants to the gold — were dead.

While it cannot be proven that their names should join the roster of people who died in connection with an apparently violent cover-up of the removal of gold from Victorio Peak, their deaths did mark the end of vigorous pursuit of the gold by active claimants.

Nearly 10 years after Operation Goldfinder failed to answer the many questions about Victorio Peak, the mystery surrounding the treasure has deepened and darkened.

References:

1 "Explorations at Victorio Peak," by Chester R. Johnson Jr., Division of Research, Museum of New Mexico, 1963. Freedom Magazine obtained copies of both the censored and uncensored reports, as well as copies of the affidavits mentioned above from the four men.

2 For the role that President Johnson played in the removal of tons of gold bullion from Victorio Peak, see Part 1.

## CHAPTER SIXTY-THREE

### SOME LAST EMAILS GIVEN TO ME

There are a number of people who are certainly trying to help me finish this book. The following copies of emails that were apparently posted on the Internet were given to me and I present this here.

## Grandmother's Last Visit
by Joanna T.

I was 19 years old and living in the dormitory at New Mexico State University. This was back in 1993. My family lived in El Paso, Texas, not too far from Las Cruces, New Mexico. My grandmother was ill. She was diabetic and my family resided with her at her home. My mom said that my grandmother was not too much of herself that day. She wasn't eating as much and was pretty quiet – and scared. So when the night time came, my grandmother kept calling for my oldest sister. My sister went in and asked what she needed. She just wanted some company and couldn't sleep, so my sister sat with her in her room so that she could go to sleep. Then suddenly my grandmother started yelling for my mom and my mom came in. She was having a heart attack, so my mom and sister started to perform CPR on her.

At this time, I wasn't aware of what was happening; I was back in Las Cruces asleep, and I was having a dream of some sort. Suddenly, I was standing alone. The lighting in my dream was gray, like a cloudy day, and cloud-like forms all over, and the floor wasn't solid like in reality. I was standing there wondering. I saw a figure at a far distance and then closer until I saw who it was in front of me. It was my grandmother, wearing her navy blue dress with little white flowers. It was her favorite.

I looked at her and she said to me with a smile, in Spanish "Ya me voy," which means "I'm leaving." I asked her in Spanish "Para adonde?" which means, "Where to?" She couldn't explain to me where, but she gave me the most beautiful hug, and it was so comforting, as if she wanted me to always remember her and pray for her.

As soon as she let go, the phone rang. I got up and it was my mom. As she was about to speak to me I said to her, "I know, mom, she passed away." My mom started to cry and I did also. The next day, when I arrived in El Paso, I told every one about my dream and we were all stunned. But I think no one could ever give me the most beautiful experience in the world, like the one my grandmother gave me.

## Unrestful Slumber Party

**by bobbyhill@earthlink.net**

My story begins back home in El Paso, Texas, when I went to visit a house where several of my friends rented a house and lived as roommates. I was told the history of the house, but I didn't really want to believe the stories. The stories were typical of ghost stories where a figure of elder woman was seen walking around the corner, a telephone cord swinging on its own, animated dolls, a face present in a lit fireplace, and so on.

The basis for this story is that an elderly woman was killed by an intruder and was discovered a while after. It was said that the chalk outline of the body was left to be covered by carpet along with other markings typical of a murder scene. I was a little uneasy being left alone in that room, because I was afraid of seeing or feeling something.

One day I decided to take up an offer to spend the night with my friends because the majority of us worked at a movie theater and decided to carpool to work the next morning. The night seemed all right as long as the lights stayed on and everybody hung around and watched the television. That night would bring the things I didn't want to know.

We got settled to get ready for bed and we decided to sleep in the room where "she" was murdered. The first thing we heard was a slow rapping on the side door and the neighbor's dog was crying mournfully. The first we did was look at each other, pick up our sleeping bags, and sleep in the next room which was the entry room. Four of us slept in front of the couch, one slept on one couch, and one on the other.

We heard the coffee table creaking as if someone was sitting on it while a knocking sound came from the wall. I made the mistake of speaking first telling this being I wanted sleep because I had to open the next day and didn't want to be disturbed.

While I was facing the room we had just run from, I heard a Christmas ornament being yanked off the tree while the TV guide flew off the table and landed on one the guys. He put the guide back on the table, only to be hit by a coaster. Then the girl laying in front of me yelled at me because she thought I had kicked the back of her knee. My knee was bent behind hers, but I would know if I had kicked her. Meanwhile, the creaking and knocking continued.

I was afraid to face the dining room so I stayed facing the abandoned room and I continued to see things fly off the coffee table. After about an hour of disruptions and my threatening we decided to see if we could recreate the sounds with what we thought was the cause.

We found an extra Christmas tree pole behind one sofa, sat it straight up and let it drop against the wall. When the sound resembled what we had been hearing, we screamed and ran into the girl's room.

Everyone got tucked into bed and I turned the lights off and as soon as I got into bed we heard a loud thud. I got out of bed and turned the lights back on only to discover an address book on the floor. It had been thrown from a dresser and against the door. I then turned off the light and laid down when I was hit on the head. Now I thought someone had thrown it, but it came from direction of the ceiling and no one could have gotten up quick enough to hit me as soon as I turned off the lights. Cursing, I got up and turned the lights to find a Disney figure from a Happy Meal in our bed. I turned off the light, threw the figure straight ahead, and was about to cover my head when I hit in the mouth very hard with something. This time I was scared and angry and everyone knew I had been hurt because I had screamed very loud. I once again turned on the light and found the figure in the bed and the head had been turned around. I knew I had a welt on my lip because it strung and it felt like it sticking out pretty far. I threw the doll in the closet and packed up my bag, because I had enough of this. Everyone else decided to follow me into the guy's room and once again we got ready for bed.

I was hit on the head with a quarter and had my sleeping yanked over my head, but after that evening nothing bothered us again. I ended with a few hours sleep and was very grumpy.

I never saw a being, but I knew that someone had done those things to me. There was no way for my friends to hit me because of the timing and the direction the object came from. I had learned my lesson never to stay in house that is haunted because I may not enjoy my stay there.

## EPILOGUE

So there you have it. El Paso has a large number of unsolved mysteries and unusual happenings that take place inside its borders. This is the second book on the spirits of El Paso that I have written as part of the Spirits of the Border Series and shall be my last for a while. The next book in this series shall be on the ghosts of New Mexico. Watch for it soon.

# PHOTOGRAPHS

# INDEX

Printed in the United States
79237LV00003B/97-123